UNOFFICIAL GUIDE TO
ANCESTRY.COM

How to Find Your Family History on the #1 Genealogy Website

NANCY HENDRICKSON

FAMILY
TREE
BOOKS

Cincinnati, Ohio
familytreemagazine.com/store

CONTENTS

PART ONE:	PART TWO:
GETTING STARTED WITH ANCESTRY.COM	DIGGING INTO RECORDS ON ANCESTRY.COM

PART THREE:
UNCOVERING ANCESTORS WITH ANCESTRYDNA

PART FOUR:
DIVING DEEPER INTO ANCESTRY.COM

The amount of information that you can find on Ancestry.com is mind-boggling, and the potential for finding your family's story is almost limitless.

INTRODUCTION

In the years since we published the first edition of this book, Ancestry.com has grown at an amazing rate. The number of records available on the site has skyrocketed, and its functionality and interface have changed, making it more accessible to even the newest genealogy searcher. In 2017, Ancestry.com surpassed the 20-billion-record mark, securing its place as the largest collection of family history records in the world. In addition, the site's number of users continues to grow: 90 million user-submitted family trees, 75 million daily searches, and more than 5 million DNA test-takers.

Using Ancestry.com's assets, genealogy researchers can begin their family history journey or dig through the cracks of seemingly impenetrable brick walls. The record collections you'll find are as varied as the people who use them. Here, you can search through the wildly popular US and UK censuses or explore obscure collections like the land records of Micronesia.

This book has something to offer for genealogists of all experience levels. If you're just getting started in genealogy, this book's early chapters will guide you through setting up your first family tree and learning genealogy research basics. If you already have a subscription and have had some level of success, you'll discover how to use more advanced search techniques to track down elusive ancestors in this book's chapters on individual categories of records.

In writing this book, I've added many records to my own family tree and met distant cousins that otherwise would have flown under my radar. I was thrilled to find my dad's photo in a high school yearbook, my great-great-great-grandfather's will, and a description of a Revolutionary War battle in which my ancestor fought. The amount of information that you can find on Ancestry.com is mind-boggling, and the potential for finding your family's story is almost limitless.

As you delve into each chapter, you'll find real-life searches you can duplicate on your own computer—think of it as looking over my shoulder as I show you how best to attack a research problem. Hopefully, each example will help you hone your detective skills to find the record collection where your family is hiding. Don't be surprised if you find another researcher who's already unearthed the exact piece of information that's stymied you for years. (Yes, it happened to me.)

One last thing: Before you begin reading this book, I want you to know that "doing" genealogy is far more than just collecting names and dates. In the end, learning about the people who came before you is an act of self-discovery. Your shared DNA will tell you some of the story, but there's so much more waiting to be found.

As you work your way through this book—and through your own genealogy problems—I invite you to get in touch and let me know how you're doing. I always love hearing about your successes. You can contact me at *genealogyteach@gmail.com* or find me with user name *genealogyteach* on Pinterest, Instagram, Twitter, and Facebook.

Nancy Hendrickson
San Diego, California
<www.ancestornews.com>

PART ONE

GETTING STARTED WITH
ANCESTRY.COM

1

LEARNING THE BASICS

Everyone has his or her own reasons for climbing the family tree. For some, it may provide the proof needed to join a lineage society like the Daughters of the American Revolution. But for others, it may be a case of simple curiosity: Who came before me? What did they do? And how am I like them?

Back in the day, learning anything about your family's place in history required a visit to a national archive, state or local government office, or family history library. You'd spend hours cranking through reels and reels of microfilm, all with the hope (but not the promise) of locating someone in your family tree. Thanks to the Internet—and one website in particular—all of that has changed.

The evolution of digital genealogy is nothing less than miraculous. Over the last several years, there's been an explosion of genealogy records online, thanks in part to individuals, organizations, state agencies, societies, and countless volunteers. However, no one has amassed as large of a collection as Ancestry.com **<www.ancestry.com>**. With fourteen billion records, it's now the world's largest online family history resource. If you want the hope (and, by some measures, the promise) of finding your ancestors' records, Ancestry.com is the place to start—and this book will show you how.

This chapter will introduce you to Ancestry.com's many services, membership options, and the basics of Ancestry.com's family trees and records system. Even if you already have an Ancestry.com subscription, I encourage you to start with chapter 1. You never know what tip might take you onto unexplored paths. In later chapters, I'll cover how to maximize your Ancestry.com membership and dig deep into the many types of records available on the site.

THE ANCESTRY.COM NETWORK

One thing that makes Ancestry.com so valuable to genealogists is its exceptionally large network of genealogy-related websites. Some are linked into Ancestry.com's site via the main navigation menu while others are stand-alone entities. Ancestry.com's holdings as of print time are:

- AncestryDNA <dna.ancestry.com>
- Archives.com <www.archives.com>
- Find A Grave <www.findagrave.com>
- Fold3 <www.fold3.com>
- Genealogy.com <www.genealogy.com>
- Newspapers.com <www.newspapers.com>
- ProGenealogists <www.progenealogists.com>
- RootsWeb <rootsweb.ancestry.com>

We'll discuss AncestryDNA in chapters 12 through 14, and Newspapers.com and Fold3 in chapter 16.

MEMBERSHIPS

Membership to Ancestry.com provides access to numerous collections and databases where you can find census, vital, military, and immigration records, as well as other members' online family trees.

If you don't yet have an Ancestry.com membership, you can join at four different membership levels:

1. **Ancestry Member:** free registration that allows you to build a family tree, use message boards, search, and access free records
2. **U.S. Discovery:** includes all US records
3. **World Explorer:** includes all US and international records
4. **All Access:** includes both US and international records in addition to Newspapers.com (150 million pages of newspaper archives) and Fold3 (450 million military records).

Your choice of membership depends on the type of research in which you're primarily interested. If you haven't yet traced your ancestors back to their immigration to the United States, the US membership is a good starting place for you.

For researchers whose family were fairly recent immigrants to America (i.e., they came to America in the late nineteenth or early twentieth centuries), the World Explorer membership can help pinpoint your family's country of origin via international records such as censuses, church, birth, death, and marriage records. The number of international records on Ancestry.com is growing, with more added as they become available. Remember, some countries have no central depository (like the United States' National Archives **<www.archives.gov>**), so those records have to be digitized by local archives.

Lastly, for researchers primarily interested in discovering military records or family information in old newspapers, the expanded All Access membership may be just the ticket. With some records (including military records), you'll find a link to Fold3's digitized version of the original record alongside its indexed information on Ancestry.com. For example, I found a Revolutionary War ancestor in an Ancestry.com index but needed to go to Fold3 to read the entire pension file. (Note: If the only thing you're interested in is your family's military history, you can subscribe to Fold3 without an Ancestry.com membership.)

Before we detail the many features of Ancestry.com, remember that some portions of the Ancestry.com site are available to anyone, whether or not you have a subscription. If you want to join as a free user, surf the site all you'd like. Any time you come to a record that's subscription-only, you'll see a pop-up box inviting you to join on a trial basis.

GETTING STARTED IN FAMILY TREE RESEARCH

If your only acquaintance with climbing the family tree is watching programs like *Who Do You Think You Are?* or *Genealogy Roadshow*, you may not know that genealogy research begins with you!

If your family lore is built around a distant relationship to Queen Elizabeth I, Jesse James, or Pocahontas, it's tempting to start research with your famous ancestor and then work your way backward to yourself. This approach can be disastrous, not to mention a waste of time. Your family legend might be based more on fiction than fact. The good news is that, if you are related to a famous person, you'll eventually find the connection based on research and evidence.

Although starting with yourself may seem counterintuitive, it's the best way to establish relationships from one generation to the next. Here are five simple steps to jump-starting your genealogy research.

Begin With You

When you climbed trees as a kid (unless you had super powers), you started on the ground and worked your way up the trunk, then out onto the branches. Genealogy works the same way.

Start on the ground (with you), climb up the trunk (your parents and grandparents), and venture out onto the branches (past generations). The higher you go in the tree, the less stable the branches. The farther you go back in genealogy, the more challenging the journey.

I know it's tempting to jump onto Ancestry.com and start searching for cool ancestors. In fact, why not take thirty minutes and do just that! Then come back and indulge me as I explain exactly why you need to take a little time to gather documents and get yourself organized. I'll wait right here.

Collect Documentation

Did you know that genealogists love telling you to "begin your search at home"? That's because you probably have more family tree "stuff" around the house than you realize, such as your birth certificate. Have you ever really looked at it? Did you know that most modern birth certificates tell the time of birth, the name of the attending physician, mom's maiden name, parents' ages, and possibly parents' places of birth? It's pretty neat to have all of that data on a single document.

Once you start amassing records about yourself (including official records such as birth certificates, marriage licenses, etc.), do the same for your parents. You've now created a solid foundation from which to build back to earlier generations. What type of documents might you have at home?

- birth certificates for you and your parents, children, and siblings
- newspaper clippings
- military documents
- school photos
- death certificates for immediate family members
- marriage certificates

TAKE YOUR TREES ON THE GO

Carry your family tree on your iPad, iPhone, or Android device. The Ancestry.com app on your device syncs with your Ancestry.com account online, making it easy to keep all of your research records up-to-date. Displays are customizable, allowing you to view your tree, photos, stories, and research hints.

If you're luckier than me, you may have journals, letters, or diaries from past generations or family bibles, awards, photographs, and wills. Do a sweep through the house and gather what you have. Then reach out to your relatives to learn even more.

To get started on your documentation, download free forms from *Family Tree Magazine* **<www.familytreemagazine.com/FreeForms>**. You won't need all of them right now—and there may be some you never use—but at the least, grab the Five-Generation Ancestor Chart and the Family Group Sheet. (You'll find them under Basic Charts and Worksheets. Fill out the family group sheet for you and your family (i.e., spouse, children, and grandchildren). You also can do this in your computer software if you've digitized your research.

Put on Your Barbara Walters Hat

Thanks to the Internet, many of your cousins, aunts, uncles, and grandparents are online. That makes doing interviews or gathering family stories so much easier than traveling to where they lived or waiting weeks for back-and-forth snail mail. If you decide to interview via e-mail, make sure the person you're interviewing wants to respond in the same way; some people don't like to type that much. If they'd rather do a phone interview, send the questions in advance so they'll have time to think about it, then record the phone interview.

If you have a smartphone or tablet, you don't even need a digital recorder to record a phone interview; you can use your device's built-in recorder or pick up one of the many recording apps on the market (most are under two dollars). One of the apps, Dragon Dictation **<www.nuance.com/dragon.html>**, will even transcribe your notes, up to one minute at a time. There are also recorder apps that will record your smartphone call (just be sure you let the person on the other end of the call know you're recording).

Can't decide which family members to interview? A rule of thumb is to begin with the oldest. Countless genealogy folks lament the fact they never interviewed an elderly relative before it was "too late." Your oldest relatives are the keepers of the family's furthest back memories. Amazingly, one of my aunts could remember her great-grandmother—a woman who was a Civil War bride!

Your oldest relative also may remember stories and weird little tidbits that you'll never find in a book or a database, such as "Grandma always wore black," or "Your dad's favorite meal was pork loin." Use the clues in these interviews to dig back further in your history and add personality to your family book or a scrapbook.

Something to keep in mind, though: Whatever stories you hear during the interviews are just stories until proven. In my experience, most family lore is actually based in fact, though the accuracy of the facts, like the telephone game, may degrade over time.

Depending on your interviewee's memory, it's possible you'll discover a fabulous clue that opens whole new research vistas. Or, you may hear a tiny bit of a story that leads you to another clue and then another. I can guarantee one thing: You'll always learn more than you expected, particularly from elderly relatives.

If you're doing the interview in person, be sure to ask if your relative has documents or photographs of the family. Most people are reluctant to let these treasures out of their hands, so be sure to bring along a portable scanner or digital camera. Again, many smartphone and tablet apps can turn your device into a scanner. Depending on the app, scans are saved in JPG (image) or PDF (document) format.

The most important thing I've learned about interviews is that a story that has absolutely no relevance to you today may be a breakthrough clue five years from now. So be sure to transcribe those interviews so you can go back to your notes in the future.

So what are you waiting for? Make a list of relatives you want to interview and the questions you want to ask them. Set up at least one interview. If applicable, download a recording app for your smartphone or tablet.

Look for More Than Just Names and Dates

As you do interviews (don't forget to interview yourself!), remember that family history is about far more than just names and dates. Just like you, your ancestors were flesh and blood "real people." They argued, had political and religious differences, brought rituals and celebrations from their country of origin, went to school, hated homework, battled illness, and witnessed great change.

The more you can uncover about the time and place of your ancestors' lives, or the more stories you can gather about them, the more likely you are to see aspects of their lives reflected in your own.

A caveat, though: Just because something is online doesn't mean it's true, and you should always check information for sources. There's a tremendous amount of erroneous genealogy information floating around the Web, and (like cute cat videos) they just keep getting passed around from person to person. Use what you find online as a jumping-off place for further investigation—not as the destination.

Get Organized

Whether you keep paper records or digital ones, find a filing system that works for you. If you continue your genealogy research over several years, trust me ... you don't want five years to get past you and all you have to show for it are boxes of paper.

It's really common in this hobby to jump in, print records, toss them in a pile, and then years later bemoan the fact that you can't find anything. With computers, this is less likely, as you can always do a system-wide search for something you saved. However, the success of the search depends on how well you named a record when you first downloaded and saved it.

Which brings me to a point about file naming: Whatever system you use to name a digital file, be consistent. Begin the file name with either the Surname or Placename, or whatever makes sense to you. Give the file name enough information (e.g., *birth, death, marriage, Ohio*) that it will be rounded up in a system-wide search.

Before you begin collecting and organizing documents and photos into folders or files, consider whether you have documents that need special handling, such as the following:

- **Photographs:** If you store photos in boxes, use ones made of acid-free materials and acid-free dividers. If you write on the back of photos (which is not recommended), use a photo-safe pen. Photos should be stored at room temperature, preferably between 65 to 70 degrees, with a relative humidity of about 50 percent.

- **Documents:** Again, store these in an acid-free environment, protected from light, heat, and high humidity. The best storage containers are acid-free boxes or archival plastic sleeves. Because of dampness issues, avoid storing documents in the attic or the basement. Try to avoid using PVC (polyvinyl chloride) plastic page-protector sheets, because they release damaging acids over time. If you store documents together, slip a piece of acid-free paper between each one. As much as you might think it's a good idea, don't laminate your documents. If fragile, they can be damaged by the high heat used in the lamination process.

- **Newspapers:** Newspapers are made of highly acidic paper, causing them to deteriorate quickly. Like other documents, store newspapers in an acid-free box or archival scrapbook, interspersed with acid-free paper.

- **Books:** Keep books out of direct sunlight as sun will bleach dust jackets and dry out leather covers. Books do best when stored upright on a shelf rather than stacked one on top of another. If stored on wooden shelves, seal the wood as unsealed wood can release acidic vapors. If a book is especially valuable, store it in an archival box.

SET A PLAN

See the *Family Tree Magazine* article at <www.familytreemagazine.com/premium/win-the-paper-chase> for good ideas on how to develop an organizational system. *Organize Your Genealogy* (Family Tree Books, 2016) <www.familytreemagazine.com/store/organize-your-genealogy-paperback> also has some great tips and strategies.

Six Genealogy Myths

1. **You can buy your family crest.** Cups, mugs, wall hangings, and other family crest doodads are available online everywhere. But "families" don't have crests—rather, individuals do. Coats of arms must be granted, and to claim the right to arms, you must prove descent through a male line of someone to whom arms were granted. Learn the truth about family crests at <www.familytreemagazine.com/premium/hark-heraldry>.

2. **The 1890 census burned to a crisp.** Actually, it didn't—it was waterlogged and lay around rotting until some unknown person authorized its disposal. But fractions survived, as well as about half of a Civil War Union veterans census. These records are available on sites such as Ancestry.com.

3. **You can find your whole family history online.** If only! Nowadays you can get lots of actual records online, including censuses, passenger lists, military records, digitized books—and on and on. But errors abound in online indexes, transcriptions, and family trees, and repositories still hold richly detailed, lesser-known records that haven't been digitized. So at some point, you'll want or need to log off and go to the library.

4. **Your ancestor was a Cherokee princess or George Washington.** Lots of families have legends about famous kin, and of course they could be true—but stories tend to get embellished and even made up over time, so research such legends before passing them on as the truth. For example, though you may have Cherokee blood, there weren't any Cherokee princesses, and George Washington can't be an ancestor because he never had children (Martha did, from her first marriage). Also, not everyone with the same last name is related, even when you go waaaaaaay back in time.

5. **The courthouse burned, and all the records are gone.** Many a genealogical dream has run smack into a courthouse fire. But the vital records, naturalizations, deeds, wills, and other records within weren't always completely destroyed. Sometimes records survived, or copies had been sent to another office, or the clerk asked citizens for copies of their records, or you can find the same information elsewhere. See *Family Tree Magazine*'s tips for beating brick walls at <www.familytreemagazine.com/premium/big-breakthroughs> and contact the county library or state archives, whose staffs may have prepared special helps for genealogists researching around courthouse blazes.

6. **Your ancestor's name was changed at Ellis Island.** This may be the biggest genealogical myth of all time. Passenger lists were created at the port of departure, and Ellis Island officials merely checked off the names on the list. (One reason why knowing your ancestor's name in the old country will help you find his passenger record.)

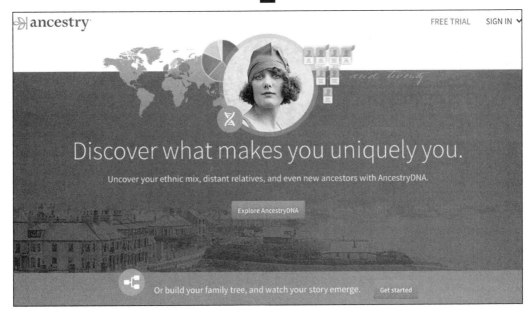

The Ancestry.com home page is where you'll start your journey.

WELCOME TO ANCESTRY.COM

Now that we've covered Genealogy 101, let's explore Ancestry.com. Although Ancestry.com is massive, it's easy to navigate once you familiarize yourself with the layout. I'll be giving several examples of real-life navigation, so go ahead, log in, and follow along.

Set Up Your Account

First, set up your account or log in at the Ancestry.com home page **<www.ancestry.com>** (image **A**). Enter your username and password, then click the Sign In button. If you already are a subscriber and have forgotten your password, click the Forgot? link for help. If you're new to Ancestry.com, click the green Subscribe button or Start Free Trial to see the available subscription plans. (Note: At print time, the All Access subscription is not offered as part of the free fourteen-day trial. However, if you click the green Subscribe button at the top right of the page, you'll see all of the subscription options.)

As noted, some sections of the site, such as AncestrySupport **<support.ancestry.com>** and family trees, are available to nonsubscribers. However, you won't be able to access the premium databases without a subscription. See chapter 2 to learn how to create your family tree online, whether or not you have a subscription.

Explore the Menu Items

Once you log in, explore all of the menu items. You'll see a menu bar stretching across the top of the page. On the far right side, you'll see an e-mail icon alerting you to messages, a green leaf with recent hints that are waiting for you to evaluate, and your username.

Here's what each of these icons do:

- **Leaf icon:** Click the leaf icon to display a list of record-based hints for people in your family tree. You'll have to create a family tree first to get any hints, but we'll cover that in chapter 2.

- **E-mail icon:** Go to the e-mail icon to read messages sent to you through the Ancestry.com system from other users.

- **Your name:** Click your name to access account information, including your member profile, preferences, and e-mail settings. If you change your e-mail address while you have an Ancestry.com subscription, don't forget to go into your profile and update the e-mail address there as well.

On the right side of the My Account Options page (under the Your Account tab), you'll find several options including updating your e-mail preferences. Click this link to subscribe to Ancestry.com's newsletters—a great way to stay informed of the latest news and collections. From My Account Options, you also can upgrade to another subscription plan.

Site Preferences, also available from the dropdown menu under your username, allows you to choose hint, community, and activity preferences. For example, you can choose whether to let other Ancestry.com members access your e-mail address or whether you want to remain anonymous. In the right-side column, you'll also find a link to connect your Ancestry.com account with your Facebook profile.

Explore the Main Menu Bar

The menu bar itself (image **B**) has several items located in dropdown menus that are accessed by clicking the appropriate tab. For example, if you click Search, other menu choices appear in a dropdown menu.

Don't worry about where to go first, as each section of the menu is covered in this book:

- Home: chapter 1
- Trees: chapter 2

- Search: chapters 3–11
- DNA: chapters 12–14
- Help: chapter 1
- Extras: chapter 1

View and Customize Your Home Page

The area below the menu is your home page (image **C**), which you can customize with a variety of modules. By default (and this may change over time), the home page contains:

1. **Recent Member Connect Activity:** When you log in to your account, your default view may contain this module. If not, you can add it to your home page. Click See More to view the items you can add to this module such as activity on your tree(s), activity on records you've recently worked with, photos saved by your connections, and other members who are saving the content you've added.

2. **Your Trees(s):** This module contains information on any tree that you've created or uploaded, along with the number of people in the tree, photos, and the last person on the tree that you viewed.

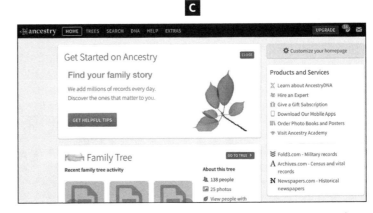

Navigate the major record collections on Ancestry.com using the Search tab, part of Ancestry.com's main menu toolbar.

Your customizable home page will give you access to various news items, tools, and shortcuts.

3. **Search:** This is a quick search box with a link to the advanced search options.

4. **What's Happening at Ancestry.com:** This provides a list of links to new records recently added to Ancestry.com's collections. Ancestry.com is constantly adding new data, so be sure to check this section often. Just because a specific record isn't online today doesn't mean it won't be there next month. I was searching for a person who lived in South Dakota in the mid-nineteenth century, and had little luck. However, a year later, I was able to track him down in a newly added index to South Dakota cemeteries (1831–2008). By the way, this particular collection (along with several others) has a link that takes you off Ancestry.com and to another site (in this case the South Dakota State Historical Society) where you can view more of the record.

In addition to the default modules, you also can add the following modules by clicking the Customize Your Homepage link at the top of the home page. From here, you can add or delete any of the default or additional modules, or move them via drag-and-drop. Here are some of the modules you can add:

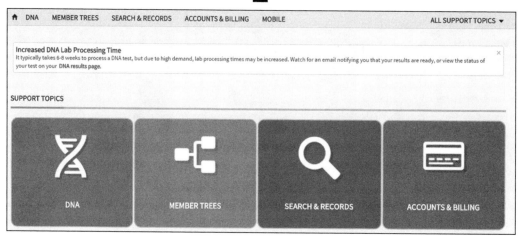

D

AncestrySupport will help you navigate every portion of the site, from AncestryDNA (see chapters 12–14) to how to get more out of your searches (see chapter 3).

- **Get Started on Ancestry**: Quick tips for using the site
- **My Quick Links**: A list of pages you view most often
- **My To-Do List**: A personalized list of tasks
- **Record Collections**: Quick navigation to key collections such as the US census
- **Jewish Name Variations**: Derivations for common Jewish first names
- **Jewish Community Locator**: Track communities through time
- **Message Board Favorites**: Your favorite Message Boards and the most recent threads posted to each

Why not stop now and set up your home page? As you become more familiar with Ancestry.com and use more features, you can always return here and reconfigure.

AncestrySupport

If you're new to genealogy and/or the site, visit AncestrySupport **<support.ancestry.com>** to enter the world's largest genealogy customer care center. From the AncestrySupport tab (image **D**), you can delve into support topics on DNA, search and records, accounts and billing, and member trees. You can also browse through the most common topics or use the search box at the top of the page to find a topic of interest.

From the AncestrySupport top menu, you can also navigate to Mobile. This is where you'll find topics on getting the most value from the Ancestry.com mobile app (available for iOS and Android devices).

Getting Started contains exactly what you might think: articles for people who are new, not only to Ancestry.com, but also to genealogy itself. Use the Search box to find free genealogy forms as well as tips on various types of research, such as British or Australian.

AncestrySupport is the place to go when you're not sure how to accomplish an Ancestry.com-related task. Potential issues could be:

- who can edit your family tree
- how to avoid duplicates in a tree
- how to split a tree
- how to add foreign letters to a tree
- interpreting your DNA test
- DNA and privacy policies

- how to find adoption records or break down brick walls

- anything to do with your account and billing

If you have any kind of problem with your account, navigating the site, or finding how to do a specific task, it's likely that you'll find the answer in AncestrySupport.

EXTRAS

On the main navigation menu, you'll see another tab: Extras (image **E**). Under the Extras tab, you can download Ancestry.com mobile apps for iOS and Android devices, order photo books and posters, enroll in online courses at Ancestry Academy, connect with ProGenealogists, and buy gift memberships to the site.

The ProGenealogists link **<www.progenealogists.com>** takes you to the website for ProGenealogists, an Ancestry.com-owned research firm. You can view information about the professional researchers available to conduct family history research, learn about the ancestry research services available, read case studies, and get a cost estimate for professional research services. Start with the section on How it Works. This gives information on exactly how you can go about working with a ProGenealogist, including topics such as setting goals and understanding outcomes.

One of the Ancestry.com sections that can benefit researchers of all skill levels is the Ancestry Academy. You'll find the link for the Academy under the Extra section of the top menu. The Academy is filled with videos and lectures on a wide variety of topics. Sections within the Academy include videos on Getting Started, Short Course Videos, and Tips and Tricks for working with Ancestry Member Trees.

Getting Started videos cover the basics. However, the Short Course videos really dig into the meat of many genealogical problems such as working with the 1790 census, researching Confederate pensions, using/applying to lineage societies, researching probate records, and dispelling

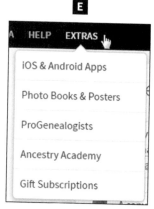

The Extras tab contains links to other Ancestry.com products and services that you may find useful, such as Ancestry Academy.

genealogy myths. Videos in the Tips and Tricks series are generally under one minute and answer the most common tree questions.

If you click on All Topics in the left column, you'll see the Academy rearranged the videos into topic areas such as Records, Methodology, and Ethnic research. If you find a video you want to come back to at a later date, click the star under the name of the video and it will be saved to your playlist (image).

Ancestry Academy offers hundreds of genealogy videos. You can even create your own video playlist.

2

USING ANCESTRY.COM FAMILY TREES

f you came to Ancestry.com with the sole goal of searching for family records, you may miss one of the most robust and popular features of the site: family trees. Creating a family tree (which you can do as a non-Ancestry.com subscriber) can open up doors to amazing research treasures as well as connect you with other people researching your tree.

If you'd rather jump into searching the records collections than creating a family tree, you're missing Ancestry.com's helpful automated features. Once you've read this chapter, created a family tree, and explored all of the parts and parcels of this section of Ancestry.com, you may have more clues for research than you'll know what to do with!

In this chapter, I'll show you how to create your first family tree, manage and add content to your tree, search other people's trees, and explore record "hints." Once we cover the basics, you'll also learn how to use Member Connect to discover and contact other people researching your family tree.

But as the song goes—"Let's start at the very beginning, a very good place to start."

BUILDING YOUR FIRST TREE

There are two ways to create a family tree: by manually inputting data or by uploading a GEDCOM file. In this chapter, I'll cover how to do both.

Do you remember the menu bar from chapter 1? If you click the Family Trees menu tab, you'll see a list of trees you've created. If this is your first tree, your dropdown menu will only have options for creating and managing trees (image **A**).

Manually Creating a Tree

If you've never used genealogy software (which creates digital trees), you'll need to start your tree from scratch by clicking Create & Manage Trees under the Trees tab, then Create a new tree (image **B**). You'll then be prompted to enter a name, birth date and place, gender, and death date (if applicable). Check the box if you want to start the tree with yourself. (You can start with any person you choose.) Note: The screen display will look slightly different depending on whether you've already created at least one tree.

Once you've entered everyone you want to include, give the tree a name, then select privacy options (see the Managing Your Trees section later in this chapter for details).

Uploading a GEDCOM to Create Your Tree

If you use genealogy software, the easiest way to create a tree is to upload your family file using the Upload a GEDCOM link that's located on the Family Trees menu tab. A GEDCOM file is the universal file format family historians use to exchange information; GEDCOM is an acronym for GEnealogical Data COMmunications. Although it appears

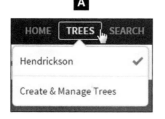

You can easily access any of your family trees under the Trees dropdown menu.

Click the Family Trees menu to start a family tree (or view trees already uploaded).

that the only type of file you can upload is a GEDCOM file (created via the Export menu link of your software), the system supports several other file formats:

- Family Tree Maker (.ftw)
- Family Tree Maker backup file (.fbk)
- Personal Ancestral File (.paf)
- Legacy (.fdb)
- Zipped GEDCOM and images (.gedz)

This means if you use Legacy, for example, you can upload that file directly to Ancestry.com without converting it to a GEDCOM file.

Click the Upload a GEDCOM link, browse your computer to locate the family file, give the tree a name, then select whether to make the tree public or private.

Once you've filled in the information, as well as read and clicked the Submission Agreement, click the Upload button.

Syncing with a Software Program

While most software programs can export a GEDCOM file that you can upload to Ancestry.com, two software programs allow you to sync your family trees between them and the genealogy megasite. Let's take a look.

ROOTSMAGIC

After working for months, independent software program RootsMagic **<www.rootsmagic.com>** added two features to its genealogy software that allow it to sync directly with Ancestry.com: TreeShare and WebHints. TreeShare makes it simple to move data between Ancestry.com online trees and your RootsMagic file on your computer, while WebHints brings Ancestry.com's famous hint system to your desktop. You can now easily transfer people, events, source citations, and—critically for researchers—pictures between the two systems.

If you have RootsMagic file version 7.5 or later, you'll see an Ancestry.com icon in the top toolbar. Click the logo and sign into your Ancestry.com account, and the system will go to work syncing the two trees. Click the box on the next screen to show only those people with differing information between the two trees (image **C**). At this point, you can go through each item and either delete it, update it as an existing event in RootsMagic or Ancestry.com, or add it as a new event in RootsMagic or Ancestry.com. Now, finally, you can ensure that your computer files are in perfect sync with your Ancestry.com trees.

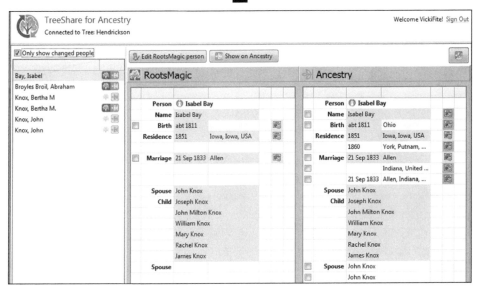

C

View, delete or accept changes between a RootsMagic file and your Ancestry.com tree.

The second new feature, WebHints, gives you the ability to access your Ancestry.com hints from inside your RootsMagic software. Click the lightbulb icon next to a person's name to view a hints box. Once you click the number of hints, another box pops up showing you where the hints are coming from. This feature makes it easy to work within your RootsMagic software instead of going back and forth between software and Ancestry.com. Go through the hints and either accept, reject or list as undecided.

FAMILY TREE MAKER

Are you a Family Tree Maker (FTM) software user? If so, you may already know that FTM 2017 can automatically sync trees between your FTM file and your Ancestry.com account. Using the FamilySync technology, your Ancestry.com tree can link to multiple FTM trees. After you upload a family tree to either Ancestry.com or Family Tree Maker, the two trees can be connected so that any changes made to one will also change the other. Syncs can be done either automatically or manually.

Like RootsMagic, FTM 2017 has several tools beyond syncing with Ancestry.com. For example, you can add up to eight different colors to an individual, perfect for those who love color-coding. Why do this? You may want to add a certain color to every ancestor whose origins were Irish or who served in the military—making it much easier to see certain characteristics at-a-glance.

Given this feature, plus a seamless integration with FamilySearch <**www.familysearch .org**> and a Photo Darkroom that restores a faded image to its original appearance, FTM may be your genealogy software of choice.

EXPLORING YOUR FAMILY TREES

After you've created your online family tree, it's time to explore how Ancestry.com displays each person in your tree. Now that the tree is uploaded, you can choose how you want to view the tree: as a Pedigree chart (viewing one person's direct line; image **D**) or by Family (viewing everyone; image **E**). The buttons to pick the view are located at the top left of your tree. In both views, a leaf icon, which represents a hint, may appear.

If you have a lot of people in your tree, you can navigate by placing your cursor on any blank portion of the tree. The cursor will change to a hand, which you can drag to different portions of the tree by holding down your left mouse button, or move the white square that's displayed in the lower left portion of your screen. At the top of your family tree page, you'll also find a Search box that you can use to quickly navigate to a specific person. If you use the Search box, be sure to look for a woman using the last name associated with her (e.g., her maiden name), otherwise she won't appear in your search results. Also watch out for nicknames.

On the main family tree page, click a person, and a box will pop up with what looks like an index card, as you can see with Ella Nora Snow (image **F**). This is a person's profile. Each profile gives an overview of the person, with salient dates of birth and death (if you know them). You can also view details about the person in several different (and exciting) ways.

Profile

To begin, click Profile or the person's name on the individual's index card, which will then open a new page. At the top of the page you'll have four choices: LifeStory, Facts, Gallery, and Hints. Along the top of the page, you'll also find three menu choices:

Search: This launches an Ancestry.com search for any record pertaining to the individual.

Tools: Access several options, including viewing notes, viewing comments, and merging duplicate information, using this dropdown.

Edit: Here you can save the individual to another tree, edit relationships, or delete the person. If you want to add an event or a new fact to the person, click the +Add icon that's displayed beneath LifeStory.

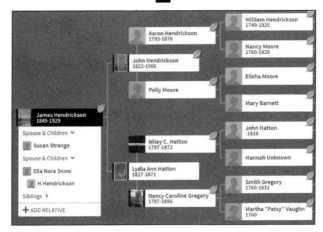

Pedigree view allows you to view more direct-line ancestors at a time, but it excludes other relatives (siblings, aunts, uncles, etc.).

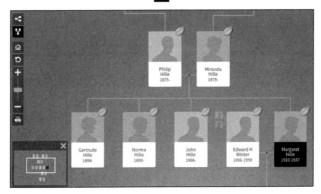

Family View displays your tree more traditionally, allowing you to see whole family groups (including siblings).

An index card shows the profile of a person in a family tree.

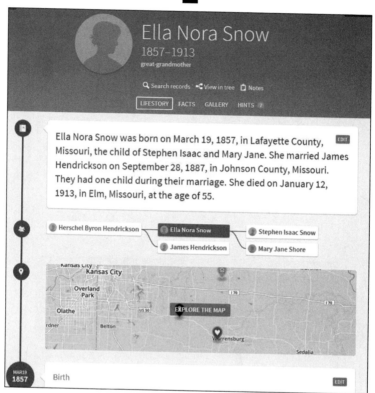

The LifeStory view illustrates the major events of a person's life in historical context.

Navigating Tree Pages Options

Now that you can navigate your way through your tree, I want to show you a menu you may have missed. Next to the name of your tree, you'll see a dropdown arrow. Click it to view several different options:

- **View Tree**: This directs you to your tree.

- **Overview**: Here you can view a summary of the data in your tree, including what content pieces (photos, stories, audio, and videos) have recently been added; the number of people, photos, and records in your tree; and a summary of that tree's hints. You can also invite other family members to view or edit your tree.

- **Media Gallery**: This lists all the media that have been added to your tree. You can filter by type (photos, stories, audio, or video).

- **All Hints**: This provides the record/tree/media suggestions that Ancestry.com has compiled for all the members of that tree.

- **Tree Settings**: Here you can edit your family tree's name or description, as well as export your data, edit privacy settings (i.e., whether your tree is private or public), and invite others to view and/or collaborate on your tree. (Note: Everyone you invite to your tree will be able to at least see it, regardless of whether or not he subscribes to Ancestry.com.)

- **Sharing**: Quickly invite friends or family members to view or edit your family tree. You can find them either by e-mail address or by Ancestry.com username.

LIFESTORY

LifeStory is a visual timeline of your ancestor's life, interspersed with historic events (image **G**). The feature includes an interactive map with pushpin icons to represent all the significant locales in your ancestor's life. Click the map to zoom in and explore. Here, you'll also find historical images that Ancestry.com added to the timeline in order to illustrate an important event that would have happened during this individual's lifetime.

To the right of each event and image, you'll find an Edit button. Click to add an image, show the event on the map, edit any information, or add new information.

FACTS

This page (image **H**) displays your ancestor's vital statistics, family members (spouse and children), and any sources you've gathered. From this page, you can also add people, search for more records, or view any notes you've attached to the individual.

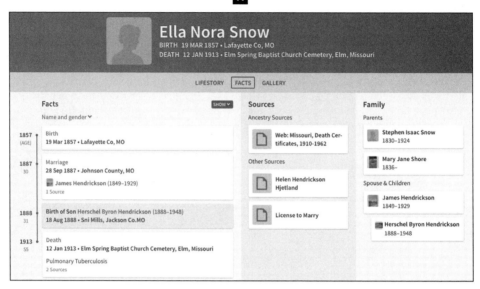

View your ancestor's life details, including sources and other relatives, under the Facts tab.

Ancestry.com's Hints feature displays suggestions for possible connections to your relatives.

As a reminder, if you like keeping your family groups (parents, children) together, you can use your software to automatically create group sheets. Or you can download a form from *Family Tree Magazine* **<www.familytreemagazine.com/freeforms/basicforms>**.

HINTS

The last menu choice is Hints. Click to open a page of hints that Ancestry.com believes are related to your individual (image **1**). The menu along the top of the hints indicates whether the hints are new. If the hints are not new, you can here see if you've reviewed them and are undecided about whether they go with your tree, have ignored them, or have accepted them.

Note you can view hints for all of your ancestors at any time by clicking the leaf in the main toolbar. This list can be sorted by Most Recent, Last Name, or First Name. You can also sort hints by type, such as photos or stories.

Under the name of each person listed in Hints, you'll see his or her relationship to you. Click the link to launch another window showing you exactly how you're related to the individual. This is a valuable tool especially if the person listed isn't someone about whom you're aware.

Additionally, on the right column is a thumbnail sketch of the tree showing the number of individuals and record types, number and types of hints as well as anyone you've invited to view your tree.

Managing Your Trees

To manage settings and information about each tree, click Trees, then Create & Manage trees. This will take you to a page where each of your trees is listed. Click Manage tree. At the top of the page you'll see three options: Tree Info, Privacy Settings, and Sharing.

TREE INFO

This section of the site will give you an overview of the tree, the tree description (good place to add your major surnames), your hint preferences, and the ability to delete your tree from Ancestry.com or export it to your computer.

PRIVACY SETTINGS

Here is where you can select to make your tree Public or Private. Ancestry.com does an excellent job of explaining what each setting does. If you want to optimize your Ancestry.com experience (i.e. maximize your ability to connect with other researchers), make your tree Public. By selecting Private, no one except people you invite can see the details in

Upload Media
Attach media to *Hendrickson*

← Back   The files you upload are visible to everyone. Privacy Settings   CHOOSE FILES

Drag or click here to upload.

Click Gallery, then Add Media to attach photos, audio, or video to a person in your family tree.

your tree. If you're concerned about information regarding living people being public, you don't have to worry. If people in your tree do not have a death date noted (or if Ancestry. com believes they are living), information about them will not be displayed, even if your tree is marked as Public.

SHARING

On this page, you can invite specific people to view your tree. Once someone is invited, you can manage her role on this page. Each invitee is given a role (guest, contributor, editor), each with a specific level of permissions.

- **Guest**: Can view your tree and leave comments
- **Contributor**: Same as guest, but can also add photos and stories
- **Editor**: Same as contributor, but can also add and edit people

SEARCH FAMILY TREES

Instead of waiting for hints to come to you, you can search member family trees on Ancestry.com. To search family trees, go to the Ancestry.com Card Catalog (under the Search tab). Under Filter by Collection, click on Family Trees, and a list of available collections will be shown on the right. For more search tips and information on using the Card Catalog, see chapter 3.

Leaves on the Go:
The Ancestry.com Mobile App

Did you know that Ancestry.com's mobile app also has leaf hints? Download the free mobile app for iPhone, iPad, or Android devices via Ancestry.com's iOS and Android link under the Extras tab. Once installed on your device, log in using your Ancestry.com username and password. You'll see your tree displayed on screen, just as though you'd pulled up the tree on the Ancestry.com website.

Tap any person with a leaf, and a page will open showing a timeline of their life events, their family (parents, spouse, children), and any images or stories in their gallery. Then tap the View Hints icon. A new page will open showing a list of all hints for this individual.

Tap any of the hints in the list to see the facts from the record compared to the facts in your tree. At this point, you can either tap the No, Maybe, or Yes button. Once you've made a choice about the hint, it can be saved to your tree or ignored.

Ancestry.com's Hints are available on mobile devices, and you can select the facts you want to add to your tree just like you can on the desktop site.

HOW TO ADD CONTENT TO YOUR FAMILY TREE

Although you can add records to your family tree via Ancestry.com's leaf icon hint system, you also can add items that make a family tree much more personal, including:

- photos
- videos
- audio
- stories

To add content, click any person's name and click Profile, then Gallery on the following page. From here, click Add Media (in the top right). Simply drag and drop whatever media files you'd like to upload onto the Upload Media page (image **J**), or navigate to where the file is on your computer by clicking in the box.

Next, add detail to your media, including the title of the image, category type (portrait, place, headstone, document), the date and location, and a description. Note: You can only add preexisting files—you can't record new audio within Ancestry.com, for example. Save the information, and (if it's an image) check the box if you want the file to be the primary photo for an individual.

Another option that's a real timesaver is the ability to connect the photograph with another person in your file. If you have a photograph of a cemetery where several ancestors are buried, you can attach the same image to each person.

What type of pictures should you add? Anything of interest relating to the individual. For example, it could be a photo of a favorite teacup, a tombstone, a family portrait, a drawing, a Civil War battle in which they fought, or a Google Earth overview of a cemetery. When adding photos of locations, add the GPS coordinates to the photo description if you know them.

Who doesn't love a great family story? In addition to media files, Ancestry.com provides a way for you to share your family legend and lore with other researchers or family members. You can type your story directly into the system or upload it using any of the following formats: .doc, .docx, .rtf, .pdf, or .txt. Individual story file size cannot exceed 15MB.

ANALYZING, USING, AND CORRECTING HINTS

Leaf icons represent hints. Some are dead ends, but others can lead you to astonishing new finds. Hints are created when Ancestry.com finds a record (official, unofficial, personal, image, photo, story, etc.) that is likely to match someone in your family tree. (Are you beginning to see why it's so important to create a tree? All this automatic matching won't happen without you putting a tree into the system.)

When a hint is found, you'll see a green leaf icon next to the person to which it relates. Hints are created when a potential match is found in:

- other Ancestry.com Member Trees

- records that other people have saved to this person in their tree

- photos that other people have added

- stories that other people have added

When you find a photo or story that matches an individual in your tree, you can easily add it to that person by clicking Save.

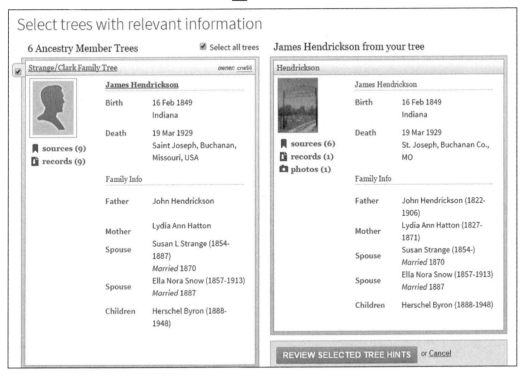

Select trees with relevant information

6 Ancestry Member Trees   ☑ Select all trees   James Hendrickson from your tree

☑ Strange/Clark Family Tree   *owner: cne56*

James Hendrickson

Birth	16 Feb 1849
	Indiana
Death	19 Mar 1929
	Saint Joseph, Buchanan,
	Missouri, USA

🔖 sources (9)
📄 records (9)

Family Info

Father	John Hendrickson
Mother	Lydia Ann Hatton
Spouse	Susan L Strange (1854-1887)
	Married 1870
Spouse	Ella Nora Snow (1857-1913)
	Married 1887
Children	Herschel Byron (1888-1948)

Hendrickson

James Hendrickson

Birth	16 Feb 1849
	Indiana
Death	19 Mar 1929
	St. Joseph, Buchanan Co.,
	MO

🔖 sources (6)
📄 records (1)
📷 photos (1)

Family Info

Father	John Hendrickson (1822-1906)
Mother	Lydia Ann Hatton (1827-1871)
Spouse	Susan Strange (1854-)
	Married 1870
Spouse	Ella Nora Snow (1857-1913)
	Married 1887
Children	Herschel Byron (1888-1948)

REVIEW SELECTED TREE HINTS   or Cancel

Select facts by checking the boxes you want to compare between your tree and a Member Tree match found by Ancestry.com.

How can you best utilize the hints on Ancestry.com? From any person in your tree with a leaf, click the leaf to see a new screen displaying each hint. If the hint relates to a record or a Member Tree, you'll have the option to review or ignore it.

When clicking the leaf icon on James Hendrickson's index card, I had nine hints. One was from Ancestry Family Trees, while the others were from record documents. After clicking the Review button for the Family Trees, a page with six trees was displayed. I selected the box for "Select all trees," then clicked the Review Selected Tree Hints button. Next, I had the option of comparing each to my own facts by checking the box next to the other person's tree (image **K**). I selected the facts I wanted to add to my tree and deselected the rest.

Reviewing hints from records is similar. After reviewing the Member Trees, I worked my way down through the records, beginning with the 1850 US federal census. I was able

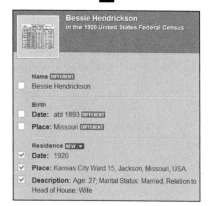

Bessie Hendrickson
in the 1920 United States Federal Census

Name DIFFERENT
☐ Bessie Hendrickson

Birth
☐ **Date:** abt 1893 DIFFERENT
☐ **Place:** Missouri DIFFERENT

Residence NEW ▼
☑ **Date:** 1920
☑ **Place:** Kansas City Ward 15, Jackson, Missouri, USA
☑ **Description:** Age: 27; Marital Status: Married; Relation to Head of House: Wife

This hint shows a new fact that was not in my uploaded family tree.

to compare the facts in the record with the data I have in my ancestor's profile (image **L**). After the review was complete, I saved the record to my own tree. Now anytime someone looks at my tree, they'll see the source for James's date and place of birth.

When reviewing and comparing information on family trees posted by others, look to see if the other user has cited his or her sources. If the facts are not cited, you'll want to use the information cautiously, since it may not be 100-percent accurate. If you think a person in the tree is a match to your ancestors, check the information provided on the tree against data you already know and have records to confirm.

When analyzing matches, you need to evaluate several fields of information. Although your tree may not have the exact date as a comparison tree, keep in mind that it's not unusual to find dates differing by a few months, days, or even years, so the trees still might be a match.

Once you begin comparing your tree against other records, you'll see labels such as New or Different. This is what they mean:

1. If the fact is not in your tree, but in someone else's tree or a record, a New label is displayed. It will be added to your tree unless you deselect the fact's check box.

2. If the fact is already in your tree but with a different value, the Different label is displayed and the fact won't be added unless you click the check box. In some instances, you may not be 100-percent sure which is correct, so you may want to click the check box, then choose to make this fact either Preferred (default) or Alternate.

3. If the fact isn't in your tree, click the edit (pencil) icon and update the fact in your tree.

4. Sometimes there's a name variation (e.g., someone has the name Henderson instead of Hendrickson). In that case, click the arrow and pick which name you want to use.

5. At times, the comparison will include the name of someone who isn't in your tree. Click the Add button to add them to your tree.

After you've edited or added facts, go back to the main Family Tree view, click on the person and you'll see that Ancestry.com has already added the new information to the person's file.

CONNECTING WITH OTHER RESEARCHERS VIA MEMBER CONNECT

Do you remember back in chapter 1 that I mentioned Member Connect? It's one of the modules you can add to your personalized Ancestry.com home page. Member Connect shows recent activity related to your family tree, depending on the filter settings you choose. From your home page, find Recent Member Connect Activity, and click See More. In the right column on the next page, you'll find several Activity Filters that you can toggle on and off.

By using the Member Connect filters, you can see any activity related to your research each time you log in to your account. Click on the Ancestry.com username to see the user's public family trees.

Let me describe an example: Under the Recent Member Connect portion of my home page, I've been alerted to new connections. Two people saved the short article I added about John Snow, and two people saved the photo I added of the Elm Springs Cemetery. When I click the username of each connection, a pop-up box shows the number of public trees each user has uploaded (if any), messages the user has posted, and the option to contact the user. (In general, if another user is downloading your stories and photos, he's doing it either because you share common ancestors or because he thinks—but isn't sure—that your information fits into his family tree.)

But why wait to be notified when new content is added? Why not take the lead and contact the other researcher using Ancestry.com's in-house e-mailing system? Click on the name of the tree owner in your Member Connect list to see a new window that lets you send a message through the system. Once the person answers your message, you'll be alerted via the envelope icon in the upper right corner of any Ancestry.com page. The number next to the envelope icon represents the number of messages waiting for you.

Connecting with other family researchers is a great way to expand your knowledge of your own family through sharing photos, stories, and research. Pretty awesome, huh? For more on collaborating with other Ancestry.com users, see chapter 15.

3

MASTERING SEARCH AND THE CARD CATALOG

W hile chapters 1 and 2 introduced you to genealogy basics and the value of family trees, this is the chapter you've been waiting for—tips for searching the thousands of collections and billions of names on Ancestry.com.

First, I'll go over search basics, from simple to advanced, and then I'll cover ways to improve your search results, including employing collection priorities, filters, wildcards, and the Card Catalog. I'll also provide sample searches, asking you to log in to your Ancestry. com account and follow along with me. Because Ancestry.com is always improving user search results, the images you see here may differ slightly from what you see when you're doing a search, but don't worry—the basic approach is the same.

As you move forward in the book, you'll see how to do focused searches on specific records of interest, such as immigration, military, census, and vital records. Keep in mind that Ancestry.com's search forms won't necessarily look the same across all record types, as the search form fields change depending on the specific collection being searched.

THE BASICS OF SEARCH

It's commonly said that being a good genealogy researcher is akin to being a good detective, gathering clues and making inferences based on them. But more than that, you also have to think critically and creatively. If you approach a search from one direction only, I guarantee you'll miss all of the results possible. That's because genealogy records are not always created in a logical, sequential, or formalized method. For example, while one record may list your ancestor as Anne Jenkins, another record may have written her name as *Mrs. John Jenkins*, *Mrs. J.R. Jenkins*, or even *Anne Presley* [maiden name] *Jenkins*.

Add to that the reality that you'll find as many spellings for a name as there are ways to break it down phonetically, and you could be looking for one person in a half-dozen different ways based on name alone. Additionally, when a US federal census gives a person's age, you have no way of knowing the exact year because this depends on what month a person was born, as well as the month the census was taken.

Consider your ancestor's location, too. Are you looking for your ancestors in the right place? Not only did the boundary lines for states change over time, but it's common for one county (or more) to have been carved out of another county. For example, Richland County, Illinois, was created in 1841 from Clay and Lawrence Counties. Lawrence was created in 1821 from Crawford and Edwards Counties, while Clay was created in 1824 from Crawford, Fayette, and Wayne Counties. I could go on, but you get the point. Your family could have lived on the same piece of property for years, but the name of the governmental entity in which they lived could have changed names two, three, or more times.

This issue of changing boundaries is typical, so be sure when you have placed a family in a specific time frame that you associate it with the correct place during the same time frame. USGenWeb <usgenweb.org> is a great place to look up county-creation dates.

As you can see, being flexible and thinking outside the box is a must when trying to track down a pesky ancestor—on Ancestry.com or any other records website.

THE ANCESTRY.COM SEARCH FORM

When you first log in to Ancestry.com, you'll see the basic search form (image **A**). This form is repeated throughout the site. If you customized your home page, the search form may no longer be at the top of the page.

Notice the calculator next to the Birth Year box. If you click the calculator icon link, a new box will open and help you calculate an estimated birth year. Remember, this is an estimate and is not exact.

If you use the basic search form, you should enter as much information about your ancestor as possible. If you're lucky, you may immediately hit a jackpot. But if you are searching for a common name, even having an approximate birth year can yield thousands of results, most of them are irrelevant. Click Show More Options next to the Search button. This will expand the search form so you can search with more information.

Let's go through each search field and discuss how best to use it in your search. Go ahead and log in to Ancestry.com now and use the search form to do a real search for someone in your family.

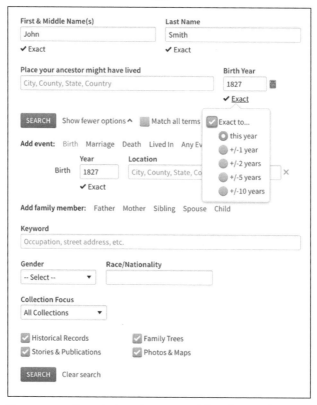

You can access the main Ancestry.com search form from nearly anywhere on the site.

(Note: You can access the search form by clicking the Search tab on the navigation bar at the top of any page, then clicking All Collections.)

Exact Searches and Default Settings

One thing you may notice is the check box option to Match All Terms Exactly (image **B**). Later in this chapter we'll try this setting, but for now, leave it unchecked. Also, as you type in the First and Middle Names, Last Name, and Location boxes, you'll see an option to set the "exactness" of the search. In the case of location, you can specify that results are restricted to the exact place. Under the name boxes, you can restrict to exact matches and phonetic matches, names with similar meanings or spellings, and records where only initials are recorded.

B

Change the Exact settings for a name field to broaden or filter your results.

What are the default settings? According to Ancestry.com, for the First and Middle Names and Last Name boxes, default settings look through all names recorded in its tens of thousands of data collections. The search then pulls out any record where the name is:

- exactly what you typed
- a phonetic match of what you typed
- a similar meaning or spelling as the one you typed
- an initial that matches the name you typed

Ancestry.com also says it may return records that do not match the first name you typed in, but strongly match other criteria. Records are also evaluated against the other criteria you provide, and are ordered based on how well all the elements in that

Records Checklist

When you start doing searches, you'll see how many record types were created during a person's life. I encourage you to make a checklist of potential records for each person you search. As you search Ancestry.com, note your findings. For starters, your checklist may include:

- ☐ home sources
- ☐ vital records
- ☐ church records
- ☐ censuses
- ☐ military records
- ☐ land records
- ☐ tax records
- ☐ probate records
- ☐ immigration records
- ☐ cemetery records
- ☐ newspapers
- ☐ mortuary records

Under each type of record, you can add subsets, as appropriate. For instance, the large category of land records can include:

- ☐ deeds
- ☐ grantee index
- ☐ grantor index
- ☐ homestead applications
- ☐ land grants
- ☐ maps

Whether your search is fruitful or fruitless, be sure to keep good research records, including a research log. Trust me on this one—three months from now you won't be able to remember if you already searched for Great-grandpa Jim in the 1920 census. *Family Tree Magazine* has a number of free forms at <**www.familytreemagazine.com/FreeForms**> that you can use to keep track of your searches.

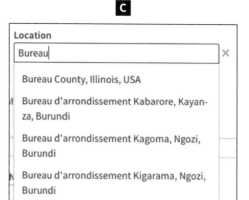

C

Location

Bureau

Bureau County, Illinois, USA

Bureau d'arrondissement Kabarore, Kayan-
za, Burundi

Bureau d'arrondissement Kagoma, Ngozi,
Burundi

Bureau d'arrondissement Kigarama, Ngozi,
Burundi

The Location box under life events will suggest place
names based on what you type in.

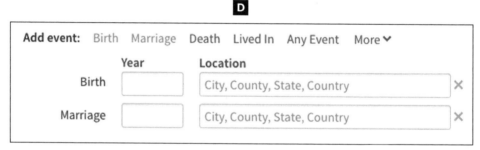

D

Add event: Birth Marriage Death Lived In Any Event More ⌄

	Year	Location	
Birth		City, County, State, Country	✕
Marriage		City, County, State, Country	✕

Ancestry.com allows you to search by additional life events. The More dropdown contains Arrival, Departure,
and Military.

record match your search. If a result matches all criteria save the name, it's worth taking
a closer look at the record.

The default setting for the Location box does not filter results, and ranks record results
based on how well the record matches the information you provided.

Names

Enter your ancestor's first, middle, and last names. Remember when I talked about different
name spellings or that a person may have used initials? The name boxes are a place on

the search form that you may have to come back to and enter the name in different ways. For instance, if your ancestor's name was John Albert Johnson, you may have to type the name as *John Johnson, John Albert Johnson, J. Johnson,* or *J.A. Johnson.* I've also seen instances when a person's middle name was listed on a census as his first name. As you do more searches, you'll become adept at editing your searches to get better results—and being on the lookout for name anomalies.

If you have uploaded a family tree to Ancestry.com, you might have noticed that, as you began typing a name into the search box, Ancestry.com tried to autofill the box with one of the names in your family tree. For example, once I started typing the name Calvin into the First and Middle Names box, Ancestry.com suggested Calvin Manlieus Dimmitt from my uploaded family tree. If the suggested person is the one for whom you're searching, just click the suggestion to autofill the search boxes.

Location

Once you begin typing the location name, the "place picker" will serve up suggested place names to help you choose the correct location. For example, when I typed *bureau* into the Location box, Ancestry.com gave me several locations with the word *bureau* to choose from (image **C**).

The autofill feature is a real time-saver, especially if you know the name of a city but not the county. Feel free to add other event dates and locations by clicking the plus sign (+) or the Add Life Events link. The more places you can add, the better the system can filter down to the best results.

Events

If you've already entered a birth year, the search form automatically adds a birth event to your search, where you can include a place if you know it. To add more life events, pick from the options listed: birth, marriage, death, and lived in (image **D**). You can access more options by clicking the More dropdown: arrival, departure, and military. Select Any Event for a life event that doesn't fall into those categories. Then, enter a year in the Year box and from the Exact to menu, pick "this exact year" or +/- 1, 2, 5, or 10 years. This tells the system the date range to limit your results to. Next, type in a location for the event chosen.

It's important that you add a date, even if it's just an educated guess. Otherwise, your search will result in people having the same name, but living across centuries. Ancestry.com has a search built into its system that will look, not only for the exact parameters you've indicated, but also for results that are "close." For example, if you type in 1800 as a date, Ancestry.com won't limit the results to those just from the year 1800 (unless you specify exact), but it will pull results around the 1800 date.

Family Member

The next section of the form allows you to (optionally) add the name of a family member (parent, spouse, child, sibling). When working with ancestors with common names, you can add the name of another person in the family to help Ancestry.com better filter the results.

Keyword

The Keyword box is another way of filtering for better results. If you know you're seeking a person with Revolutionary War service, enter the keyword *revolutionary war*. Putting quotation marks around keywords (such as *"revolutionary war"*) tells Ancestry.com to search for that exact phrase. (Note that it's not necessary to capitalize words in the search boxes.)

Gender and Race/Nationality

This line gives you the opportunity to select Gender and Nationality. This is a field you can usually leave blank, as it is not as important as other fields in helping to narrow your search.

Collection Focus

The last section of the expanded search form gives you the opportunity to target your search more precisely by narrowing your results to a specific collection: namely, to the records for a particular place. I highly encourage you to use this option if you know where a person lived. For example, if an ancestor lived his entire life in Canada, you can select Canada as the collection focus to view only records that have been specifically identified as Canadian records. Optionally, you can choose All Collections.

If your ancestor lived in multiple places (such as first in the United Kingdom, then Canada, and then the United States), do multiple searches, each with a different collection focus.

Using Wildcards

Wildcards are special characters you can use in search fields (such as name and location) to enhance your searches. You can use either an asterisk (*) or a question mark (?) in Ancestry.com searches, but the first or last character must be an actual letter.

The asterisk replaces multiple characters. The question mark replaces only one character. When you use a wildcard you must have at least three letters plus the wildcard. That means *ou or ?ou won't work, but *oud or ?oud will.

Collection Types

At the bottom of the search form, you'll see four collection types: Historical Records, Stories & Publications, Family Trees, and Photos & Maps. Check the boxes next to the type of records you want searched. If you're just beginning, check all of the boxes to get as many results as possible. But if you know you're looking only for photos, for example, only check the Photos & Maps box.

After you've filled out the expanded search form for your own ancestor, come back here and let's do a search together.

SEARCH FILTERS

Filters can increase or decrease your relevant search results. In a broad sense, any time you add information to a search form, you're telling Ancestry.com to refine the focus of the search; each time you delete a field (like a state name) from a search form, it broadens the search. When you get too many results, add more information in the search form; when you get too few results, decrease the information provided.

Using Sliders

Ancestry.com uses slider filters (image **E**) to broaden or narrow search terms. In addition to adding or removing information from search forms, you can filter results using these sliders. Once you search for an individual and click a record category to search, the search results page will show relevant sliders in the upper left corner for the search information you entered.

To test out this slider feature, I entered only the following search terms in the expanded search form:

- first name: Herschel

- last name: Hendrickson

- location: Missouri

- date of birth: 1888

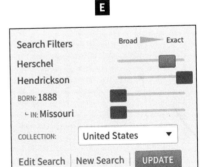

E

Use slide filters (along the left column of the search results page) to limit your search results to more (or less) specific matches for your terms.

Explore by Location

If you scroll to the very bottom of the search page—or go to <search.ancestry.com>—you'll see an Explore by Location section. This section contains a list of the names of the states as well as a clickable map of the United States.

Click on any state to see all of the collections associated with that state, a history of the state, and state research resources. For anyone doing US research, you'll find a bonanza of information. Each option (collections, history, resources) is located on the tabs at the top of each state's page.

Under the Collections tab, you can view a list of record collections. Click on any of the collections to search that specific collection. In this example, I clicked on the "Florida Marriage Collection, 1822–1875 and 1927–2001" collection.

Under the History tab, you can read a brief overview of Florida history, see the famous people associated with the state, and view a list of articles to help you with research in the state. For Florida, these include:

- "Florida Family History Research"

- "Counties of Florida"

- "Research in the Deep South"

- "Why Southern Research Is Different, Part I and Part II"

- "What Do You Know About the 1885 Census?"

As you can see, this can be an incredibly valuable resource.

Under the Resources tab, you can see an overview of how to do research in the state. Here, you'll find information on when the federal census was first taken in the state and the dates the state began collecting vital records, as well as links to local libraries, genealogical societies, and historical societies.

At the bottom of the right column you'll find a box titled More Help. In the example for Florida, this section links to a Florida map (use the scroll on your mouse to zoom in and out), Florida message boards, and a Florida member directory. The links to Understanding Records and Handwriting Help will take you to AncestrySupport.

The search results page gives me the option of either broadening or narrowing the search results by moving the sliders to the left (broadening results) or to the right (narrowing results).

How much do the sliders help in refining results? Leaving all sliders at the Broad mark, we receive more than eighty-six thousand results. By moving all of the sliders (except Missouri) farther right toward the Exact mark, we narrowed that down to just four—all of them my grandfather.

Using sliders, you can quickly filter down to far more relevant results. Remember to employ the slider filters to your searches in all collections on Ancestry.com.

For now, this will give you a little guidance on employing filters in your searches. Later in this chapter you'll learn how Ancestry.com power users employ filters to find the collections with the highest probability of success.

Using Categories

Another way of filtering is to confine results to specific categories (also called collections). Here's how to do that.

Using the expanded search form, search as you usually would. For this example, I searched for my grandfather, Herschel B. Hendrickson, by entering his name, gender, birth date and place, and collection focus. The search engine returned more than ten thousand hits. The results are not very helpful unless the top ten (or so) are matches. But, if you look at the left column next to your search results, you'll see the results divided by category under the slider filters (image **F**).

Most of the categories still show thousands of hits, so find a category that interests you and click on it. In this instance, I clicked Military. Like magic, another list appears—all subsets of the Military category.

Although I still have many, many search results, my hope is that anything remotely matching my grandfather will be among the top findings. When I clicked the subcollection of Draft, Enlistment, and Service, guess what? Grandpa was the very first one listed.

When I clicked the image, I saw a copy of his WWI draft registration card. Pretty neat, don't you think?

Common Search Problems (and Strategies for Overcoming Them)

It's frustrating when you've searched using every possible spelling, date, and place variation and still come up

All Categories	
> Census & Voter Lists	2,306
> Birth, Marriage & Death	3,878
> Military	10
> Immigration & Emigration	487
> Newspapers & Periodicals	4
– Pictures	291
> Stories, Memories & Histories	19
> Directories & Member Lists	5,000+
> Court, Land, Wills & Financial	869
– Family Trees	4,504

You can also limit your results by category and (by clicking on the appropriate arrow) subcategory.

empty-handed. If this is happening to you, your search may be failing for one of four different reasons:

1. **Record errors.** Back in the day (pre-Internet), I remember going to a genealogy library, searching for a book that indexed early Kentucky marriages. The book had two sections: one an alphabetical-by-surname listing of brides, and the other a listing of grooms. Can you guess what I discovered? My bride was listed, but her groom was not. For some reason, his name was missed when the book was being compiled. Or, it's possible his name was missing from a record from which the compilation was created. If something like this happens to you, don't stop if you can't find the name you're looking for; instead, shift your search to someone else in the family.

2. **Transcription errors.** If you've ever looked at a document with pre-twentieth-century handwriting, you'll appreciate the accuracy of the Ancestry.com transcriptionists. Even on today's printed materials, it can sometimes be difficult to discern whether a number is a 3 or an 8, a 7 or a 1. Although transcription errors are fairly uncommon, you will find them as you search. Oftentimes someone else has already caught the error and posted a note through the Ancestry.com system asking for a correction (image **G**). When you find an error, you can do the same.

3. **The record may not exist.** We've all faced this dilemma. No matter how hard we've searched, the truth is that the record we're searching for never existed or that it existed but is now lost. Any number of things could have happened to the record: It could have been destroyed in a courthouse flood or fire, been stolen, or (most likely) been misfiled. My sister and I spent one very hot, dusty afternoon in a storeroom at a Missouri courthouse looking through probate records for our great-great-grandfather. It's a miracle we even found records, given the courthouse's poor filing system. In another instance, a friend of mine was battling with a local courthouse that wanted to destroy old records to make room for newer ones. While your search strategies may be perfect, the record simply may not exist.

4. **The record isn't online.** We like to think that every single genealogy-related record has been transcribed or scanned and is sitting online just waiting to be discovered. Unfortunately, this isn't true. While billions of records have been uploaded to Ancestry.com, with an average of two million more records added daily, one can only imagine the millions that are waiting to be added. In addition to new records, Ancestry.com constantly updates existing collections with even more information. To access newly added or updated records, visit <ancestry.com/cs/recent-collections> (image **H**).

Name:	Schwer Blasius	
	[*Blasius Schwer*]	
	[*Schwer Schwer*]	
Age:	30	
Birth Year:	abt 1830	
Gender:	Male	
Birth Place:	Baden	
Home in 1860:	Worth, Cook, Illinois	
Post Office:	Blue Island	
Family Number:	393	
Value of real estate:	View image	

Household Members:	**Name**	**Age**
	Schwer Blasius	30
	Wilhlne Blasius	27
	Mary Blasius	3
	John Blasius	2
	Margot Blasius	1

VIEW

📄 View blank form
✏ View/Add alternate info
⚠ Report issue

SAVE ⌄   Cancel

H

New and Updated

U.S., Indian Wills, 1910-1921

Beaver County, Pennsylvania, Obituary Records, 1920-1969

(UPDATED) U.S. WWII Draft Cards Young Men, 1940-1947

(UPDATED) 1840 United States Federal Census

(UPDATED) Web: Tennessee, Supreme Court Case Index, 1809-19

California, Voter Registrations, 1900-1968

Unfortunately transcription errors sometimes occur, throwing off your search results. However, you and other Ancestry.com users can catch the error and submit corrections. This record has two transcription corrections (note the two alternate spellings beneath the name field).

Ancestry.com continues to add new records collections to its database and update existing collections. Check the site's list of new and updated collections every so often.

Although genealogy searches can present a variety of challenges, these three can be particularly confounding:

1. searching for an ancestor with a common surname

2. searching for maiden names of female ancestors

3. nicknames

Here are search strategies for all three.

SEARCHING FOR AN ANCESTOR WITH A COMMON SURNAME

If a Smith and/or a Brown lives in your family tree, identify as much about their lives as possible. That way, when you're searching Ancestry.com, you'll have far more information to add to search forms than simply *John Smith*. You can gather information from a variety of sources.

First, go to *Family Tree Magazine*'s free forms page at **<www.familytreemagazine.com/freeforms/basicforms>** and download the Biographical Outline. Use this form (or something like it) to make notes regarding your ancestor's education, military service, marriage(s), children, illnesses, religious milestones, migrations, residences, jobs, family events, land purchases, court appearances, death, and burial.

Fill in as much information on the chart as you can, using family stories, interviews, newspaper articles, local church records, military records—any type of publication or formal record that mentions your ancestor. Armed with a bounty of data, you'll be able to filter down to more relevant results, as well as be in a better position to identify search results that relate to your own family. Think of it this way: While there may be a zillion John Smiths, there won't be a zillion John Smiths who fought in the Civil War and who also had a wife named Rebecca, a son named John, a birthplace of Highland County, Ohio, an 1835 date of birth, and an 1862 date of death.

Next, follow the person via a census trail. Once you locate an ancestor in one census, look for him in earlier and later census records. Verifying the John Smith in Highland County, Ohio, in 1810 is the same one in 1820 will take perseverance, as you'll have to calculate if the number and ages of other people in the household fit into your John's family as it looked ten or twenty years earlier. After 1850, each household member was named. (See chapter 4 for more on census records.)

The problem can get even more frustrating when a family with a common surname also used common first names for their children (e.g., William, John, Martha). In this case, you have to gather as much information as possible about each family member. To do this with as much accuracy as possible, I encourage you to go back to the *Family Tree*

LEARN THE GENEALOGY LINGO

If you're not sure "first cousin once removed" means, read up on all the different cousin designations (second cousin, first cousin once removed, etc.) on FamilyTreeMagazine.com **<www.familytreemagazine.com/premium/now-what-cousin-confusion>**.

I'm Related to Royalty (or Someone Famous)

I've lost track of the number of e-mails I've received saying that family legend has it that the person is related to (fill in the blank). The blank is usually someone like:

- Billy the Kid
- Pocahontas
- Wyatt Earp
- King Richard the Lionheart
- A *Mayflower* passenger
- Abraham Lincoln
- Queen Elizabeth I

Ancestry.com's We're Related app suggests how you're related to famous individuals.

In some instances, these claims may be true. However, some are easily dismissed as some famous people (like George Washington) didn't have any children. In any case, the genealogies of many famous people are actually online, making it fairly easy to see if your branch fits anywhere into the tree. In fact, you can use Ancestry.com's Search form to find most famous people's family trees—they're typically in a user's tree (but may not have sources). Warning: The chances of finding your royal connection in someone's unproven (and unsourced) family tree may be high, so don't run out and get fitted for your crown right away!

For those interested in researching these famous roots, Ancestry.com released a mobile app titled We're Related. To use it, you'll need an Ancestry.com family tree and a Facebook account. Once you log into the app, Ancestry.com tries to find ways in which you could be related to a famous person. Once Ancestry.com finds what it believes is a connection, the famous person appears in your app, along with your relationship to one another and the direct line from which you both descend. For example, We're Related tells me that I'm a fourth cousin, nine times removed of John Adams. Once I tap the connection, I can see that we're both descended from an earlier John Adams (1555–1604), but our lines separate in the preceding generation. Note that this is dependent on the data in your tree (and the app fills in a lot of gaps in your research without much data to back it up), so take the app's suggestions lightly.

Magazine forms and download the Family Group Sheet. Make a sheet for the parents and for each sibling. Once you've completed this, you'll have a good way to make comparisons. Here are two more quick tips:

1. If you're lucky, your common-surname ancestor married someone with a non-common surname (like my Faulkenberry family). If this is the case, start searching for the uncommon name—this can lead to a successful search.

2. If you're unlucky enough to find two people with the same name living in the same town at the same period of time, make a comparison chart between the two. As I've stated before, the more information you can fill in, the more obvious it's going to be which of the two people belong in your tree.

SEARCHING FOR MAIDEN NAMES OF FEMALE ANCESTORS

The female ancestor hunt has always been a challenging one. But thanks, in part, to the variety of records on Ancestry.com, you have a far better chance of tracking down a maiden name than you ever did in the past. Records that can include maiden names are:

1. **Marriage records:** If you can find a marriage record, you'll find a maiden name. This is probably your fastest route to success.

2. **Military pensions:** If a woman filed for a widow's pension, she had to provide proof of the marriage. That means if you find a pension record, you're likely to find a marriage record as well.

3. **Headstones:** It's possible to find a woman's maiden name on a tombstone. In one instance in my own family, not only did the record list my ancestor's maiden name, it also listed the county in Kentucky where she was born.

4. **Censuses:** You'll like this idea. It wasn't atypical for a widow to move in with her parents or siblings, or for a woman and her husband to move in with parents or in-laws. You'll often find these people listed on a census living in the same household, with the relationship clearly noted.

5. **Church documents:** Here, be on the alert for birth records, church memberships, baptisms, and funeral records.

6. **Wills:** Let's say you find a will for your great-great-grandpa, but you don't know anything about several of his children. It's possible you'll find them mentioned in the will, including the names of married daughters. If you find this, then you know the daughters' maiden and married names.

7. **Death certificates:** A death certificate can include the deceased's maiden name as well as the maiden name of her mother.

8. **Naming patterns:** While not really records, these can provide excellent clues. If a child has a surname as a middle name, you can almost always bet this middle name is a surname in either the mother or the father's family. In my family, Robert McClelland Hume's middle name is the maiden name of his mother, Sarah McClelland.

9. **Obituaries:** An obituary may not give the deceased woman's maiden name, but it may name her male siblings, thus giving you the maiden name (unless they were step-siblings).

SEARCHING FOR NICKNAMES

I can almost guarantee that somewhere along the line you're going to find a census record and wonder whether if it's "that one ancestor" with a similar name. While, today, we use nicknames that are simply a shortened form of a name (e.g., Rob, Bob, Tom, Jim), our ancestors were far more creative in the nicknames they used. Here are a few examples:

Male nicknames		Female nicknames	
Full name	Nickname	Full name	Nickname
Adolph	Dolph	Abigail	Nabby
Benjamin	Jamie	Ann	Nanny or Nancy
Elias	Lee	Beatrice	Trixie
Harold	Harry	Elizabeth	Libby
Jacob	Jay	Florence	Flossy
Lawrence	Lonny	Isabel	Nibby
Zachariah	Zeke	Margaret	Madge

Consult these resources for additional help determining possible nicknames:

- USGenWeb: Common Nicknames **<usgenweb.org/research/nicknames.html>**
- Connecticut State Library: Nicknames **<www.ctstatelibrary.org/node/2329>**
- Genealogy Today: Nicknames **<genealogytoday.com/genealogy/enoch/nicknames.html>**

Card Catalog
Searchable listing of all record collections

Title

Keyword(s)

SEARCH   or   Clear All

Filter By Collection

Census & Voter Lists	615
Birth, Marriage & Death	+1000
Military	+1000
Immigration & Travel	514

Results 1-25 of 32,877   Sort By Popularity ▼

Title	Collection	Records	Activity
📄 Public Member Trees	Family Trees	2,147,483,6 47	
📄 1940 United States Federal Census	Census & Voter Lists	134,484,64 8	
📄 U.S. City Directories, 1822-1995	Schools, Directories & Church Histories	1,560,284,7 11	
📄 1930 United States Federal Census	Census & Voter Lists	124,964,07 3	UPDATED
📄 1920 United States Federal Census	Census & Voter Lists	107,684,89 0	
📄 1900 United States Federal Census	Census & Voter Lists	77,277,539	

You can use Ancestry.com's Card Catalog to find specific records collections you would like to search. This image shows the Card Catalog's homepage, which defaults to listing collections by popularity.

THE ANCESTRY.COM CARD CATALOG

Still having problems locating people in your family tree? No need to worry, because Ancestry.com offers a nifty way to delve into those millions of online records via its Card Catalog (image **I**). The link to the Card Catalog is located under the Search tab on Ancestry.com's main toolbar. Click it, and find Card Catalog towards the end of the dropdown menu.

Do you remember the card catalog drawers at the library—the ones where you could look up a single title or find categories of books? The Ancestry.com Card Catalog works the same way. It's a listing of all the collections on the site, searchable by title or theme. With more than twenty billion records currently in more than thirty-two thousand collections, the Card Catalog will help you filter searches in a way that's impossible if you only use the global search.

CLEAR YOUR SEARCHES
Each time you begin a new search, remember to click the Clear All link located by the Title/Keyword search boxes, otherwise the system will remember your filters from the last search and apply them to your new search.

Non-People-Specific Collections

Did you know that Ancestry.com has collections that don't have a search box for "name"? In fact, you may be wondering why you'd want to search a collection that wasn't specific to an ancestor. Don't worry—there's a method to my madness.

Some of the collection types aren't indexed by a person's name. These include maps, atlases, ships (under immigration), or historical postcards (under pictures). However, that doesn't mean they don't have great value to you, especially when it comes to learning more about the places and times in which your ancestors lived.

Later in this chapter, I'll search the Card Catalog for collections related to railroads. In it, I found a business directory along the A, T, and SF routes that listed places in Missouri, including my hometown of St. Joseph. Although I didn't have family living in town in 1889, they were in the nearby countryside. Skimming through the businesses gave me quite a sense of what my family would have seen when they went to town. This was kind of like taking a stroll back in time.

Because the businesses in this directory have business names and addresses, I can actually use Google Maps <maps.google.com> or Google Earth <earth.google.com> to "fly over" and see if any still exist. The biggest surprise to me? The fact that so many services no longer exist today—at least not in a large city, including:

- horseshoer
- confectioner
- boot maker
- blacksmith
- cornice maker
- piano maker
- fish market (although we do have one here in San Diego!)

Even more surprising was the number of saloons! I guess they were the Starbucks of the 1880s.

The postcard collection is another of the not-to-be-missed collections of "non-people." Search by location and also by keyword. In my case, I searched for *Missouri* with keyword *St. Joseph* and found several old postcards, including a great linen one of the Pony Express Motel where my dad installed a new heating system sometime in the 1940s or early 1950s.

When you do a global search, Ancestry.com will comb through all of its records trying to find relevant matches—many of which may have no connection to your family. If I do a global search for *John Hendrickson*, born in Indiana, I get more than seventy-one thousand hits. However, using the Card Catalog, I can find collections that are specific to my search. For example, I may only want to search a collection of Indiana birth records or Indiana marriages. This kind of search is doable using the Card Catalog and its filters.

Something to keep in mind, though, is the Card Catalog search is a search for a *collection—not for an individual*. Once you find the collection relevant to your search, click on the name of the collection and, from that point, you can do an ancestor search. Later in this chapter, I'll walk you through the process.

What if you've delayed getting an Ancestry.com subscription because you're not sure it has the records you want? Use the Card Catalog (available to nonsubscribers) to check out all the collections of interest—both for your US and international research.

The catalog contains a listing of all collections on Ancestry.com. The catalog has two main columns: The right column lists the names of collections, while the left column has title and keyword search boxes, as well as several filters.

The default view in the right column is a list of collections sorted by popularity. As you can see, "Public Member Trees" is the most popular, while the "1940 United States Federal Census" is second, followed by "U.S. City Directories, 1826–1995." Note the Records column displays the number of records in the collection, and the Activity column indicates if a collection has been updated recently.

You can change the default view by clicking the down arrow next to Sort By and selecting to sort by Database Title, Date Updated, Date Added, or Record Count (the latter of which you will probably never use).

Once you've found the collection(s) you want to search, click your mouse on the collection. Now, go ahead and search it just as you would when using the global search. Note, too, that each collection will have unique search boxes. For example, while I could search the Civil War draft registration records by name only, I also had the option to add to my search parameters, marital status, and congressional district—options you may not see in other collection search forms.

Be a creative investigator when selecting collections, and don't forget to read the description before you decide that it's not one you want to search. For example, there's a collection in this category (subset Africa) titled "Slave Registers of Former British Colonial Dependencies, 1812–1834." While you may think this collection (with more than two million records) relates only to Africa, if you read the description, located below the search form, you'll find that many of the records are from the Caribbean. Following the outlawing of the slave trade from Africa to the British colonies, registers were done of so-called "legal slaves," who had been traded prior to the Abolition of the Slave Trade Act (1807).

Card Catalog Search Boxes

In the left column on the main catalog page, you'll find two search boxes: One is for searching for a collection by title, and the other by keyword(s). If you want to see all

Results 1-25 of 212		Sort By Popularity ▼		
Title		Collection	Records	Activity
🗋 Texas, Death Certificates, 1903-1982		Birth, Marriage & Death	4,814,88	
🗋 Texas Birth Index, 1903-1997				
🗋 Texas, Marriage Index, 1814-1909 and 1966-2011				
🗋 Texas Death Index, 1903-2000				
🗋 Texas, Birth Certificates, 1903-1932		Birth, Marriage & Death	2,285,12 3	

Texas, Marriage Index, 1814-1909 and 1966-2011

Published on Ancestry   5/31/2005

Updated   7/25/2013

This database is a collection of marriage indexes from the State of Texas, USA, covering the years 1814-1909 and 1966-2011.

Hover over a collection to view details about it, such as a brief description and the dates it was published and updated.

collections specific to one location, you can get a fairly comprehensive list by typing the name of the place in the Title box.

If you hover your mouse over any title in the results, a pop-up box will give a brief description of the collection, including when it was originally published on Ancestry.com and when it was last updated (image **J**).

If you're unsure of what name Ancestry.com may have given a collection, use the Keywords search box (image **K**). For example, one of the people in my family line worked for the railroad, and I wanted to see what kind of railroad-related collections might be on Ancestry.com. When I entered *railroad* in the Keyword box, the search resulted in sixty-five collections, including employment records and a business directory of principal towns along the Atchison, Topeka (A and T routes) and Santa Fe, Mexico (SF route), in 1889.

Use the keyword box to search for collections when you are unsure of the collection's name.

Card Catalog Filters

Ancestry.com's Card Catalog has four sets of filters in the left column: collection, location, date, and languages. You can use one or many filters in combination to narrow your collection search. Let's explore each.

Overview of the Card Catalog Categories

Ancestry.com has a handful of main collections categories, along with several subsets of each. Here's an overview of the types of collections you can expect to find in each category, with the exception of Family Trees (which we covered in chapter 2).

Census and Voter Lists (chapter 4): As you might expect, this collection includes censuses from the United States (both federal and state), the United Kingdom (listed under Europe), and Canada. You'll also find collections relative to Australia, Europe, Mexico, Africa, Asia, South America, and Oceania.

Birth, Marriage, and Death (chapter 5): Vital records are favorites among genealogists because one record can hold many clues. A marriage record, for example, can contain the name of the bride's father, the county where the marriage took place, and the name of the minister and witnesses.

Military (chapter 6): The Military collection has several subsets, running the gamut from enlistment and pension collections to photos and histories.

Immigration and Travel (chapter 7): Along with passenger lists, bordercrossings, and passports, you'll also find collections of ships' pictures, and citizenship and naturalization records.

Newspapers and Publications (chapter 8): Here you'll find newspapers, magazines, and obituaries from the United States, Canada, United Kingdom, Ireland, Australia, Oceania, and New Zealand.

Pictures (chapter 9): Although the number of picture collections is relatively small, the number of photos within them is not! The "U.S. School Yearbooks" collection alone contains more than 372 million records.

Stories, Memories, and Histories (chapter 9): Knowing that Great-great-grandpa Steve Snow migrated from North Carolina to Missouri is one thing, but finding a story about his beekeeping is quite another. This category is among my favorites, primarily because it contains so many county histories that captured the early history of a county in stories, biographies, maps, and statistics.

Maps, Atlases, and Gazetteers (chapter 8): In case you're wondering about the difference in these three: A map is simply an illustrated to-scale visualization of a place; an atlas is a collection of maps; and a gazetteer contains geographical and statistical information about an area.

Schools, Directories, and Church Histories (chapter 10): If you've never used a city directory, you're in for a treat. A city directory is an alphabetical list of people in the area along with their address and occupation. A telephone directory is like today's Yellow Pages, including name, address, and phone number. Note, too, that the City Directory contains professional status (e.g., student or traveling salesman).

Wills, Probates, Land, Tax & Criminal (chapter 11): While genealogists rely on researching census, birth, death, and marriage records, legal documents are probably among the least explored. Too bad, as they can contain a wealth of information about the family, such as who was left out of a will.

Reference, Dictionaries, and Almanacs (chapter 8): This group of collections is like having the best genealogy reference library on your own computer. Dictionaries & Encyclopedias is a catchall subcategory with materials ranging from geography to English and Welsh surnames to early settlers of Maryland. Again, this is a category that you'll want to filter by keyword.

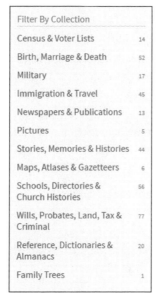

Filter By Collection	
Census & Voter Lists	14
Birth, Marriage & Death	52
Military	17
Immigration & Travel	45
Newspapers & Publications	13
Pictures	5
Stories, Memories & Histories	44
Maps, Atlases & Gazetteers	6
Schools, Directories & Church Histories	56
Wills, Probates, Land, Tax & Criminal	77
Reference, Dictionaries & Almanacs	20
Family Trees	1

Title

Keyword(s)

civil war

SEARCH or Clear All

Filter Titles

✖ Military

✖ USA

✖ Illinois

✖ 1860s

✖ Draft, Enlistment and Service

Filter by category to sift through the various categories of records collections.

You can use a combination of keywords and filters to search for records collections.

FILTER BY COLLECTION

Ancestry.com organizes its collection into subject categories. Earlier, you learned how to filter a global search by record category. You can do the same thing in the Card Catalog. This filter allows you to find collections that fall into specific record types (image **L**). The number by each type of category represents the number of collections within that category, not the number of records. Because so many categories have more than one thousand collections, you'll probably want to use the filter in combination with one of the other filters (image **M**).

FILTER BY LOCATION

The location filter has ten main geographic areas; once chosen, some of the areas have several subset filters (i.e., if you choose USA as a filter, you'll have the option of filtering further by state). Europe has several subsets, including the United Kingdom, which alone contains more than one thousand collections. Be sure to click each of the major location filters, as some areas are included as subsets in places you may not expect (e.g., you'll find the Federated States of Micronesia as a subset of the USA, but Micronesia as part of Oceania).

FILTER BY DATE

You can filter either by a century (1600s to 1900s) or per decade within each century (e.g., 1910). If you are fairly certain of the decade in which a record will fall, this filter will be a huge help to focus in on relevant records.

FILTER BY LANGUAGE

Ancestry.com has collections in English, French, Spanish, German, Italian, and Swedish. If you're only doing US research, you probably won't need to use this filter. But once you get into international records, it's one you may want to employ.

Once you've filtered your search by collection type (e.g., Military) and then by location and date, you'll be close to finding a collection that will return a few dozen, rather than a half-million, hits.

I was interested in finding Civil War records for a pesky ancestor. First, I searched for keyword *Civil War*; that returned 532 collections. Next, I used the filters to choose Military as category and USA as location. Why did I filter by location? Because I didn't want British or Canadian records appearing in the search results. Those filters took me down to four hundred collections.

I knew (via family story) that my ancestor was in an Illinois regiment. Under USA, I selected the Illinois subset. This narrowed my search to ninety-eight collections. Still too many to easily go through. Lastly, I filtered by date (1860s), as I knew the Civil War was from 1861 to 1865. I still had ninety-five collections in the results. What to do?

I went back up to the Military filter and choose the subset: Draft, Enlistment, and Service records. As you can see, Military has several other subsets (as do most collection types). Finally, with this last filter, I narrowed the collections down to fifteen—a number I could easily search.

Sample Card Catalog Search

Let's search the entire Ancestry.com Card Catalog for any collections that might have information on Mercer County, Kentucky—the birthplace of both my third and fourth great-grandfathers. To filter the collection results, I entered Kentucky in the Title box and Mercer in the Keyword box. The search returned four hits. Two of the collections had marriages; one had deeds; and one had tax, criminal, and land records.

Next, I searched for family information in all four collections. One of the marriage collections had six Hendrickson records, all of them members of my family. These, I saved for later research. I was hoping to find a Hendrickson as a witness in a deed book—but no luck. Although I struck out when it came to stories here, I did pick up information on several marriages to track down.

When you view a record image on Ancestry.com, you have several options for saving or enhancing it.

WHAT TO DO WHEN YOU'VE FOUND A RECORD

When you find the record you're searching for, you have several options for what to do next: view, save, or correct.

Viewing Records

Many items you find will have images of the original records. Ancestry.com has Viewer Tools that are available when examining any original record. Once you've found a record, click View Image; this will open a new page (image **N**). In the case of a census record, one of the first things you'll notice is the family unit is highlighted in green, while the individual you were searching for is highlighted in yellow.

On the far side of your screen is a slide-out window with three tabs: Detail, Related, Source. Detail is a summary of the actual record, Related is a list of suggested records that probably relate to the individual. Source is an actual source citation. If you use a genealogy software program, copy the source citation into your software. This ensures that several months or years hence, you'll know exactly where the record was located.

Next to the slide-out window is a vertical line of controls. From top to bottom:

- full screen (this allows the record to fill your entire screen)
- right-pointing arrow (closes the slide-out window)

- tools (looks like a crossed hammer and wrench)
- zoom in and out

Now let's look at each of the tools. Click the tool icon to open a pop-up window. Your options are:

- print
- download
- share
- rotate left
- rotate right
- flip horizontally
- flip vertically
- invert colors
- settings
- help & tips, feedback
- report problems

One of the most useful tools in this group is the invert colors tool. If you're working with an image that's difficult to read, you can often get a better view by inverting it from black on white to white on black. The unfortunate reality, though, is that some images are just too faint or too damaged to see clearly.

You'll notice that Share and Settings have downward pointing arrows; this indicates another menu under each of these two items. Click the downward arrow on Share, and you'll see that you can share the image via e-mail, Facebook **<www.facebook.com>**, Google+ **<plus.google.com>**, and Twitter **<www.twitter.com>**.

The additional menu items under Settings are on/off toggles that allow you to customize how you want records displayed.

Saving Records

On the top right of your screen, you'll see a green Save button. Click this to save the record to someone in your family tree or to your computer. When you click Save Record to Someone in My Tree, a new box will appear, asking which family member (or new person, if not already in your tree) to save this to. As you begin typing the name of the person to whom the record is attached, the Ancestry.com system will automatically show you the people in your tree with that name. Select the correct person to attach the record.

Correcting a Record

I guarantee, as you work your way through various genealogy records, you'll find errors. In census records, for example, those errors may have been made by the enumerator, the transcriptionist, or your ancestor.

Spelling is one of the most common errors you'll encounter. In some instances, though, misspellings aren't really errors—just your ancestor using creative spelling. People living in the nineteenth century didn't give as much weight to correct spelling as we do today. In fact, President Andrew Jackson said, "It is a damn poor mind indeed which can't think of at least two ways to spell any word." And journalist H.L. Mencken noted that, "Correct spelling, indeed, is one of the arts that are far more esteemed by school ma'ams than by practical men." With that prevailing attitude, it's no wonder that surname spellings are so harum-scarum.

One example I have found of a transcriptionist error is the one in the 1850 New York census for the family of Daniel Hendrickson. The enumerator spelled the name correctly, but the transcriptionist wrote it as *Hendickson*. A pencil icon will appear next to an error previously caught and corrected by someone.

How do you correct a record? Once the person's record is displayed, in the left column, you'll see a pencil icon that says Add Alternate Information. Click the icon and a pop-up box will give you the option to add or correct the information.

PART 2

DIGGING INTO RECORDS ON
ANCESTRY.COM

4

MAKING THE MOST OF CENSUS RECORDS AND VOTER LISTS

W hether you've been chasing ancestors for a week or a lifetime, census records were probably the first genealogy tool you learned to use. Censuses are valuable because they place a person in a specific place during a specific period of time. Once you know when and where a person lived you can begin to delve into birth, marriage, death, land, and other legal records.

In this chapter, you'll learn where and how to search US federal and state censuses, as well as censuses in the United Kingdom and Canada.

WHAT CAN A CENSUS TELL YOU?

A census record can tell you much more about your family members than their names, ages, and where they were born. In a single page of a 1900 US federal census in Chicago, for example, I found the birthplace of the individuals listed, and it showed exactly why America was called a melting pot. The countries of origin of the people living on the block were:

- Canada

- France

- Germany

- Ireland

- Italy

- Russia

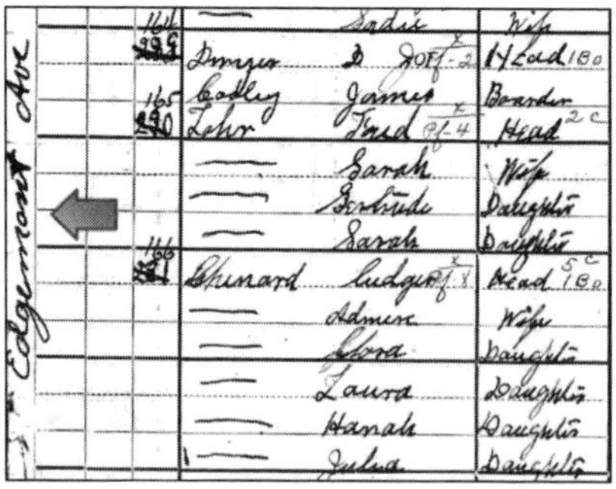

Look for a street address along the left side of a federal census record.

And, in that same block, professions included:

- carpet cutter
- dressmaker
- horseshoer
- laborer
- office boy
- painter
- teamster
- typesetter

This information alone tells you that the family lived in a neighborhood of immigrant blue-collar workers. Next, use Google Earth <earth.google.com> or Google Maps <maps .google.com> to type in the address (found along the left side of the census image; image).

If your ancestor lived in a city in the early part of the twentieth century, there's a good chance his house has been replaced by a business building. Why? Because early settlers would have lived in what is today a downtown area, and homes have likely been razed for commercial buildings.

For more details on using Google Earth with the David Rumsey Historical Map <www.davidrumsey.com> overlays to view old city maps, see chapter 8 in my e-book *Discover Your Family History Online* <www.familytreemagazine.com/store/ discover-your-family-history-online-ebook-w5974>.

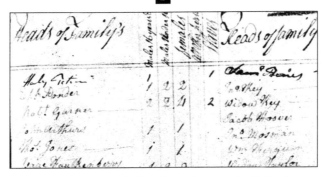

Some federal census records, like this one from 1790 South Carolina, can be hard to read.

SEARCHING CENSUS RECORDS

In chapter 3, you learned how to access specific collections, as well as search through broad record categories. You can use that knowledge to search census records via:

- category
- card catalog
- collection
- location

Searching by Broad Category

From the Search dropdown menu, choose Census and Voter Lists. You can now use either this search screen or filter your search by specific categories (US federal, UK census, Canadian census, or century) using options in the right column.

Also in the right column, Ancestry.com gives you links to what the system thinks might be helpful when searching for ancestors in census records. Find these links under More Help in the bottom of the right column.

If you're not sure when an ancestor lived in a particular state, use this broad search screen to see if any of the results contain information that will help narrow your search.

SPELLING VARIATIONS

If you have difficulty locating your ancestor, try several spelling variations. It's possible that your ancestor spelled his name for the censustaker differently than you spell it today or that the enumerator spelled the name phonetically. It's also possible the enumerator misheard the name, or that whomever transcribed the census misread the handwritten information. If you've seen some of the original census images, you'll understand how easy

This 1920 federal census record from Missouri misreports my ancestors' surname as "Deering."

it would be to make this mistake. Throw on top of that how difficult it is to read some of the census images—like image **B** from the 1790 South Carolina census—and you'll appreciate that the transcription errors are so few!

The bottom line: Be creative in how you spell surnames. In both the 1790 and 1800 South Carolina censuses, you'll find my ancestral surname listed as Faulkenberry, Falkenbury, Faulkinbury, Falconbury, Faulkenburgh, and Faulkenbery. If you find an error, you can correct it (see chapter 3).

WILDCARDS

If trying various spellings still returns too many hits, you can use wildcards in your search by including an asterisk (*) or a question mark (?). If you want to search for names that differ by only one letter, use the question mark wildcard. A search for *Hendricks?n* returns both Hendrickson and Hendricksen. Use an asterisk for zero to five unknown characters. *Hendri*on* returns Hendrickson, Hendrixson, and Hendrixon, as well as other variations. Names must contain at least three non-wildcard characters, and either the first or last letter can be a wildcard (but not both). That means *hen** is okay but **end** isn't.

MISREPORTED INFORMATION

Another place you might find errors is in the place of birth or via a misinterpreted relationship. Both could have been due to forgetfulness or erroneous information given by a family member who wasn't sure about the answer. In the 1920 Missouri census, my grandmother, Nora Roselan Dearing, is listed as Deering—not a problem as it's a common mistake (image **C**). However, the familial relationships listed here are a bit misleading. You might assume Nora is Ola's daughter, but she's actually her stepdaughter. Unfortunately, unless you knew the family you wouldn't realize that Ola was not Jacob's first wife. Don't make assumptions about relationships.

If you can't find an ancestor in a census, use Ancestry.com's Card Catalog or list of census years to directly access the census by year in which your ancestor is missing.

Additional Census Search Tips

Sometimes it will take more than one search attempt to find the ancestors you're looking for in a census. In addition to spelling variations, try these strategies to find your elusive family members:

- **Fill in as many Ancestry.com search boxes as you can**. Available boxes will vary from year to year. For example, the difference in search box options for the 1790 US census and 1860 US census is like night and day.

- **Don't specify "exact" in your search.** Even if you know the exact name, place, and more, don't check the Exact box. As you saw earlier, errors can be made by enumerators, transcriptionists, and respondents, so the information recorded in the census may not exactly match what you know about your ancestor.

- **Try searching by first name only.** Use this strategy if you can't find someone by surname. I found an ancestor by filling in his first name, his state, and the first names of his parents.

- **Use name initials.** It's possible that a census used initials or a middle name instead of a first name. In the 1900 Missouri census (image **D**), my grandfather, Herschel Byron Hendrickson, is listed on the census as H. Byron, although, according to my aunt (his daughter), he never went by the name Byron. A mystery.

- **Track your searches.** You'll find blank research forms at <ancestry.com/download/charts#ancchart> (image **E**). What you can't find one day may be

D

Your ancestors (like my grandfather, Herschel Byron/"H. Byron" Hendrickson) may have gone by his initials or middle name, rather than his full name, in the census.

E

Track your census searches using Ancestry.com's research forms.

something you can find on another day. You never know exactly when a new collection will appear, when a collection will be updated, or when you'll learn something new that will make a census search successful.

- **Keep track of the neighbors.** It's amazing, once you get into genealogy, how often a neighbor will show up as a witness on a will, in a land deed, or as the future husband of someone in your family. When you save census information, be sure to save a page ahead and a page behind your own family's records. The neighbors' names may mean nothing today and everything tomorrow.

US FEDERAL CENSUS RECORDS

Beginning in 1790 and continuing to the present, the United States has taken a population census every ten years. Early census records (1790–1840) contain only the name of the head of household along with information about the number of other people living in the home, grouped by ages (e.g., three free white males between the ages of ten to fifteen, and one free white female age forty-five or older).

Beginning in 1850 (the Golden Year for genealogists!), the censustaker (enumerator) noted the names of every person living in the home. Additional information gathered from 1850 onward varied, but could include ages, race, relationship to head-of-household, ability to read and write, employment, value of property, whether a renter or a homeowner, birthplace, and parents' birthplaces. Download blank census forms to see what questions were asked in each census year at <www.ancestry.com/download/charts#ancchart>.

Ancestry.com's US federal census holdings include transcriptions of all available records from 1790 to 1940. Due to privacy concerns, census information cannot be released for seventy-two years from the date of the census; this means the 1950 census won't be available until the year 2022. Included in the US federal census holdings are:

- Population Schedules, 1790–1940 (including the fragments of the 1890 census, the majority of which was destroyed in 1921)
- Veterans Schedule of 1890
- Mortality Schedule, 1850–1880
- Indian Census Rolls, 1885–1940
- Selected Non-Population Census Schedules, 1850–1880
- Slave Schedules

Consider current and life events. If you can't find your family on a census when you're sure they should be in a specific place, check to see if something untoward was happening at the time of the census. Who knows if disease, financial hardship, war, or a death or marriage in the family forced your ancestors to temporarily or permanently leave a place.

Special US Censuses

To view all census collections, go to the Card Catalog and type census into the Title box. There, you'll find close to five hundred census-related collections, with more than three hundred of them for the United States.

Let's look at some of the most popular special US censuses.

MORTALITY SCHEDULES

From 1850 to 1880, individuals who died in the previous year were counted on a special census. These census reports show cause and month of death, birthplace, profession, race, and martial status. This collection also includes mortality schedules from Colorado, Florida, and Nebraska, which were conducted in 1885.

If you find an ancestor on a mortality schedule, skim down the list to see the causes of the other people's deaths. It's possible, by doing this, that you may find an ancestor who died during an epidemic. Or you may discover a lot about the nature of where your ancestor lived! Take the 1850 Calaveras County, California, mortality schedule from the Gold Rush era as an example. Causes of death were:

- shot accidental
- burnt by Indians
- murdered
- stabbed
- delirium tremons [sic]
- shot
- dysentery
- murdered by Indians
- fever

Compare this in the same time period to more-populated Sacramento County, and you'll find the majority of the citywide deaths were due to cholera.

Back to Calaveras County. Something fascinating was the place of birth of the miners. A glance down this list will show you that the whole world, indeed, poured into California in hopes of getting rich on gold. Birthplaces included:

Name:	Red Woman
Date of Birth:	abt 1792
Age:	95
Gender:	Female
Tribe:	Oglala Sioux (Sioux)
Agency:	Pine Ridge
State:	Dakota Territory
Last Census Number:	4647
Census Date:	1887
Neighbors:	View others on page

✏ Add alternate information
⚠ Report issue

SAVE ⌄   Cancel

US Indian census rolls search results show tribe, agency, and state.

G

4651	American Horse	Father	m	48
4652	Sleep	Wife	f	42
4653	Charles	Son	m	5

US Indian census rolls also include age and relationship to the head-of-household.

- Indiana
- Kentucky
- Mississippi
- New York
- Ohio
- Tennessee
- Chile
- France
- Germany
- Ireland
- Mexico
- Peru
- Scotland

1890 VETERANS SCHEDULES

This record collection documents Civil War veterans and their widows. Given the destruction of the 1890 general census, this index can help fill in the gap, providing key information for certain individuals. Learn about the 1890 Veterans Schedule in chapter 6.

Collection Highlight: Dawes Commission Records

If you have Native American ancestry, the Dawes Commission collections on Ancestry.com may aid your research.

In 1887, Congress passed an appropriations bill (called the Dawes Act) that ceded tribal title of Indian lands to the United States. The lands were then divided and given to individual members of the Five Civilized Tribes: Cherokee, Creek, Choctaw, Chickasaw, and Seminole. Tribal members were required to apply for official enrollment to receive a share of common property. The Dawes Commission allowed individuals to claim membership in only one of the tribes, even though several tribal members had ancestry that reached back into more than one tribe.

The records that resulted are known as the Dawes Rolls. Ancestry.com has three collections related to these records, including the "U.S. Native American Enrollment Cards for the Five Civilized Tribes, 1898–1914." This Dawes Commission collection contains more than one hundred thousand names of applicants.

Other collections such as the "Dawes Commission Index, 1898–1914" include indexes for documents such as birth, death, and marriage records. Search the index to discover the name of the applicant, gender, and "blood degree" (such as one-eighth Cherokee).

1930 CENSUS OF MERCHANT SEAMEN

As one of the more interesting censuses, this one was taken in April of 1930 (October of 1929 in Alaska) and included merchant seamen serving on US flag merchant vessels. The census included everyone aboard ship except officers who had permanent housing ashore.

The information gathered is extensive. Besides the typical name, race, age, and birthplace, the census included name of ship, home port, address of wife or next of kin, whether the seaman was a veteran, marital status, whether he could read and write or speak English, and whether naturalized or alien.

US INDIAN CENSUS ROLLS

If you think you have Native American ancestry, start your search at the collection "U.S., Indian Census Rolls, 1885–1940." These special censuses include a wealth of genealogical information, including the name of the tribe, name, age, birth date, reservation, census date, and relationship to head-of-household.

Information about the tribe, agency, and state are noted in the search results (image **F**), while the image of the census roll itself contains the name, age, and relationship to head-of-household (image **G**).

The more information you have about the person, the better, because many people have similar names. For example, type the name *Horse* or *Bear* into the search form as either

Browse this collection

To browse this image set, select from the options below.

State

California ▼

Schedule Type

Agriculture ▼

Year

1850 ▼

County

Calaveras ▼

Locality

Calaveras District

Comfort

Not Stated

Use the Browse This Collection function to select the non-population schedule of interest.

I

NAME OF OWNER, AGENT, OR MANAGER OF THE FARM.						
Allen Johnson	120	70	4,000	30	2	
William Primm	200	60	6,050	100	14	
J. M. Terry	80		1,200	10	2	
George H. Doom	60		1,200	30	3	
Elisha Primm	220	75	7,500	350	13	1

Agricultural schedules provide valuable details about your ancestor's farm and belongings.

a first or surname, and you'll probably be surprised at the number of results!

(Note: If you have the Ancestry.com All Access membership, you can access additional Native American records at Fold3 <www.fold3.com>.)

NON-POPULATION SCHEDULES:

These records from 1850 to 1880 provide agriculture, industry, and social statistics. In particular, explore the "Selected U.S. Federal Census Non-Population Schedules, 1850–1880" collection to find information about agriculture, industry, and manufacturing for twenty-one US states. You can find the collection by searching the Card Catalog by Title.

Once on the collection's page, use the Browse This Collection function (right side of the screen) to select the state, schedule type, year, and county (image **H**).

The agricultural schedule (image **I**), for example, lists the person's name along with columns for number of acres, number of livestock (which is broken down further by type, such as horse, sheep, and cattle), and types and amount of produce. The amount of detailed information about the person's holdings is amazing, ranging from bushels of peas and beans to the value of orchard products.

If your ancestor happened to own a business, check the Industry schedules. These schedules detail the value of the business, the number and wages of employees, months in operation, and the nature of the business.

The amount of information varies per schedule year. If you find your ancestor in one year, be sure to search the years previous and following.

US STATE AND COUNTY CENSUS RECORDS

While the federal government conducted censuses every ten years, several states conducted their own statewide censuses more frequently. Some, but not all, of these state censuses are available on Ancestry.com, including:

- Alabama State Censuses (1820–1866)
- California Spanish Mission Censuses (1796–1798)
- Colorado State Census (1885)
- Florida State Censuses (1867–1945)
- Illinois State Censuses (1825–1865)
- Iowa State Censuses (1836–1925)
- Kansas State Censuses (1855–1925)
- Minnesota State Censuses (1849–1905)
- Mississippi State and Territorial Censuses (1792–1866)
- Missouri State Censuses (1844–1881)
- Nebraska State Census (various years and county coverage)
- New Jersey State Census (1895)
- New York State Censuses (1880–1905, partial coverage)
- North Dakota State Censuses (1915–1925)
- Oklahoma Territorial Census (1890 and 1907)
- South Dakota Territorial Census (1885)
- South Dakota State Census (1895)
- Washington State Censuses (1857–1892)
- Wisconsin State Censuses (1895–1905)

Information varies by state and year. For example, if you're looking for family in the 1935 Florida state census, you'll find their address, ages, highest levels of education achieved, birthplaces, and occupations. By comparison, questions on the 1885 South Dakota census are similar to a federal census, with data for parents' birthplaces, whether the person has an illness or disability, and if he was blind or "insane." You'll also find plenty of clues about where

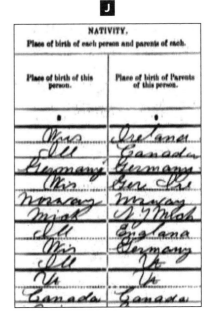

State censuses can give you information about your ancestors and their parents in years not covered by federal censuses.

Enumeration District Maps

Many genealogists rank censuses among the most useful records. But in addition to census returns, researchers can access another great resource from the census-taking process: enumeration district maps.

What are enumeration districts? Since 1880, the US Census Bureau has divided states into numbered enumeration districts (EDs) to organize enumerators' efforts. Each ED was sized such that one censustaker (enumerator) could count the population there in a day. You can find ED numbers for your ancestor's hometown using the Unified Census ED Finder tool <stevemorse.org/census/unified.html>.

The Census Bureau created ED maps that display the boundaries and numbers of each ED. On many ED maps, ED numbers are larger and lighter than the other type on the page. ED boundaries are usually along city ward boundaries, roads, or railroad tracks.

ED maps are valuable companions in census research, providing a visual representation of how enumerators conducted their research. They're also useful for genealogists, particularly when you compare them to contemporary street maps to see where your ancestor's neighborhood was and where he lived in relation to another family. Some maps also label local landmarks such as churches and schools.

In addition, the size of your ancestor's ED reflects how many people lived within it. Geographically smaller EDs have a greater population than do larger EDs, making them helpful when indicating population size and density. For example, in an enumeration district of Allen County, Ohio, the city of Lima has ED numbers 2-21 through 2-56, while EDs surrounding the city cover large swaths of land.

Most surviving ED maps are at the National Archives and Records Administration <www.archives.gov>. On FamilySearch.org <www.familysearch.org/search/collection/2329948>, you can browse a collection of these maps from the censuses taken between 1910 and 1940, organized by state and county.

to search for previous generations, such as places of parents' birth, shown on the 1905 Wisconsin state census in image **J**.

Among the earliest censuses are those taken at the California Spanish Missions beginning in 1796. The only information in these records is name, date of enumeration, and age.

Although not strictly census records, you can find early (Colonial) records by using the Card Catalog and searching for *state name records* (e.g., *Pennsylvania records*). Here, you'll find church, pastoral, and biographical records.

UK CENSUS RECORDS

Do you have British ancestors? Then jump into the UK censuses. These include censuses from England, Scotland, Wales, the Channel Islands, and the Isle of Man from 1841 to 1911. Like the US censuses, the information in UK records varies from year to year—with some years only including head-of-household and number of males and females, and other years providing names of every person in the home, ages, birthplaces, occupation, and relationship. Download blank UK census forms at **<www.ancestry.com/cs/census-forms>**.

While US federal census records are held for seventy-two years from the date of the enumeration, British law precluded release before one hundred years. In the early twenty-first century, that was changed to ninety years to provide for the release of the 1911 census.

When searching for your family in this collection, note that names can be misspelled (just like on US records) and ages can be inaccurate, depending on which month the census was taken. If you can find the family in each census, you can compare the information in each to find any discrepancies or where information remains the same.

As with all indexes, check the original census image (when available) to make sure the information was correctly transcribed.

Searching UK Census Records

Let's do a sample search. You'll find a link to the U.K. Census Collection in the right-side column of the main Census and Voter Lists page. Use this link (or the Card Catalog) to navigate to the 1871 census.

One of the first things you may notice on UK census images is a variety of marks or abbreviations. According to Ancestry.com:

> The clerks who compiled and reviewed the census data made a variety of marks on the records. Unfortunately, many of these tally marks were written over personal information and some fields, such as ages, can be difficult to read. On the other hand, some of these marks can be useful because they designate separate households. In a small parish, a double slash (//) might indicate a new household and a single slash (/) might indicate a non-related person living in the house (such as a servant or lodger). In larger parishes, a double slash (//) might indicate separate buildings and a single slash (/) might indicate separate households within the same building.

Located at the bottom of the 1871 census search form is a list of common abbreviations used, such as *SCH* (scholar) and *NP* (nephew).

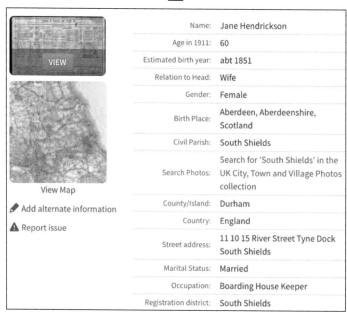

K

NAME and Surname of each Person	RELATION to Head of Family	CON-DITION	AGE of Males	AGE of Femal
Edward Morton	Head	Mar	32	
Helena do	Wife	do		35
Ann Tylyman	Mother in law	Widow		66
Mary C. Langhorne	Servant	Unm		11
George Newsome	Boarder	do	52	
James Tymers	Head	Mar	53	
Mary Tymers	Wife	do		56
Eln. do do	Servant	Unm		16

This UK census record shows the relationship of each person to head-of-household.

L

Name:	Jane Hendrickson
Age in 1911:	60
Estimated birth year:	abt 1851
Relation to Head:	Wife
Gender:	Female
Birth Place:	Aberdeen, Aberdeenshire, Scotland
Civil Parish:	South Shields
Search Photos:	Search for 'South Shields' in the UK City, Town and Village Photos collection
County/Island:	Durham
Country:	England
Street address:	11 10 15 River Street Tyne Dock South Shields
Marital Status:	Married
Occupation:	Boarding House Keeper
Registration district:	South Shields

VIEW

View Map

✐ Add alternate information

⚠ Report issue

Search results of the 1911 UK census show a thumbnail highlighting the enumeration area.

A client with the surname Testerman wanted to know if anyone from the family might have been in the United Kingdom by 1870. I performed a search of the 1871 England census and surprisingly (at least to me), only one person with that name was listed—an Ann Testerman living in the home with her daughter and son-in-law.

As you can see from the image of the UK census record (image **K**), the census gives us Ann's relationship to the head-of-household as well as her age and marital status ("condition"). Notice, too, the double slash marks that indicate a new household.

A handy feature of searching the 1911 UK census on Ancestry.com is that a thumbnail of the area enumerated is also shown (image **L**). Click the thumbnail to bring up a full-size image.

Once you find a record you want to save, you can do so by using the Save Record to Someone in My Tree option listed in the left column under Tools.

If you're searching for Scottish censuses, you can view transcribed results, but not the actual images. (As Ancestry.com has not received permission to do so through the General Register Office for Scotland.) You can, however, view records at the ScotlandsPeople website <www.scotlandspeople.gov.uk>.

CANADIAN CENSUS RECORDS

We often think of Canadians as nineteenth-century immigrants from the United Kingdom. However, among the earliest Canadians were *voyageurs*—fur trappers and traders who came to Canada as early as the seventeenth century.

In addition, people born in Canada or who immigrated to Canada may have crossed the border and become American citizens at some point in their lifetime. That means it's likely that your search will take you back and forth across the United States–Canada border. A 1900 Cook County, Chicago, Illinois, census of the Joseph Brooks family showed Joseph as being born in England while his wife, their oldest child, and the wife's parents were born in Canada.

MAP IT OUT

If you're new to Canadian genealogy, pick up a Canadian map. Not only will it help you trace migration within Canada, it will also help in discovering the bordering US states where Canadian ancestors may have settled.

Canada has a long history involving both France and England. Exploration by both countries began in the late fifteenth century, but France officially ceded its territory to the United Kingdom after the French and Indian War. Although it's part of the British Commonwealth, Canada remains bilingual at the federal level, with records dating back to the mid-seventeenth century. The first Dominion census was taken in 1871 and has continued every ten years since.

Because of Canada's rich English and French heritage, it's possible your family has Métis ancestors. These people trace their ancestry to mixed First Nations (native) and European heritage. You may find Métis ancestors who are descendants of either First Nation and voyageurs or First Nation and English or Scottish parents.

Ancestry.com's Canadian census holdings include indexes and images for every decade from 1851 to 1921, as well as censuses of Manitoba, Saskatchewan, and Alberta from 1906 and 1916. Don't forget to download your blank Canadian census forms at <**www.ancestry. com/cs/census-forms**>.

Searching Canadian Census Records

Let's use Joseph E. Brooks (a printer) and Anna Wilson, who married in 1882 in Toronto, as an example for searching the Canadian census records. (For more information on finding their marriage record, see chapter 5). I want to find as much information on the young couple as possible. Sadly, their marriage didn't take place until 1882, and they just missed the 1881 census as a married couple. We know, too, that their first child was born in Canada was born in 1885, but the second child in 1888 in Illinois—so they wouldn't be on the 1891 Canadian census either.

You'll find a link to the Canadian Census Collection in the right-side column of the main Census and Voter Lists page. Use this link (or the Card Catalog) to navigate to the 1851, 1861, 1871, 1881, 1901, 1911, and 1921 Canadian censuses, among other censuses.

Going backwards, I first searched the 1881 census (image **M**). I found Joseph living with his mother, Christina, in this census; however, the father listed on Joseph and Anne's

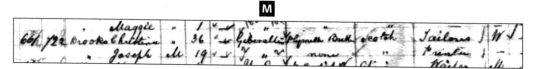

The 1881 Canadian census lists Christina Brooks as a widow.

marriage certificate was not on the census. Christina listed Gibraltar as her place of birth, but Scotch as origin for herself and her son. Interestingly, the transcriber listed her place of birth as Mediterranean. Also of interest is Christina's marital status, which is listed as *W* (widow).

Once I found Christina in the 1881 census, I went back to the 1871 census and found her living in a household of servants with *M* (married) as her marital status. Joseph's birthplace is now listed as Malta and Christina's as Gibraltar. On this census, Christina and Joseph are living in a thirteen-member household of mostly servants. Christina does not appear on the 1861 census or 1851 census. Because Joseph's wife, Anne, has too common a surname (Wilson) and not enough other known information to reliably find her on the census, I put that search on the back burner.

After you find a Canadian census record you're searching for, you can view the original record, as well as save it to your tree.

If you need help with Canadian census records, the Library and Archives Canada has excellent tips for researching Canadian censuses at **<www.bac-lac.gc.ca/eng/census/Pages /census.aspx>**.

OTHER INTERNATIONAL CENSUS RECORDS

Although US, UK, and Canadian census collections are by far the largest, you can still locate other international censuses. The second largest group of European census records (behind the United Kingdom) are for Germany, but all of them are written in German. There are some Eastern European records in English and four French censuses are in French. Australia and New Zealand (collected together in "Oceania") have about a dozen census collections.

One "international" collection that might be of interest to US researchers is "The Census Tables for the French Colony of Louisiana from 1699 Through 1732." This is an invaluable resource for those who have French ancestors from Louisiana.

5

DELVING INTO BIRTH, MARRIAGE, AND DEATH RECORDS

H ave you ever thought about documenting your own birth, your parents' marriage, or your grandparents' death? Records that document life events are the building blocks for genealogical research, providing evidence about key events in a person's life. The documents within this group are known as vital records or (in countries with civil registration) civil records.

Vital records are the official records maintained by governmental agencies at a city, county, or state level. These include birth certificates, death certificates, marriage licenses, and divorce decrees. While vital records are now routine, they weren't always. State-mandated registration of births didn't begin for most US states until the latter part of the nineteenth century or early part of the twentieth century. Prior to that time, records (if any) were kept at the county level, with dates of record-keeping varying wildly. In Pennsylvania, for example, records of births, marriages, and burials began in 1692, while in Wyoming, very few birth and death records were kept prior to 1906, even at the county level.

Vital records can contain far more information than just a date and a place name. In the best cases, they can contain a mother's maiden name, an address, the name and length of an illness, a religion, a place of burial, info about military service, the number of siblings, the name of a presiding minister, and age.

ANCESTRY.COM'S VITAL RECORDS

Ancestry.com currently has more than one thousand US birth, death, and marriage collections, as well as over one hundred Canadian and hundreds of European records collections. In some cases, your search will yield links that take you to an image of the actual record, while others will contain an excerpt or transcription. If copies of a record are available for purchase, you'll see a link to an order form. When viewing an original image that's difficult to read, don't forget to use the Tools options (top right corner of original image).

Although Ancestry.com's vital records collection is called the Birth, Marriage, and Death collection, it covers a variety of documents. Let's look at some of the most important:

Birth

A birth record (image **A**) typically shows the name and gender of the child, place of birth, and name of parents. Occasionally a record will contain the parents' place of birth. Earlier records may simply record a name, date, and parents' names.

Death

Death records (image **B**) often show the name of the deceased, age at death, illness or accident causing death, length of illness, attending physician, place of death, marital status, name of parents and their birthplaces, name of spouse (if any), occupation, and name of the person providing the information.

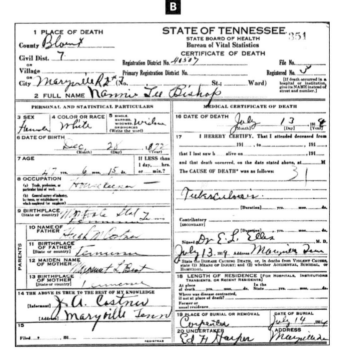

A

This birth record, from a collection of Pennsylvania church and town records, shows the person's name, birth date, and parents' names.

B

This death record sample (from the "Tennessee Death Records, 1908–1958" collection) contains the usual information, as well as the maiden name of the deceased and the name of the undertaker.

Divorce

These records document the dissolution of a marriage. While some records merely state names and place, others can contain far more information. For example, the "Connecticut Divorce Index, 1968–1997" states race, number of marriages, level of education, number of children, decree date, birth state, and location of the superior court.

Social Security Death Index (SSDI)

An often-overlooked source of information, the SSDI contains names of deceased people from 1935 to 2014, who applied for (and were assigned) Social Security numbers. You'll find more information about the SSDI in the Social Security Death Index sidebar.

Cemetery

These records may include tombstone inscriptions, death indexes, and perhaps birth and death dates and the names of surviving family members.

Church

Church records contain birth, baptismal, marriage, and burial records. In some instances, you also can find information about family members.

Obituaries

Obituaries are excerpted from newspaper records and vary depending on the newspaper. Most often, you can expect to find the person's name, date of death, and name of the newspaper. Other records show publication date, age of the deceased, and a link to a non-Ancestry.com site where you can find more information. Present-day obituaries tend to include basic facts about people (names, dates, places). However, older obits (from the early twentieth century, for example) can often give you insight into the person herself. This is part of the obituary for Nancy Dimmitt from 1930:

> She united with the Christian church in middle age and as long as her health permitted she never missed a Sunday School or church service, often going when she was so weak she could hardly get there and back. Or [sic] never missed a chance to do a Christian's duty. Besides these children she leaves 22 grandchildren, 42 great-grandchildren, and a host of friends who will miss Grandma Dimmitt.

Baptism and Christening

At the least, you'll find the name of the person being baptized, as well as the date. You'll get a bonus if the collection has the names of the parents and godparents, and the date of birth. Non-US baptisms will probably show parish and county.

Burial and Grave Records

Although it doesn't contain official (government) records, Ancestry.com's Birth, Marriage, and Death category search results often include useful links to off-site databases such as Find A Grave **<www.findagrave.com>** and BillionGraves **<www.billiongraves.com>**. If you've been doing genealogy research for any period of time, you've probably run across at least one of these sites.

Find A Grave is a database of worldwide burials, currently totaling more than 160 million entries. Membership to the site is free, and all members can create a memorial, submit data, add flowers and photos, or search the database at no charge. When you click on an Ancestry.com search result for Find A Grave, the next screen will include the pertinent data, with a link to click over to the site (image **C**). The Find A Grave page (image **D**) can

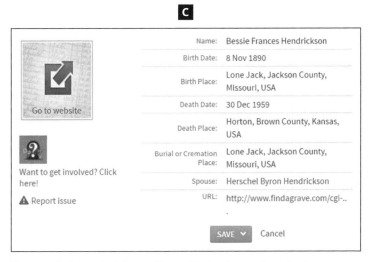

The arrow indicates the full record is on a third-party website and not on Ancestry.com.

Social Security Death Index (SSDI)

As noted earlier, the SSDI is a database of deceased persons who applied for and were assigned a Social Security number (SSN), received benefits, and whose deaths were reported to the Social Security Administration. The benefits most often paid to a person listed in the database were retirement (old age pension) or disability.

If you know a person's date and place of birth (but not where or when they died), the SSDI is a good place to begin your search. Conversely, if you know a place and date of death (but not birth information), you can find that, too. For example, I knew the place of death of my Great-aunt Dollie West, but I didn't know when she was born. I quickly found her listing in the SSDI, and learned that she was born on May 15, 1897, seven years after my grandmother (her sister).

When searching the SSDI, you'll notice an option to order a copy of the original application. You can request copies of original applications online or in writing. To order online, follow the directions and link to Form SSA-711, which you'll need to fill out in order to get your copy of original form SS-5. Fees vary depending on whether you have the person's SSN (which you should have if you found the person in the SSDI, unless it was a recent death).

The index currently contains more than ninety-four million records. If the information is available, you can find:

- last name
- first name
- SSN
- state of issue
- birth date
- death date
- last residence
- lump sum payment

Because of privacy issues, you won't see the SSN of anyone who died within the past ten years.

Another Social Security collection is the "U.S., Social Security Applications and Claims Index, 1936-2007." Providing more detail than the SSDI, the Application and Claims Index contains data for forty-nine million people. Additional information includes the names of the claimant's parents.

Name:	Dollie West
SSN:	496-10-2107
Last Residence:	64070 Lone Jack, Jackson, Missouri, USA
BORN:	15 May 1897
Died:	Apr 1971
State (Year) SSN issued:	Missouri (Before 1951)

No Image
Text-only collection

🛒 Request copy of original application

✏ Add alternate information

⚠ Report issue

SAVE ∨   Cancel

Ancestry.com links you to a page where you can order the original Social Security Death Index.

include images, birth and death dates, relationships, user-added flowers, and newspaper articles. It all depends on who created or added to the record.

You can also go directly to the Find A Grave Index database by clicking on Card Catalog, then typing Find A Grave in the Title box.

BillionGraves uses technology (free Android and iPhone apps) to capture images of headstones with their GPS locations. The images are then uploaded to the website. Once uploaded, you (or other users) can transcribe the records into a searchable format. Using the BillionGraves smartphone app (image **E**), you can take photos (which will include GPS coordinates) as well as search already uploaded data.

INTERNATIONAL VITAL RECORDS

If you search Ancestry.com's Card Catalog, you'll see that Ancestry.com has an extensive collection of international vital records, particularly from Europe and Canada. Don't be surprised to find records that look nothing like vital records in the United States—not only in form, but also in what's contained in the record.

For example, a marriage record from the "Ontario, Canada Marriages, 1801–1928" collection provides information on the July 1882 marriage between Joseph Brooks and Anne Wilson (image **F**). The record shows that Joseph was born in Quebec, was a printer, and had parents named Christina and Henry Brooks. It also shows that Anne, age nineteen,

D

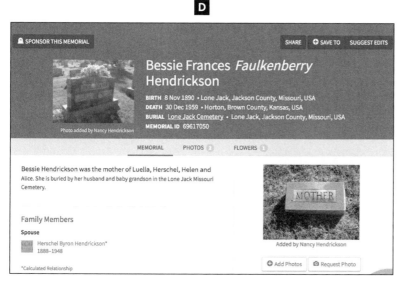

Find A Grave, one of Ancestry.com's subsidiary sites, hosts millions of online memorials that contain tombstone photos and information about the deceased.

E

BillionGraves links tombstones with GPS to allow you to put burial sites on a map.

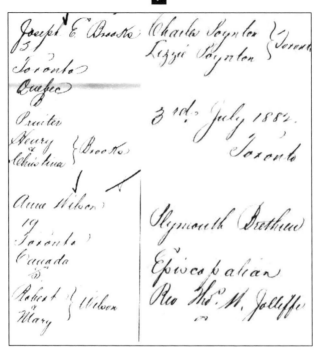

The marriage record for Joseph Brooks and Anne Wilson gives a lot of detail about the couple's marriage in Ontario.

| View Record | John Hendrickson | 1838 | Jul-Aug-Sep | Newcastle upon Tyne | Northumberland | 🛒 Order a Birth Certificate for John Hendrickson |
| View Record | John Frederick Hendrickson | 1841 | Oct-Nov-Dec | Poplar | London | 🛒 Order a Birth Certificate for John Frederick Hendrickson |

My search for John Hendrickson in the "England & Wales, Civil Registration Birth Index, 1837–1915" collection returned two results.

was born in Canada to Robert and Mary Wilson. The record goes on to name the witnesses (Charles and Lizzie Poynton of Toronto), the name of the minister, and the religious affiliation of the groom (Plymouth Brethren) and the bride (Episcopalian). Now that's a record filled with clues!

England and Wales

As excellent as Canadian collections like the one we just mentioned are, among the best known of the international vital records is the FreeBMD (birth, marriage, death) collection, which covers England and Wales. FreeBMD **<www.freebmd.org.uk>** is an ongoing project to transcribe the civil registration index of births, marriages, and deaths for England and Wales. Frequently referred to as the GRO Index ("GRO" from the government department, the General Register Office responsible for it), the system has been in place since 1837. The system required births, marriages, and deaths be registered in the area where the person lived. The GRO holds the original records; copies of the records can be ordered online **<www.gro.gov.uk/gro/content>** or through Ancestry.com.

The collections for England and Wales Civil Registration records on Ancestry.com are separate: one each for births, marriages, and deaths, with dates ranging from 1837 to 2007. Birth records include surname, name of the child, the registrar's district, and volume and page number where the original record was recorded. In the marriages collection, you'll find names, date, district, county, and volume and page number. Likewise, the death index includes names, district, and volume and page numbers of the original recording. In all, you'll find transcriptions of alphabetical ledgers, each compiled quarterly after all records are received by the GRO.

Do a sample search along with me for a birth of John Hendrickson, born about 1838. In Ancestry.com's Card Catalog, choose the "England & Wales, Civil Registration Birth Index, 1837–1915" collection, then use the search form to enter John's name and approximate birth date. The results include two John Hendricksons, one born in 1838 and the other born in 1841 (image **G**).

STUDY OLD HANDWRITING

For tips on deciphering these records, consult Ancestry.com's "Tips for Reading Old Handwriting." To find the guide, go to **<support.ancestry.com>** and enter *old handwriting* in the search field.

SURNAME of Parent	NAME (if any) or SEX of CHILD	SUP. REGISTRAR'S DISTRICT	Vol.	Page
		134		
Hendley	Thomas Barnett	Grantham	XIV	351
Hendrey	Isabella Frances	West	I	396
Hendrickson	John Frederick	Poplar	II	310
Hendrie	Eleanor	Liverpool	xx	831
Hendley	Mary Ann Elizabeth Grant	Alverstoke	VII	21

Ancestry.com's collection of English and Welsh civil records provide citation information that you can use to order copies of the original records. John Hendrickson's entry from 1841 is third from the top.

When you click to view the record, you'll see that the first John was born in the third quarter (July-August-September) in Newcastle upon Tyne, Northumberland; his birth was recorded in volume 25, page 326. The second John was born in the fourth quarter (October-November-December) 1841, Poplar, London, with the birth recorded in volume 2, page 310 (image H).

Once you click on either of the listings, you'll also notice the Page Tools (left column) has three options: order a birth certificate, search for John in the UK census collection, and search for John in the *London Times*. Click the second option, pick the appropriate census year, then do a census search. If you pick the third option, the *London Times* link will display a list of possible matches in the publication's database. It's possible there will be no links for "good matches" if there isn't enough information to effectively do the search. (Note that, if you want a copy of the birth certificate, you'll need to pay a fee. The order form is prefilled from the information in your ancestor's FreeBMD listing.)

When using any of the FreeBMD collections, don't forget to click over to view the image, just to ensure that the transcription displayed in the search results is correct.

Other International Records

While many people reading this book will have UK ancestry, don't miss checking the Card Catalog for other international birth, marriage, and death collections if your family lived or immigrated to other parts of the world. A sampling of what you can find includes:

- "New Zealand, Notices of Deceased Estates, 1880–1950"
- "Sweden, Church Records, 1500–1941" (in Swedish)
- Paris marriage banns (in French)

- Italian civil registrations (in Italian)

- Norwegian burial records (in Norwegian)

- "Lübeck, Germany, Marriage Banns, 1811–1871 (in German)"

- "Nuevo Leon and Tamaulipas, Mexico, Selected Parish Records, 1751–1880

FINDING VITAL RECORDS

As with all other records on Ancestry.com, you can do a global search of the Birth, Marriage, and Death category, or you can search within individual collections that comprise the category. The broad category is searchable via the dropdown Search menu located at the top of each page. You can narrow the collection search by choosing a category, which will take you to a new search form.

You also can search individual collections, which you can find in the Card Catalog (see chapter 3 for more information on using the Card Catalog). For example, if you want to narrow your search to Indiana births, type *Indiana* in the Title box of the Card Catalog, then filter (if desired) by Collection, Location, Date, or Languages. Once you filter by state you can further filter by county. Remember, though, that the more you filter, the less likely you'll find results. If your search returns no results, remove some of the filters.

Sample Search

Although Hendrickson is my surname, it's the side of the family I've had the most problem researching—particularly when it comes to finding more about the women and any details about their lives. A case in point is Ella Snow, wife of James Hendrickson. Using the Birth, Marriage, and Death category, I entered Ella and James' names and their approximate date of marriage. Search results included a cemetery listing from Find A Grave, as well as probable matches in the "Missouri Marriage Records, 1805–2002" collection.

Within the Missouri marriage collection, I discovered James and Ella's marriage took place on September 28, 1887, in Independence, Jackson County, Missouri. Along with the

TAKE YOUR RESEARCH TO CHURCH

If you're searching for your roots in Mexico, Roman Catholic parish records are the best source of family information.

★LICENSE★TO★MARRY★

STATE OF MISSOURI, }
COUNTY OF JACKSON, } *ss.*
Office of Recorder of Deeds at Independence, Mo. }

To any Judge, Judge of a County Court, Justice of the Peace, or any Licensed or Ordained Preacher of the Gospel—GREETING :

The provisions of the act entitled "An Act in Relation to Marriage and Marriage License," approved March 26th, 1881, having been satisfactorily complied with, you are hereby authorized to join in matrimony Mr. *James Hendrickson* 38 , years of age of the County of *Jackson* and State of *Missouri* , and *Ella Snow* 30 years of age of the County of *Johnson* and State of *Missouri* Witness my hand and seal of office at Independence, Mo., this 24th day of Sept A. D. 188*7*

R.S.Hinde Recorder of Deeds.

By *John Hinde* Deputy.

Ancestry.com collections can contain a variety of marriage records, such as marriage licenses and applicants.

Application for License to Marry, the collection also had an image of the License to Marry (image **I**) and included the name of the minister, J.N. Cobb, who was a "licensed minister of the gospel." Of note was the fact that the groom lived in Jackson County, while the bride resided in Johnson County. James was thirty-eight and Ella was thirty.

•   The bride's and groom's ages were red flags for me. I was almost certain that one or both of the couple had been married previously, as thirty and thirty-eight were ages far too advanced for a first marriage during this time period.

I skimmed through several James Hendricksons in the Missouri marriage collection until I found a marriage record for a nearby county—Cass. (Jackson, Johnson, and Cass all border one another.) The marriage date was July 20, 1870—a year when James would have been only twenty-one. But what really caught my attention was the name of the bride: Susan Strange. Why? Because I had found previous Strange and Hendrickson marriages in my family history. Even more interesting was the notation in the 1870 marriage records for Cass County, Missouri, was a marriage on July 21 for Anna Hendrickson and William Groves.

I knew James had a sister named Anna. With further research, I found James in the 1870 census (Cass County) living in the Groves's household with another sister and brother-in-law (Martha and Mike Keller). Guess who was living right next door? Sixteen-year-old

Susan Strange. From a single red flag (ages listed in a marriage record), I was able to track down a previous marriage for James, although (to date) I have found no record of Susan's death.

Vital Record Search Strategies

In addition to searching in specific collections, you can use these strategies to improve your vital records searches on Ancestry.com.

SEARCH MULTIPLE COLLECTIONS

If you can't find an ancestor using the global search (and you know the state in which the event took place), go to the Card Catalog and search for an applicable collection from that state. For example, I couldn't find a marriage record from Tennessee when using the global search, so I went into the Card Catalog, pulled up the collections with the word *Tennessee* in them, and searched "Tennessee State Marriages, 1780–2002." Still no luck. Next, I searched the "Tennessee Marriage and Bible Records" collection. Another strikeout. Finally, I searched through "Tennessee, Marriages, 1851–1900," and there it was! The marriage record of my great-great-grandparents, Calvin Dimmitt and Nancy L. Marcus, married on July 30, 1864, in McMinn County, Tennessee. Now that I know the county, what else might I find? Possibly birth, death, or other records.

SEARCH FOR NAME VARIATIONS

When searching for the marriage record for my great-grandparents Sarah Dimmitt and Francis Faulkenberry, I went directly to the collection "Missouri Marriage Records, 1805–2002." There I found the record, although my ancestors' names were noted as *F.A. Faulkenberry* and *Jossie Dimmitt*.

How did I know these were the people I was searching? Francis Faulkenberry's middle name was Albert (F.A.), and Sarah Josephine Dimmitt was known by her nickname of Josie. Interestingly, the name of the presiding official was J.D. Faulkenberry, Justice of the Peace. Is this Francis's brother, Jacob David? More clues to research.

As I looked at this record image, I noticed it clearly shows the bride's name as Josie, not Jossie. I clicked the link to Add Alternate Information, then chose my reason for an alternate name a "transcription error," then submitted it for correction

SEARCH FOR THE BRIDE OR THE GROOM (BUT NOT BOTH)

Many online lists of marriages are transcriptions of microfilms or books. Typically, you'll find a listing by groom, then another one by bride. If you don't find your ancestor on one list, try the other. I have found instances when a marriage record wasn't in the list of grooms, but was in the list of brides.

As with all records, you're going to find a variety of spellings for all vital records. If not a spelling mistake, you may find a mistranscription or simply an omitted fact or data point. If you keep your search flexible and move seamlessly between various collections and types of records, it's much easier to piece together the facts that make up your ancestors' lives.

6

WORKING WITH MILITARY RECORDS

Humans have taken up arms from the earliest recorded history to the present, and Americans have participated in many wars and conflicts. Even the earliest colonists in America were fighting, with the French and Indian Wars flaring up over seventy-four years and four separate stages of conflict.

If your ancestor was between the ages of seventeen and fifty-five during any of those struggles, there's a high likelihood that he served in the military for at least awhile. For your Revolutionary War ancestor, the time in service may have been only a few months. For your WWII family member, the enlistment was typically "for the duration of hostilities."

American military records are housed in the National Archives and Records Administration (NARA) **<archives.gov>**, while Canadian records are at the Library and Archives Canada **<www.bac-lac.gc.ca>**. You also can find records in various state and county libraries and archives as well as in US federal censuses. The types of military records kept at an official level include indexes to service records, pension files, death and/or casualty lists, draft registrations, and enlistment records.

In this chapter, we'll explore Ancestry.com's American military collections, as well as international records of military service.

Before we begin, let's take a look at the major American military conflicts for which records are available so you can determine which your ancestors might have served in. The following chart lists the year of US involvement in major military conflicts, plus the range of birth years for soldiers who fought in them.

Name of conflict	Dates	Birth year
Revolutionary War	1775–1783	1720–1765
War of 1812	1812–1815	1757–1798
Mexican-American War	1846–1848	1791–1831
Civil War	1861–1865	1806–1848
Spanish-American War	1898	1843–1881
World War I	1917–1918	1862–1901
World War II	1941–1945	1886–1928
Korean War	1950–1953	1895–1936
Vietnam War	1965–1973	1904–1958

An easy way to determine which of your ancestors may have served in the military is to use your genealogy software and filter the collection by dates of birth. For example, to choose the ancestors who might have served in the War of 1812, filter your collection to select all males born after 1756 but before 1799. Each genealogy program has its own filtering system, so check your program's Help files for instructions on filtering. When I created a filtered list in Legacy Family Tree <www.legacyfamilytree.com>, I had more than five dozen potential War of 1812 soldiers. Eighteen of those are direct ancestors with the remainder in peripheral lines. I now have a great starting place for my War of 1812 search in Ancestry.com's records.

MILITARY RECORDS ON ANCESTRY.COM

Ancestry.com has nine categories of military records. I'll go through each category and detail what information you can expect to find. Before we get started, note that some collections are included in more than one record type.

Draft, Enlistment, and Service

Here, you'll find more than two hundred collections that cover draft, enlistment, and service records dating from the Revolutionary War through the Korean War. The following are collections you'll likely want to explore:

Begin Your Soldier Search at Home

As I mentioned in chapter 1, start your ancestor search at home—before going to Ancestry.com. If your father or grandfather served in World War I, World War II, the Korean War, or later conflicts, it's possible you'll find discharge papers, awards, disability claims, or photographs to help narrow down research objectives. We have my dad's purple heart, combat infantryman's badge, and medical records.

You may also have heard family stories about an ancestor's military service. For example, my grandmother told stories about how her grandfather was wounded in the Civil War's Battle of Shiloh in Tennessee. That piece of information opened up a new research direction for me.

If you have photographs of an ancestor in uniform or wearing civilian clothes with a military insignia or medal, scan the image and enlarge it to see if it holds clues about his service. If you don't know what insignia was used during specific time periods, Google terms like *union civil war uniforms*, *union insignia of the civil war*, or *confederate insignia*. These searches will yield plenty of images—hopefully enough to help you identify at least a branch of service. Once you've found all available at-home records, it's time to move to Ancestry.com.

- "Civil War Draft Registration Records, 1863–1865": This collection contains lists of individuals who registered for the draft. Records show birthplace, residence, race, age, profession, prior military service, and registration class. Class I includes men ages twenty through thirty-five, as well as ages thirty-six through forty-five who were unmarried. Class II contains everyone else who registered.

- "Union Soldiers Compiled Service Records, 1861–1865": Compiled service records are cards that record information about a soldier. You may find dates that he was sick, on leave, absent without leave, or in a hospital. Typically, you'll at least find the soldier's name, rank, and unit.

- "World War I Draft Registration Cards, 1917–1918": This is an invaluable resource, as WWI registrations include approximately 98 percent of the men under age

WWI (and WWII) draft registration cards are among the most consistent military records. WWI draft registration covers an estimated 98 percent of US men who were under the age of forty-six at the time.

forty-six. In each entry (image **A**), you can find the ancestor's name, age, address, race, occupation, place of employment, nearest relative, and physical description.

- "World War II Draft Registration Cards, 1942": This was the so-called "old man's" draft registration, as it was limited to men who were born on or before April 28, 1877, and February 16, 1897. This registration wasn't done to enlist men in active military service, but rather to assess skills that could be used in the civilian work force.

CONSULT THE PHOTO DETECTIVE

If you've found photos but aren't sure of when they were taken, check out Maureen Taylor's *Photo Detective* blog at *Family Tree Magazine*. Maureen's blog posts are all about identifying time periods in photos based on several things, including hair styles, clothes, and poses <**www.familytreemagazine.com/articles/news-blogs/photo_detective**>.

- "U.S. World War II Army Enlistment Records, 1938–1946": This collection contains information about 8.3 million men and women who enlisted in the United States Army during World War II.

- "U.S. Rosters Of World War II Dead, 1939–1945": This collection contains casualties from all branches of the service. The records include the serviceman's name, religion, race, service number, branch of service, rank, date of death, and name and location of cemetery. (Note: This collection is also included in the Casualties category.)

Casualties

Records in this collection include burial records, deaths, veterans interred overseas, with casualties ranging from colonial muster rolls through Vietnam, and grave sites to the present. International records are also in this collection, including a German WWI casualty list (in German), a New Zealand WWI casualty list, and a Canadian war graves register.

Want to find a few well-known figures? Look in the "Vietnam War, Casualties Returned Alive, 1962–1979" collection, and you'll find U.S. Senator John McCain, a Vietnam War naval aviator held as a prisoner of war for six years. The "U.S. Burial Registers, Military Posts, and National Cemeteries, 1862–1960" collection has a handwritten list of officers' remains removed from the Little Bighorn battlefield (including George Armstrong Custer).

Another interesting collection is "U.S. Vietnam War Military Casualties, 1956–1998" (image **B**), which includes individuals who died from both hostile and nonhostile incidents and as well as those who died while missing in action (MIA) or as a prisoner of war (POW).

Collections of casualties from a number of states are part of the Casualties category. Records may include newspaper clippings, burial records, and more. Here are just a few:

B

Name:	William Clifton Hoover
Birth Date:	4 Dec 1939
Death Date:	10 Jun 1965
Age:	25
Home City:	San Diego
Home State:	California
SSN/Service #:	4841380
Death Date:	10 Jun 1965
Casualty Country:	Republic of Vietnam (South Vietnam)
Service Branch:	Department of the Navy
Component:	Regular (RA, USN, USAF, USMC, USCG)
Rank:	SWF2
Military Grade:	SWF2
Pay Grade:	Specialist Fifth Class (U.S. Army) or Sergeant (U.S. Army, U.S. Marine Corps) or Staff Sergeant (U.S. Air Force) or Grade/Rate Abbreviations With First Column: Any Entry; Second Column: Any Entry; Third Column: 2; Fourth Column: Blank (U.S. Navy, U.S. Coa
Province:	Military Region 2 - Phu Yen
Decoration:	Not Available
CN:	Republic of Vietnam (South Vietnam)
Unit:	USN MCB 11
Service Occupation:	SWF2
Data Source:	Coffelt Database

Search for casualty records, such as this one from the Vietnam War, on Ancestry.com.

- "California World War I Death Announcements, 1918–1921"
- "Iowa Civil War Soldier Burial Records"
- "Maine Compiled Military Records, 1812–1865"
- "Panama Canal Zone, Gorgas Hospital Mortuary Records, 1906–1991"
- "Illinois Revolutionary War Veteran Burials"
- "Columbus, Franklin County, Ohio: Camp Chase Cemetery"

Soldier, Veteran, and Prisoner Rolls and Lists

The information in military records varies greatly, depending on the collection. You can typically find a name, birth (or death) date, and place of birth. Some collections will include the name of a person's spouse and children (particularly pension files) or details of military service (pension applications).

One example of a POW collection is the "Andersonville Prisoners of War" collection. Andersonville was a Confederate Civil War prison camp that housed forty-five thousand Union soldiers. This collection contains records compiled by the National Park Service of camp inmates between 1863 and 1865. Information typically includes name, rank, unit, and state. Some records may include capture information.

Pension Records

Military pension applications and records can include names and birth dates of the veteran, spouse, and children, as well as proof of marriage or dispositions (legal statements) made by the soldier's family or friends. In the latter case, a veteran may be too old or forgetful regarding details of his military service. In those instances, warrants were given on behalf of the veteran. Some pension records are federal, while others are state-specific.

The "U.S. Civil War Pension Index: General Index to Pension Files, 1861–1934" collection has the most records of all the pension records collections on Ancestry.com. The 2.3 million records include images of the original pension index cards. Other collections are primarily from the United States and cover the Revolutionary War, World War I, and World War II. A few UK and Canadian pension collections are available, too.

Histories

As you would expect, this category contains histories of regiments, battles, wars, state-specific military records and rosters, correspondences, and chronicles. If you had a Civil War soldier, don't miss searching the "American Civil War Regiments" collection, where you'll find a complete history of the regiment (including names and dates of battles, plus the number of men killed, wounded in action, or dead from disease or accident).

Awards and Decorations of Honor

Although it's a fairly small collection, this collection contains the twenty-seven volumes of books that reference the names of over two hundred thousand Union soldiers who were buried in national cemeteries, soldiers' lots, and garrison cemeteries. You'll also discover several UK collections in this subcategory, such as this listing from the "U.K. Army Roll of Honour, 1939–1945."

News

Here, you'll find collections with military news from the *Stars and Stripes* newspaper, German publications, a British war honors scrapbook, and the "Abraham Lincoln Papers" (twenty thousand documents written by Lincoln held at the Library of Congress). Another interesting collection in this series is the "New York World War I Veterans' Service Data, 1913–1919." Most of the documents in this collection contain information about soldiers from New York State who served in World War I, including:

- name
- birth date
- enlistment details
- branch of the military
- unit
- discharge information

Disciplinary Actions

Was your military ancestor ever in trouble with his superiors? Find out here by searching collections dating back to Revolutionary War courts-martial. Among the collections is

A Military Records Success Story

Genealogy researcher Bill Krause shared this first-person success story:

A family story tells that my second great-grandfather, George Byron (Dutch) Proper, was killed during the Civil War at the Battle of Petersburg, Virginia, on April 12, 1865. I was puzzled, because Robert E. Lee surrendered at Appomattox Court House on April 9, 1865. This meant that my second great-grandfather had died three days after the war had officially ended.

To explore this mystery, I searched for and found his military records on Ancestry.com. The records showed he had enlisted in the 179th New York Volunteers in September 1864 and had been killed in battle on *April 2* at Petersburg in the last great battle of the war—not three days after the war ended, as I had originally thought based on information from my family.

I was able to view records of the regimental hospital, showing he died from wounds related to artillery fire. The census records that I found on Ancestry.com showed his youngest daughter was two years old when he died. She would grow up to become my great-grandmother.

Other census records showed my great-grandmother named her second son after one of her uncles, leading me to speculate he had stepped in to act as a father figure for his fallen brother's children. Thanks to Ancestry.com, I was able to print these records and share them and stories with my grandchildren. I probably could have found these records from other sources (such as the National Archives), but I wouldn't have found them as easily or conveniently as I was able to using Ancestry.com.

C

Date of Grant	County in Which Situated	Names of Former Proprietors	Number of Acres	Names of the Purchasers	Sum Sold for
	Anson	Henry E. McCulloch	64	William Bowman	30:—:—
	"	" " "	58	" "	20:—:—
	"	Walter Cunningham	100	Samuel Younge	57:—:—
	"	James Cotton	300	" "	50:—:—
	"	Walter Cunningham	200	Benjamin Robenson	61:—:—
'84 June 5th	"	Robert Palmer	200	Spruce McCoy	80:—:—
5	"	" "	300	" "	100:—:—

EXTRACTS OF ALL SUCH GRANTS OF CONFISCATED PROPERTY AS ARE RECORDED IN THE OFFICE BY THE SECRETARY OF THE STATE OF NORTH CAROLINA

Some military records convey the hardships of those who fought. This sample record from "The Loyalists in North Carolina During the American Revolution" collection indicates that Loyalists (colonists who sided with Great Britain during the American Revolution) had property confiscated in North Carolina.

one of "The Loyalists in North Carolina During the American Revolution." The records in this collection (such as the one in image **C**) describe in great detail the hardships they encountered, their land that was confiscated, and their attempts at gaining financial restitution from Britain.

Photos

Of the more than sixty collections in this category, one that really stands out to me contains more than 250 United News newsreels. Each averages about ten minutes in length and consists of military footage from 1942 to 1946. Each of the newsreels has a thumbnail sketch of subject matter, such as:

> Part 1, naval guns bombard the beaches of Leyte and carrier-based planes bomb the island defenses. The amphibious assault begins. Shows Gens. MacArthur and Wainwright and Adm. Halsey. Part 2, Red Cross personnel pack food parcels for Americans imprisoned in Germany. Part 3, cadets parade at Uruguay's military academy in Montevideo. Part 4, a MARK I calculator at Harvard University solves math problems. Part 5, Marines capture pillboxes and dugouts on Peleliu Island. Part 6, the 5th Army breaks through the Gothic line in Italy behind artillery and tanks.

Other collections in this category offer gravestone photos from national cemeteries, images from US wars and conflicts, soldier photographs, narrative and photos from former slaves, and British Royal Aero Club pilots' photos and flying certificates.

INTERNATIONAL MILITARY RECORDS

Ancestry.com also has a healthy selection of international military records, with the largest group from the United Kingdom, followed by Germany (though several of these are in German). UK records cross the centuries and include military service in the French and Indian Wars, the Boer War, and World Wars I and II, along with service and pension records. If you're primarily interested in international military records, use the Card Catalog (see details in chapter 3) to filter to the record collections of interest. You'll need the World Explorer membership to access most international military records.

Among the excellent collections are ones that cover UK WWII prisoners of war, WWI service and pension records, and WWI casualties. Canadian military records stretch back to the 1700s and include records from the War of 1812, Revolutionary War, and World War I. Record types include pension files, Loyalist claims, muster lists, and grave registers.

Applications for the Sons of the American Revolution (SAR) and Daughters of the American Revolution (DAR) can contain detailed genealogical information, which was used by applicants to prove their relationship to Revolutionary patriots.

SAMPLE SEARCH: FINDING MILITARY RECORDS ON ANCESTRY.COM

Let's do a search for service records. But first: Put on your detective hat. We're trying to find out if there are any military records relating to my ancestor John Knox, born July 31, 1744, Rich Square, Northampton County, North Carolina. John Knox would have been the correct age for military service during the Revolutionary War, but the Knox family was historically Quaker (and thus, opposed to violence). Are there any records showing that he served?

In this section, we'll go step by step, and you can use this search as a template for doing your own military record searches. This search is also an example of how deeply you can begin to solve a genealogy problem by weaving back and forth between Ancestry.com and other sites such as Google <www.google.com>.

Under the Search dropdown menu, select Military to scour the collection for John Knox. My search found several results with that name, but none were part of my family line. However, while viewing search results that pointed to other users' family trees, I found a tree containing my Knox family. What caught my eye was a notation for a Sons of the American Revolution (SAR) application based on the patriot service of John Knox of Rich Square, Northampton County, North Carolina. To be considered a patriot by the SAR or Daughters of the American Revolution (DAR), the organizations require that a person gave some kind of service to the Army—but not necessarily in a combat role. Perhaps John wasn't a Quaker at the time, or maybe he didn't serve in a combat role? Only more research can tell.

Having used on the main search form, I moved on to specific collections that may relate to information I know or suspect about my ancestor. I wanted to learn more about the SAR application notes in the Member Trees, so I searched Ancestry.com's collection of "U.S. Sons of the American Revolution Membership Applications, 1889–1970." The SAR application (image **D**), neatly typed onto a form, included this notation about John Knox: *Named on a list for commanding officer under Col. Allen Jones, May 20, 1775.*

With that in mind, I turned to other sources for more information on what I had already learned. Taking the information from the SAR application, I Googled the term *John Knox Col. Allen Jones 1775*. Among the search results was a PDF document titled "A History of Rich Square Monthly Meeting of Friends, 1760–1990." That history listed the fact that John Knox was an Elder, which meant he belonged to the Quaker church. In the May 20, 1775, meeting notes, it states:

> Also it appeared to this Meeting that Col. Allen Jones, the commanding officer of this county, requests to have a list of all male Friends from the age of Sixteen to Sixty Years in order that they may be exempted from being called on to act under the Militia Law according to an Act of Assembly in that case made and provided. Therefore John Knox is appointed to make out a list in order to be presented to the Colonel.

I still had one question: Was the list on which John Knox (under Col. Allen Jones) was named related to those who served or those who were exempt due to their religious beliefs? The SAR application listed supporting evidence in the following sources:

1. *Encyclopedia of American Quaker Genealogy* by Hinshaw, Vol. 1, pages 167, 168, 217, 244, and 347

2. *Biographical Record of Bureau, Marshall, and Putnam Counties, Illinois,* pages 168–169

3. *North Carolina Revolutionary Army Accounts*, Vol. 6, folio 4, page 33

I decided to check all three, if possible.

I went back to the Ancestry.com Card Catalog to see if the sources noted are available through the website. The first source, the *Encyclopedia of American Quaker Genealogy* by Hinshaw is. This encyclopedia contains monthly Quaker meeting notes. Volume 1 has records from North Carolina. This collection is searchable by name, as well as volume and page number. Page 217 contained a wealth of information:

- John's wife's name (Pharaby)
- the names and birth dates of their children

- the names and birth and death dates of John's parents
- the names and birth and death dates of John's siblings

Page 244 contained more than three-dozen references to the family, all taken from the Rich Square monthly meeting notes. Among the most interesting:

- On May 20, 1775, John was on a list for commanding officer Col. Allen Jones. (This date and notation is the same as that given on the SAR application.)
- John was "con" [condemned] for misconduct for being a judge at a race.
- The date of John's marriage to Pharaby

Having learned so much about the Knox family, I returned to non-Ancestry.com sources for more background information. I still had the same question: What was this "list" that was used in the SAR application? I searched Google for anything to do with the Rich Square, North Carolina, meeting and found the same history of the meeting I had found earlier, but this time one of the lines in that history stood out to me:

> Also it appeared to this Meeting that Col. Allen Jones, the commanding officer of this county, requests to have a list of all male Friends from the age of Sixteen to Sixty Years in order that they may be **exempted from being called on to act under the Militia Law** [emphasis mine] according to an Act of Assembly in that case made and provided. Therefore John Knox is appointed to make out a list in order to be presented to the Colonel.

It seems John was on the list of people who were *exempt* from military service, not of people who were a part of military service! But being a stickler for verification, I searched Google for more information about Col. Allen Jones and the Rich Square people. I found another reference:

> Francis Beaman [senior] and his wife Mary were received by the Friends at Rich Square Monthly Meeting in Northampton County, North Carolina, in January 1764, having satisfied the preparative meeting (Hinshaw, Vol. I, page 229)... In 1775 Francis was on the list of exemptions prepared by the Monthly Meeting at the request of Col. Allen Jones of the local militia.

It appears that the list "proving" John's service to independence was actually a list of people exempt from that service.

Armed with this new information, I went back to Ancestry.com's *Encyclopedia of American Quaker Genealogy* collection and searched for *Col. Allen Jones*. There I found more than a dozen other notations exactly matching that of John Knox: "[name of person] on list for commanding officer Col. Allen Jones."

I searched Google to see if a digital copy of the *Biographical Record of Bureau, Marshall, and Putnam Counties, Illinois*, was available online. Eureka! Not only did I find the book online <archive.org/details/cu31924028804932>, I found a biography of John and Pharaby's grandson, William. The biography notes that five of William's brothers served in the Civil War along with four of his nephews.

I now have nine members of the family who should have Civil War records in the Ancestry.com collection of Civil War draft, enlistment, and pensions. (Looks like the next generation of the Knox family weren't Quakers.)

One last thing about this biography (and why it's a good idea to always check facts): William's biography notes that two of the nephews "died soon after their return home from effects of starvation and disease while incarcerated in Libby prison." Using Ancestry.com's 1890 Veterans Schedules (a special census of Civil War veterans), I found James and John M. Jr. listed, so clearly those two did not die soon after the war. What happened to Joseph and William?

After exhausting my Ancestry.com search, I went to Fold3 <www.fold3.com> (an Ancestry.com property that specializes in military records—see chapter 16) and found that Joseph was sent to the hospital on March 10, 1862. On March 12, 1862, he was "left sick" in the hospital in St. Louis, and discharged at Corinth, Mississippi, on January 3, 1863, for "disability." His disability papers say he had an "affliction of the chest said to be the result of measles." The papers went on to note that he had chronic bronchitis, the sequel to a bout of measles.

Back at Ancestry.com, I found a Joseph Knox of the right age and residence on the 1870 census; however, I've found no trace of him following that record.

And the other nephew, William? What of him? At Fold3, I found that he had been discharged on March 3, 1862, on a surgeon's certification of disability. I cannot find William on either the 1870 census or the 1890 Veterans census.

Are Joseph and William the two nephews who perished soon after the war? Neither of their service records indicates being a prisoner at Libby prison, but clearly both had medical problems.

Check offline sources to locate more information. Let's go back to my original problem of John Knox, the Quaker, and his Revolutionary War service. The third reference, *North Carolina Revolutionary Army Accounts*, wasn't online. I telephoned the North Carolina State Archives, who then sent me to the Government and Heritage section of the State Library of North Carolina, then onto the Genealogy section.

The librarian was kind enough to look up John Knox in that reference, and found three references of payment but couldn't access the original records, which are stored in the archives. She sent me the names of local researchers for hire to complete the research.

Of interest, though, she did tell me that North Carolina gave the equivalent of payment IOUs to people other than soldiers, such as someone who gave a barrel of apples or whiskey

Finding Military Service in a US Federal Census

Sometimes, you can use multiple kinds of records in conjunction with each other to take your research to new heights. For example, you can use US federal census records to identify if, when, and where your ancestors served in the military. Four US federal censuses contained information about military service:

1. The 1840 census shows surviving Revolutionary War pensioners and/or their widows.

2. The 1890 special veterans census lists Union veterans or widows (though only a partial census remains). This census includes: name of surviving service member and widow, rank, regiment, enlistment date, discharge date, length of service, address, and disability (if any).

3. The 1910 federal census asks if the respondent was a survivor of the Union or Confederate Army or Navy.

4. The 1930 federal census shows military service in any major war through World War I. If military service is noted, use the chart at the beginning of this chapter to approximate the conflict in which the service member may have served. With that information in hand, use the Military category in the Card Catalog to filter down to the most appropriate collections.

to the army, or provided blankets and care of the sick. Remember, as I learned earlier, a patriot can be someone who provides service to the military. Is it possible that John Knox was among these patriots? I don't yet know.

USING PENSION FILES

If you can't find service records for an ancestor, start searching pension files. Pension files can contain a massive amount of detailed information about the person's military service. More than just about any other type of military record, pension files give an insight into the person not found in "just names and dates."

Let's look at another search example. In this case, the ancestor in question is David Faulkenberry from South Carolina. Although family lore places him as a Revolutionary War soldier, a search of Ancestry.com's "U.S. Revolutionary War Rolls, 1775–1783" collection was fruitless. However, David did show up in "Revolutionary War Pension and Bounty-Land Warrant Application Files, 1800–1900." This bountiful find included several pages of testimony and affidavits.

I knew David lived in South Carolina, but I tracked him down in Tennessee when he applied for a Revolutionary War pension (1833). From the pension files on Ancestry.com (image **E**), I learned that David personally appeared before a justice of the peace in Rutherford County, Tennessee. The affidavit shows that he stated his age was eight-five or eight-six and that he entered the service before the engagement of Hanging Rock, South Carolina.

Revolutionary War pension file excerpts, like this one from Fold3, can attest to details of a person's wartime service.

With this information from my Ancestry.com search, I did a quick search at Wikipedia <www.wikipedia.org> to learn more about the battle. The Wikipedia entry said the "Battle of Hanging Rock took place on August 6, 1780, [was] a three-hour battle that caused some men to faint from thirst and heat." An interesting side note—and, of course, one I wondered about Faulkenberry taking part in—was "A group of Americans came across a storage of rum in the British camp and became so drunk they could not be brought back into the battle."

According to the testimony, David was a drafted militiaman and after five or six months of service was discharged but then recalled for another five- or six-month tour. He was also in the army at Gates' defeat at the Battle of Camden (August 16, 1780, near Camden, South Carolina). He was sergeant of a guard detail to watch wagons. Twenty or so years after the war, he moved to Clarke County, Georgia.

David's son, Jacob Faulkenberry (sixty-two years old at the time), also appeared in court, submitting an affidavit that stated his father was "in full vigor and perfect exercise of his memory" to give details of his service. Jacob further said that after Gates' defeat, his father was ordered to collect property (guns, baggage, etc.) that had been left by the retreating army. David is crippled in both of his hands, caused by "being cut to pieces" by Tories, and also wounded by a ball at the same time. A neighbor who knew David for forty years also appeared in the document. When his memory was still good, David had told the neighbor in detail about his service. Another neighbor and a clergyman swore to David's good character.

NAME OF SOLDIER:	Metzger, Adolph				
NAME OF DEPENDENT:	*Widow,* Metzger, Frederika				
	Minor,				
	Mother Metzger, Anna M.				
SERVICE:	C. 2 US Cav.				

DATE OF FILING.	CLASS.	APPLICATION NO.	CERTIFICATE NO.	STATE FROM WHICH FILED.
	Invalid,			
1867 June 21	*Widow,*	148888	99563	
	Minor,			
1890. Nov 12	*Mother*	493.601		Germany

This Civil War pension index card for Adolph Metzger, found in "General Index to Pension Files, 1861–1934," notes the names of both his mother and wife.

Because pension files can have so much personal information, be prepared for the unexpected. Case in point: I was curious to learn more about a cavalryman named Adolph Metzger, who was killed December 21, 1866, in Dakota Territory, near Fort Phil Kearny. If you're a history buff, you may have read about the fight that goes by the name the Fetterman Massacre. In brief, Captain Fetterman (against orders) led the eighty-one men under his command into a trap set by about one thousand Sioux, Cheyenne, and Arapaho warriors. None of the men—including bugler Adolph Metzger—survived.

I went to Ancestry.com and searched the Civil War records. I easily found Adolph in the "U.S. Army, Register of Enlistments, 1798–1914" collection, serving as a bugler in Company C, 2nd Regiment, Cavalry, during the Civil War. Later I searched "U.S. Civil War Pension Index: General Index to Pension Files, 1861–1934" and found that Adolph's widow, Frederika, filed for a widow's pension in 1867. Surprisingly, there was also an 1890 pension filing from Adolph's mother, Anna, still living in Germany. Of course, I wanted to know more.

This sent me again to Fold3, as the site has many complete files. I searched for a widow's pension and found several pages of pension files for Frederika (image **F**), including a copy of her marriage certificate (August 2, 1864). She was awarded an eight-dollars-a-month widow's pension.

Interestingly, Anna's 1890 claim was among the files I found. The letter (written in German) was translated, and both the original and translation are part of the lengthy file. Anna claimed that Adolph would never have married without telling his parents (which he did not do) and that she was entitled to his Army pension. Her claim was rejected.

You really never know what you'll find in those military pension files!

7

USING IMMIGRATION AND TRAVEL RECORDS

U nless you have Native American heritage, your ancestors were among the tens of millions of immigrants who left Europe, Asia, Oceania, South and Central America, and Canada to make their way to the United States. Your family may have heritage steeped in the lore of County Kildare or may have lost to time the memory of a country of origin.

While Ellis Island is the most iconic immigration port in America, it certainly was not the first port of entry. With Europeans sailing to American shores as early as the sixteenth and seventeenth centuries, Ellis Island was two to three hundred years down the road. In fact, Ellis Island didn't open until 1892, just in time to welcome the surge of immigrants arriving in the early part of the twentieth century.

In 1819, the United States Congress passed legislation requiring arriving ships to carry a passenger manifest. The law, which took effect in 1820, made it mandatory for manifests to be presented to the customs house before anyone could depart the ship. Over time, those records came under the purview of the National Archives and Records Administration (NARA) <www.archives.gov>.

As tempting as it is to log into Ancestry.com and head directly to immigration records, you need to know an approximate date when your family immigrated to effectively find your immigrant ancestor. For example, if you found your ancestor on the 1880 federal census, it's a sure bet they didn't come through Ellis Island. In addition, knowing (or suspecting) a country of origin will help you to search the probable ports in which they entered the United States. So hang in there and let me cover some immigration basics and the major periods of immigration to the United States first.

A BRIEF LOOK AT AMERICAN IMMIGRATION

Europeans came to America far earlier than what we consider the eras of immigration. French trappers explored much of present-day Canada, the Spanish had long-held settlements in Florida and the Southwest, and the Russians and British vied for supremacy in the Pacific Northwest.

Beyond those early explorers, America witnessed approximately three major eras of immigration. The first is during what we call the Colonial Era, beginning around 1600 and continuing for approximately two hundred years. During this era, colonies were established along the Eastern seaboard, with the most important being Jamestown, Virginia (1607), New England (1620—think *Mayflower*), and New Amsterdam (1624). Colonists were primarily English, Dutch, and German.

The second main era is from 1800 until about 1900. This is when the potato famine rocked Ireland, when free land beckoned Scandinavians to the Great Plains, and when Chinese workers came to build the transcontinental railroad. It was also during this era that the California Gold Rush attracted newcomers from every corner of the globe.

As German and Irish immigrants hit America's shores, many found steady work by joining the Army. A report compiled by the Adjutant General covering the years 1865 to 1874 showed half of all recruits were foreign-born: 20 percent were from Ireland, followed by 12 percent from Germany. If you're having trouble finding your Irish or German ancestor's immigration records, you may have more luck searching for them in the military (see chapter 6).

The last major immigration era began around the turn of the twentieth century. This was the heyday of Ellis Island and the great immigration from Eastern and Southern Europe, including many Jews seeking asylum from the pogroms in their homeland. Between 1892 and 1954, Ellis Island processed more than twelve million third-class and steerage immigrants. If your ancestors were of a higher social status (traveling first or second class), they would have been processed onboard steamships entering New York Harbor, not at Ellis Island.

BEGINNING YOUR SEARCH

Knowing the approximate date and probable ports where your ancestors arrived will help immensely as you search Ancestry.com immigration records. If you don't already know the date or port of entry, you can use other genealogical records to help narrow your search.

Once you have that information, check out the records we'll detail in this section.

Using Naturalization Records

One type of record that can be helpful in finding ancestors is the naturalization record. Naturalization is the process by which a foreign-born person becomes an American citizen.

Naturalization records, such as this Declaration of Intention for Joseph Brooks, can be key in connecting you with other key details.

While a voluntary process, it is required for US citizenship. Naturalization records can provide you with clues to finding the name of the immigrant's ship, age, place of residence, and place of birth.

Your ancestor first had to declare his intent to become a US citizen and renounce his allegiance to a foreign government. The record created from this was called a Declaration of Intention (image **A**). Early Declarations of Intention typically included the name of the person filing the intention, country of birth, application date, and signature. Records after 1906 were more detailed, noting physical description, birthplace, occupation, and (most importantly) the date and port of immigration. Beginning in 1929, a photo was also

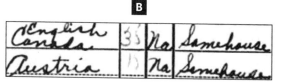

The 1940 US federal census notes a person's immigration status using an abbreviation. *Na* indicates the person is a naturalized citizen.

required. Three years after filing a Declaration of Intention, a person could file for a Petition for Naturalization. Once a petition was granted, a certificate of citizenship was issued.

Although naturalization laws were first established in 1790, the government has granted various people groups exceptions throughout history. First, from 1790 to 1922, wives of naturalized men were automatically granted citizenship. And up until 1940, children under the age of twenty-one automatically became naturalized citizens upon their father's naturalization. Strangely, if a female US citizen married an alien, her citizenship was revoked. A second change to the law came about in 1824. From 1824 to 1906, foreign-born children who had lived in the United States five years before their twenty-third birthday could file for both their Declarations and Petitions at the same time. Additional exceptions were granted for military service, as, in many instances, a veteran could file a Petition for Naturalization without filing a Declaration of Intention.

Currently, Ancestry.com has more than two hundred thousand records in a collection titled "New York, New York County Supreme Court Naturalization Petition Index, 1907–1924." Records may include important information such as birth location, occupation, spouse information, and witness names and addresses.

Using the US Census

Did you know that, in some instances, you can find immigration information in the federal census? Beginning in 1900 and continuing through 1930, the census required foreign-born people to declare their year of immigration and whether they were naturalized. On the 1920 census, respondents were asked for the year of naturalization. The 1940 census (the most recent census available) asks for citizenship of foreign-born people, with the following codes used (you'll find this in column 16):

- Na: Naturalized (image **B**)
- Pa: Having first papers
- Al: Alien
- Am Cit: American citizen born abroad

Note that, on the 1940 census, a foreign-born person from Canada and Ireland was required to state whether he or she was Canada-French, Canada-English, or from the Irish Free State (Eire) or Northern Ireland (part of the United Kingdom).

Lastly, the 1870 US federal census had a column for "Male citizens of the U.S. aged 21 years and upwards." If a foreign-born male checked this column he would have been naturalized prior to 1870.

Although the census can serve as a clue to finding the ancestor on a passenger list, censuses often have inconsistencies in how immigration and naturalization questions were answered. One ancestor I was researching gave three different dates of immigration on three different censuses.

You'll also find birthplace information on the census, which is a huge help when doing immigration research. But again, inconsistencies abound. I've seen one person state his place of birth as Malta, England, Gibraltar, and Madrid. So if you find a birthplace on one census, be sure to check other census years for verification.

One other way the census can help in locating a country of origin is to check the censuses that ask for the person's mother tongue. While this is not an infallible method, it definitely can be a clue. If your ancestral search takes you to Canada, be aware that the mother tongue can be listed on a census as *Can (English)*, *Can (Fr.)*, or *English (Irish)*.

If your family arrived in America before 1820 or before the period when immigration status was requested on the census, you'll need to consult other records in your search. We'll discuss these later in this chapter.

Ports of Entry

Again, we all think of Ellis Island when we think about the immigrant experience, but don't limit your search to New York City. Other popular ports of entry included:

- San Francisco, California (called "Angel Island"; arrivals came primarily from China)
- Baltimore, Maryland (a favored pre-American Revolution port)
- Boston, Massachusetts
- Castle Garden, New York City (operated until Ellis Island opened)
- Charleston, South Carolina (records from 1820)
- Philadelphia, Pennsylvania (major port of entry beginning in 1815)
- Port Townsend, Washington (arrivals from China)
- St. Albans, Vermont (arrivals from Canada)

AN OVERVIEW OF ANCESTRY.COM'S IMMIGRATION RECORDS

Ancestry.com has the world's largest online collection of immigration records. In addition to arrivals in America, you also can find collections of immigrant lists from Canada, the United Kingdom, and Australia. Those with Canadian or Mexican heritage may find family in one of the bordercrossing collections.

Ancestry.com's Immigration and Travel category has six major subcategories:

1. Passenger Lists

2. Crew Lists

3. Border Crossings and Passports

4. Citizenship and Naturalization Records

5. Immigration and Emigration Books

6. Ship Pictures and Descriptions

Each subcategory has its own unique records. Some contain images, original documents, digitized copies of books, or just simple indexes. You can do a global search of the entire Immigration and Travel category or search each collection individually.

To do a global search of these collections, select Immigration and Travel from the Search tab in Ancestry.com's main menu or go to the Card Catalog, then select Immigration and Travel (in the left column) and click the Search Entire Immigration and Travel Category link.

But first, let's look at what you can find in each subcategory.

Passenger Lists

As noted earlier, the US government required ships to present a passenger manifest list beginning in 1820. Early passenger lists included only basic information about immigrants, such as name, age, occupation, nationality, and gender. After 1892, immigration passenger lists added details such as last town of residence and final destination in the United States; the latter often included the name of a friend or relative in the states. Additionally, passenger lists noted whether the person could read or write, his general state of health, and his race. After 1906, you'll also find a physical description. While details vary from ship to ship and era to era, you can expect to find:

- full name

- date of birth

- birthplace

- last residence (city and country)

- occupation

- associates already in America
- intended destination in America
- traveling companions

When searching passenger lists, don't stop with just finding your ancestor's name. Check out the names of other people on the list, and you're likely to find other family members or neighbors. These same people probably lived close to your relative during a census, later married into your family, or witnessed a legal document.

You also can find annotations on a passenger list such as an X by the name of someone who was detained. Passengers may have been held due to a health condition or a woman may have been held until her husband or a relative came to get her. If you're interested in learning more about passenger list annotations, check out the great (and free) guide online at <**www.jewishgen.org/infofiles/Manifests**>.

In the Passenger Lists subcategory of Ancestry.com, you'll find records from around the world, including US, Swedish, German, Australian, Canadian, and Irish collections. I suggest using Ancestry.com's Card Catalog to filter by Passenger Lists and Location (image **C**). Remember the caveat from chapter 3—be creative in your filters. For instance, if you filter passenger lists by Location: Asia, you'll turn up two seemingly odd choices:

- "Netherlands, Dutch East India Company Passenger Lists to India, 1699–1794" (in Dutch)
- "Israel, Sarajevo Survivors Who Went to Israel, December 1948"

Knowing that Ancestry.com can select curious categories for collection, you may want to add a keyword to your search filters.

Crew Lists

This group of collections contains, not only crew lists, but also passenger lists, masters' and mates' certificates,

C

Filter Titles

❌ Immigration & Travel

❌ Passenger Lists

Filter By Location

Australia	23
Canada	21
Europe	57
Mexico	1
USA	150
Africa	2
Asia	1
North America	164
Oceania	23

When researching passenger lists, consider filtering by location using the Card Catalog.

Passenger lists aren't the only manifests worth researching. Crew lists provide valuable information about the shipmaster and his crew.

and crew lists of airplane departures. The latter contains indexes to passengers and crews departing or arriving from various cities, including Seattle, Miami, San Diego, and Honolulu. Some of the crew lists span several decades, others only a few years. Image **D** from the collection "Dorset, England Crew Lists, 1863–1914" lists the names of the shipmaster and the crew, age, place of birth, name of ship, date and place of joining and discharge from the ship, capacity (e.g., master, mate), date, and place and cause of death or leaving the ship.

Border Crossings and Passports

The most common collections you'll find in this group are bordercrossings to and from the United States, Canada, and Mexico. Also of great interest are passport applications. This group of collections also includes a few oddball records that you may not expect (remember to use the keyword filter!), such as internal Lithuanian passports (which, despite the name, are really identity cards rather than passports).

"Border Crossings from Canada to the U.S., 1895–1956," detail the person's name, age, residence, race, physical description, and destination (image **E**). Crossings in the collection "From Canada to U.S., 1895–1956," have records for crossings into many of the US states bordering Canada:

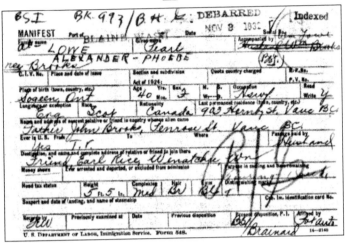

Immigrants often came to Canada or Mexico before making their way to the United States, so look for bordercrossing records like the ones found in "Border Crossings: From Canada to U.S., 1895-1956."

- Idaho
- Maine
- Minnesota
- Montana
- New York
- North Dakota
- Vermont
- Washington

If you're unsure of which state your ancestor might have crossed into, search for a map of the United States and find the state closest to where he lived in Canada. This makes for a good starting point.

US passport applications can provide a high level of detailed information about your ancestor, such as birth date and place, birth date of father, occupation, destination, and physical description. The description itself has more information than you're likely to find elsewhere, such as shape of nose, mouth, chin, and face. Even if your family never applied for a passport, it's fun to look up famous people like Franklin Roosevelt, who applied for a passport when he was assistant secretary of the Navy.

Prior to 1941, US citizens were not required to have passports for travel abroad, except for a few brief periods around the time of the Civil War and World War I.

Citizenship and Naturalization Records

Ancestry.com has an impressive collection of naturalization records, ranging from records by state, records of intent (mentioned earlier), consulate applications, and oaths of

Ancestors from Canada

It's not unusual to find ancestors who originally immigrated to Canada, then came to the United States. The Library and Archives Canada maintains a website with genealogical resources, including immigration records <www.bac-lac.gc.ca/eng/discover/immigration/immigration-records /Pages/introduction.aspx>.

Prior to April 1908, people could move freely across the border from the United States into Canada; no record of immigration exists for those individuals. You can, however, search the 1881 and 1891 Canadian censuses (for free). These records will give a place of birth, which means, if your ancestor originally immigrated to Canada and was there for either the 1881 or 1891 censuses before coming to the United States, you can find his place of birth. Search the census at <www.bac-lac.gc.ca/eng/search/Pages/ancestors-search.aspx>.

To learn more about your Canadian ancestors, begin investigating the official sites such as the Archives of Ontario or the Library and National Archives of Quebec (Bibliothèque et Archives nationales du Québec).

allegiance. Several of these collections are indexes only, while others contain images of original documents.

Again, make wise use of the Keyword search box to keep results within practical limits. Also, you'll find collections that you may not realize fit the definition of citizenship and naturalization, like California's Great Register (titled "California, Voter Registers, 1866–1898" on Ancestry.com). The register lists eligible voters, including their date and place of naturalization. Compiled at the county level, the Great Register was published every two years from 1866 to 1898.

Immigration and Emigration Books

This category contains a hodgepodge of passenger lists, records from the Emigrant Savings Bank, criminal registers, records of wives and children of Irish convicts in Australia, and even lists of early Scots Colonists to America. Given its diversity, this category is best searched by making liberal use of keywords and filters.

Ship Pictures and Descriptions

You may not find your ancestors' ships in this collection, but you can find a ship that looked very much like the one on which they booked passage. While this subcategory only contains a few collections, it has millions of records—so give it a go.

If you choose the collection "New York Port, Ship Images, 1851–1891," you can choose a specific year, month, or even ship name. The collection "Passenger Ships and Images" is not searchable by person's name, but rather by location, history, or year. A search for ships

Ancestry.com boasts a host of ship pictures, giving you valuable information about ships that brought immigrants to the New World (such as the *Acropolis*, pictured here).

into Charleston, South Carolina, for example, returned several ships spanning decades—like this one of the *Acropolis* (image **F**), built to transport immigrants from Greece to the United States.

SEARCHING FOR IMMIGRATION RECORDS

You've now learned about the variety of collection within the Immigration and Travel category, so let's take a look at how to find these types of records—first by searching the whole category, then by searching individual collections.

Sample Global Search

I want to search for an eighth great-grandfather, Johannes (Breul) Broyles, who I think came to America in the early 1700s—an unproven fact I discovered in a family genealogy. When I did a global search within the Immigration and Travel category for Johannes, Ancestry.com returned thirty hits, with one Hans and most others Jacob (the name of Johannes's son). The surnames:

- Broyles
- Breul
- Broile
- Broyl
- Broyle

Based on Johannes's approximate date of birth, all of the relevant hits came from the same collection: "U.S. and Canada, Passenger and Immigration Lists Index, 1500s–1900s." Johannes's date of entry into the United States was 1717.

Attached to his record in this collection were "Wife Ursley; Son Conrad; Daughter Elizabeth; Son Jacob." This matches information I had of a wife named Ursula and children Conrad and Elizabeth. The record further states:

Florida Genealogy

US history is often complicated, and knowing what parts of the country belonged to which global power during your ancestor's time is critical to learning about them. If your research takes you back to pre-statehood Florida (1845), for example, you may have to turn to Spanish, French, or British records when searching for your family.

The first written records in Florida begin with the Spanish in 1513, but by 1562 the French had established a colony near present-day Jacksonville. In 1702, English settlers attacked the Spanish at St. Augustine, while the French captured Pensacola a few years later.

The British, who had taken control of Cuba during the Seven Years' War, traded it back to Spain in exchange for Florida, which was then split into East Florida and West Florida. Both remained loyal to Britain during the American Revolution. In 1784, Spain regained control of Florida but formally ceded it to the United States in 1821. Have fun untangling that mess of family records!

Date of arrival at the colony at Germanna, Virginia. In 1725 the entire colony moved to the Robinson River near the foot of the Blue Mountains, in present Madison County [Virginia].

What type of search do you think is called for next? I'm unsure about the discrepancy of the first name (Johannes vs. Jacob), so further research is warranted. With the mention of the Germanna Colony, I'm fairly certain researching the people who came to that colony will take me back to the Broyles's country of origin. Because of this, I went back to Ancestry.com's Card Catalog, cleared my filters, and did a simple search of the entire catalog for the keyword *Germanna*. I received two hits, both genealogies of early German families in America. One of them, the genealogy of the Kemper family, included a scan of the genealogy, with a section devoted to the Germanna Colony.

Of great interest was the information that colonists were looking for "skilled miners out of Germany" to come and work in the iron mines. I didn't find Johannes named among the surnames, probably because this document was about a group of men who came to Germanna in 1714, while Johannes was among the 1717 arrivals.

Searching a Single Collection

You've just seen the process for searching the entire collection, now let's focus on a single collection. My target for this search was to find immigration or naturalization records for Albert Einstein. Per Wikipedia <www.wikipedia.org>, Einstein came to the United States in 1933 from Germany. Which collection should I use to start my search?

After browsing the list of Immigration and Travel collections in Ancestry.com's Card Catalog, I chose "New York Passenger Lists, 1820–1957." Amazingly, I found only one

| EINSTEIN √ | Albert | 54 | ✓ | M | Scientist | Yes | German | Yes | Switz'ld | Hebrew |

You can find famous immigrants in Ancestry.com's collection. Albert Einstein arrived in the United States in October 7, 1933, and his passenger list record notes he's a Hebrew scientist from Switzerland.

H

B 620	
Family name	Given name or names
Brooks	Joseph Edward
Address	
1917 Congress St.	Chgo.,Ill.
Certificate no. (or vol. and page)	Title and location of court
P-159201 C.N.4335953	U.S. Dist. Chgo.,Ill.
Country of birth or allegiance	When born (or age)
Gibralter-Gr. Britain	Apr. 15, 1861
Date and port of arrival in U.S.	Date of naturalization
	Nov. 18, 1937
Names and addresses of witnesses	

I found this naturalization record for Joseph Brooks in an Ancestry.com collection, but more records of him have eluded me—for now.

Albert Einstein, and luckily I knew his birth date and date of immigration. I quickly found him listed as a passenger on the *S.S. Westernland,* sailing out of Southampton on October 7, 1933 (image **G**).

Einstein is listed as a scientist, a citizen of Switzerland, and belonging to the "Hebrew" race. His last permanent residence was listed as Belgium. I checked all instances of Einstein in the collection and found him on other passenger lists, including one from Bermuda to the United States in 1935 and another in 1932, sailing from Bremen, Germany, to the United States on the *MS Oakland.*

WHAT TO DO IF YOU GET STUCK

As robust as Ancestry.com's immigration collections are, there will be times when you can't find someone in a record. Let me give you an example and then suggest some alternative strategies.

In chapter 5, I found the marriage of Joseph Brooks and Anna Wilson in 1882 Toronto, Canada, records. I next found the couple in Chicago on the 1900 US federal census. According to the census, the couple came to the United States in 1888. In addition, the code "Na" (naturalized) was noted next to both of their names. This told me that they had come to the United States and been naturalized by 1900 at the latest.

However, when searching immigration records for both Joseph and Anna, I found information related to this family in the "U.S. Naturalization Record Indexes, 1791–1992" collection (image **H**), which show the date of his naturalization as 1937.

I next looked in the collection "U.S. and Canada, Passenger and Immigration Lists Index, 1500s–1900s," but I doubted the Joseph Brooks I found was the correct one. The only information here was an arrival date in 1894 in Wisconsin. Does Wisconsin seem like a strange place to enter the United States? Yes it does, considering that Joseph lived in Toronto.

If you pull up a map of the United States, you'll see that Toronto is right across Lake Ontario from New York, so it seems more likely I'd find Joseph and Anna in a border-crossing record or a ship's passenger list going into New York. However, no such luck.

What's next? Other options for research:

- other Ancestry.com users' family trees

- obituaries

- newspapers

- stories

- legal documents

If those options fail, try these search strategies:

Learn native language spellings. If your ancestor came from a non-English speaking country, learn how his name would have been spelled in his native language. Check ethnic heritage websites that list surnames to find the original spelling.

Use wildcards. To use wildcards when searching for a surname, replace questionable letters with an asterisk. This will help when looking for a surname that is spelled differently than you think it should be spelled. My uncle, whose father was a Norwegian immigrant, has the surname Hjetland. While the name looks as though it should be pronounced "ha-jet-land," the correct pronunciation is "yet-lan." Think about how you'd use wildcards to track down this name in immigration records.

Consult the censuses. Use the US federal censuses or even state censuses to get an approximate year of immigration. Remember that the year noted on the census may not be exact.

Check bordercrossing records. It was less expensive for immigrants to go to Canada first and then immigrate to the United States, rather than to go directly to the United States. A close friend of mine told me that her parents, natives of Wales, first went to Canada and then on to the United States—so it seems that this might have been more common than I thought.

Research the history of an area. Borders, names, and territorial ownership have changed over time, particularly after wars. For example:

- Ethiopia was once called Abyssinia.

- Austria, Hungary, parts of the Czech Republic, Poland, Italy, Romania, and the Balkans were part of the Austro-Hungarian Empire until World War I.

- Myanmar was once called Burma.
- Newfoundland was a self-governing Dominion until becoming a Canadian province in 1949.
- The Republic of Texas gained independence from Mexico in 1836 and was annexed to the United States in 1845.
- Florida has existed under Spanish, French, and British control. (See the Florida Genealogy sidebar for more.)

Look to other records for early arrivals. If your ancestor arrived in the United States prior to 1820, you may have to use other sources to discover the country of origin. One of my favorite sources to check is a county history or a family genealogy. In one county history I discovered a reference to the family coming to the United States from Wales. In a genealogy, another branch was mentioned as having Irish roots.

Find male relatives first, then the rest of the family. If you find a male immigrant ancestor traveling without his family, this may be his first trip to America. Search later passenger lists, as he may have stayed in America long enough to put down roots or make enough money to go home and bring the rest of the family to the United States.

Use Ancestry.com's message boards. Did you know that Ancestry.com has nearly two hundred thousand message boards with more than twenty-five million messages? If you're having problems with an immigrant ancestor, discovering a country of origin, or unsure of how a family member might have spelled his name in the old country, start posting on one of the message boards.

You cans search the boards **<www.ancestry.com/boards>** in several ways, including by:

- content
- surname
- locality
- topic (immigration is one of the topics)

Message boards are a feature of Ancestry.com that you may not have previously explored. In the Immigration topic section, for example, you can search boards about tracing specific nationalities (e.g., Polish immigrants). Here, you'll find answers to problems such as "I found my ancestor's date of arrival in the United States on his naturalization papers, but couldn't find him in any immigration database."

8

DIGGING INTO NEWSPAPERS, PUBLICATIONS, AND MAPS

Newspapers, publications, and maps, along with reference material, are four major categories of printed works that may name your ancestor, describe a major event in your family's town, mention your family tree in a genealogy publication, or pinpoint locations in your family's life.

In this chapter, you'll learn about this group of Ancestry.com collections and how best to use them in your research.

NEWSPAPERS

Ancestry.com has more than one thousand collections of newspapers. Some contain indexes, while others have full text. The site includes US newspapers from all fifty states plus the District of Columbia. You'll find several publications from the United Kingdom and Canada, with a smattering of papers from Europe. Ancestry.com also owns Newspapers.com **<www. newspapers.com>**, one of the largest databases of digitized historical newspapers; we'll discuss this more in chapter 16.

Newspapers of old are much like newspapers of today—they report on events. These events include, but are not limited to:

- marriages
- deaths
- politics
- local news
- national news

- weather
- world events
- financial news
- school awards
- retail ads

While newspapers contain a tremendous wealth of information about a specific time and place, genealogists use these most often to search for obituaries. Obituaries (image **A**) can be the equivalent of a mini-biography, much like those found in old county history books. They may tell the circumstances of a person's death, and the names and ages of the spouse, children, parents, and siblings. You also may find the name of the funeral home, cemetery, and church where the service was held. Not all obits include a cause of death, but many do. Even if the cause of death isn't noted, you may find a clue in more recent obituaries based on the family's request for donations to organizations like the American Heart Association.

Other genealogically relevant information may include a mention of military service, place of employment, and membership in any organizations. In one detailed obituary I found on Ancestry.com, I learned the deceased was a devoted New York Yankees fan, loved fishing, was an Army veteran, and was predeceased by his three brothers, all of whom were named.

You can choose from a few ways of searching Ancestry. com's newspaper records. We'll start with how to search in the "United States Obituary Collection," then how to search for individual newspapers by titles or location.

Searching the US Obituary Collection

To get to this collection, click on the Search tab, then go to the Card Catalog. From there, select the Newspapers & Publications category. Next, find the "United States Obituary Collection, 1930–2017," a collection with more

MRS. CUSTER DEAD IN HER 91ST YEAR

Widow of Famous General and Indian Fighter of Post-Civil War Days.

KEPT HIS MEMORY ALIVE

"Boots and Saddles" and Other Books by Her Reviewed Deeds of Gallant Cavalry Chief.

Mrs. Elizabeth Bacon Custer, widow of General George A. Custer, famous Indian fighter of post Civil War days, died at 5:30 yesterday afternoon in her apartment at 71 Park Avenue after a heart attack that occurred Sunday evening.

Obituaries, like this 1933 one of Elizabeth Custer (wife of the famous general), are like mini biographies.

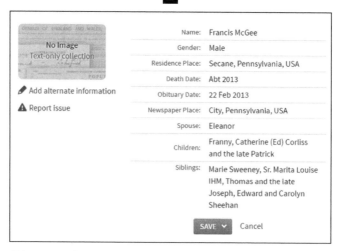

B

Name:	Francis McGee
Gender:	Male
Residence Place:	Secane, Pennsylvania, USA
Death Date:	Abt 2013
Obituary Date:	22 Feb 2013
Newspaper Place:	City, Pennsylvania, USA
Spouse:	Eleanor
Children:	Franny, Catherine (Ed) Corliss and the late Patrick
Siblings:	Marie Sweeney, Sr. Marita Louise IHM, Thomas and the late Joseph, Edward and Carolyn Sheehan

Obituary records on Ancestry.com will provide you with a summary of the text, including the names of any children or siblings that the obituary mentions.

than thirty-seven million records (and recent obituaries from hundreds of newspapers, with more added daily).

Right-click the link to open the search form in a new tab. The search boxes allow you to enter name, birth and death dates and locations, or newspaper title. Fill in whatever information you have, then begin the search. If you don't get any results, try removing or adding filters to expand or narrow the search.

To help you determine if the person in the search results is from your family, the results page lists other people mentioned in the obituary along with the name of the city where the newspaper was located. This gives you a quick way to gauge if the names are relevant to your family search.

When you click on the record link, you'll see a summary of the obituary (image **B**). Note that, in some cases, family members are also named in the summary.

Searching Newspapers by Location

When you've finished searching the "United States Obituary Collection" (or if you don't know enough about your ancestor's area to search by newspaper), go to the Card Catalog and clear any previous filters. Next, begin applying filters for location and/or date. If you apply the filter for the United States (and you're positive of the state in which a person died), go ahead and also apply the state filter. Once you've selected a state, you'll have the further option of filtering by city.

Click the name of the city to bring up a list of newspapers included in the collection. Some cities (like New York) might have several collections, while others may only have a few. San Diego, for example, has only one newspaper collection on Ancestry.com: "San Diego Union-Tribune Obituaries, 1993–1994."

You also can search by newspaper name in the Title or Keyword search box. You don't have to use the full name of the paper in the search boxes.

If you have UK or Irish heritage, be sure to search the more than one-million names in the "United Kingdom and Ireland Obituary Collection."

Searching the Historical Newspapers Collection

Ancestry.com has a fine collection of historical newspapers (see the "Historical Newspapers, Birth, Marriage, and Death Announcements, 1851–2003" collection); however, these are limited geographically. To date, records in this collection pertain only to:

- *The New York Times* (1851–2001)
- The *Los Angeles Times* (1881–1984)
- *The Boston Globe* (1872–1922)
- The *Chicago Defender* (Big Weekend and National Editions; 1921–1975)
- The *Chicago Tribune* (1850–1985)
- *The Hartford Courant* (1791–1942)
- *The Washington Post* (1877–1990)
- *The Atlanta Constitution* (1869–1929)

Search this collection by name, event date, event, keyword, or newspaper title.

PERIODICALS & MAGAZINES

Periodicals and magazines make up a separate section of the Newspapers & Publications category. Periodicals and magazines are both printed at regular intervals, but periodicals are often published less often than magazines, such as a quarterly journal. The Periodicals & Magazines subcategory comprises sixty-nine collections, with the majority of them from the United States and Canada.

The Periodicals & Magazines subcategory has a handful of eclectic journals (e.g., the *New South Wales Police Gazette*), but its strength lies in its genealogy journals, such as:

- *Genealogies of Virginia Families*
- *Virginia Genealogical Society Quarterly*

C

Uffington.

[1796, *Part I., p.* 105.]

Inclosed (Fig. 2) is an exact delineation of the figure called the White Horse, as it appears at about a mile distance from the hill on which it is cut, supposed by Wise* and other antiquaries to be a monument of the West Saxons, made in memory of a great victory obtained over the Danes, at Ashdown, near it, by King Alfred, A.D. 871. Thus Mr. Pye, in his "Poem of Farringdon Hill,' describes it :

> "Carved rudely on the pendant sod, is seen
> The snow-white courser stretching o'er the green ;
> The antique figure scan with curious eye,
> The glorious monument of victory !
> There England rear'd her long-dejected head,
> There Alfred triumph'd, and invasion bled."

After this manner our horse is formed, on the side of a high and steep hill, facing the north-west. His dimensions are extended over an acre of ground or thereabouts. His head, neck, body, and tail consist of one white line ; as does also each of his four legs. This is done by cutting a trench into the chalk, of about 2 or 3 feet deep and about 10 feet broad.

J. STONE.

"The Gentleman's Magazine Library, 1731–1868" collection contains this description of Uffington, an ancient site in Britain.

D

BALLARD NOTES

Thomas Ballard b. 1630; buried March 24, 1689. Clerk of York County in 1652 and for many years later. Burgess from James City in 1666, member of the council in 1675, speaker of H. of B. in 1680. His case as a creditor of "Bacon the rebel" was in 1686 represented to the King by the council. Married Anne ——, who died Sept 26, 1678. William Thomas of York Co, whose wife was Anne ——, calls Ballard "son-in-law" and Sarah Henman and Jane Hillier wife of John Hillier, "daughters-in-law." Ballard's wife was captured by Bacon, and placed, with other ladies of the Council, upon his breastworks before Jamestown, where their white aprons warned Berkeley from attack. Capt Robert Baldrey

The Periodicals & Magazines category includes published genealogies that may include information about your own ancestors.

- *Pennsylvania German Pioneers*

- *Genealogies of Pennsylvania Families*

- *North Carolina Historical and Genealogical Register*

- *Maine Historical and Genealogical Register*

To search the Publications & Magazines subcategory, return to the Card Catalog, clear filters, and filter by the subcategory Newspapers & Publications, then Periodicals & Magazines. Because this is a relatively small group of records, begin by searching the entire category. You'll find the link above the listing of all of the collections within this category.

Unless you have families who were early settlers in the states with genealogy publications, you may not find a family member by name. However, adding keywords to your search might at least ferret out some article about a place in which the family lived.

From the Card Catalog, you also can filter the Periodicals & Magazines subcategory by location. If you filter by location, you'll see Ancestry.com has a couple dozen collections from Europe, with eleven of them from the United Kingdom. One of the more interesting UK collections is "The Gentleman's Magazine Library, 1731–1868." First published in London, the magazine has biographies, stories, essays, articles, poetry, and descriptions of historically important places (image **C**). In addition, it included announcements of births, marriages, and deaths. The publication has been scanned using optical character recognition (OCR), which converts the image to text so it can be searched.

Likewise, the *Genealogies of Virginia Families* are scanned, and I was fortunate to find a section on my Ballard family line in more than one of the volumes (image **D**).

Even if you don't find your ancestors listed in periodicals or magazines, you can learn some wonderful social history lessons from them. For example, if you had working-class UK ancestors, take a bit of time to read through some issues of the *Penny Magazine* (1832–1844). Geared toward the workingman, the magazine cost one penny and was (per Ancestry.com) "meant to provide means for those unable to receive formal teaching to educate themselves." In it, you'll find discussions about poetry, historical events such as the Battle of Hastings, and Mr. Shakespeare.

MAPS, ATLASES & GAZETTEERS

Maps, atlases, and gazetteers are among my favorite research tools. Without maps, I wouldn't be able to trace migration patterns, see changing boundary lines, and understand the geography of where the family lived, as well as figure out its location relative to other towns, counties, and states. Look at a map, and you'll get a real understanding of migration routes and patterns. The easiest routes were clearly along coasts or down rivers. Pull out a present-day atlas and try to imagine it without roads. You'll quickly see how your ancestors traveled and why they ended up in certain locales. If you ever "lose" a generation, you can use maps to help speculate on a possible new home.

One of my early research mistakes was not using a map when trying to track down information about my family tree. I swore I did everything possible to find a great-great-grandfather in the county where he lived, but came up short on every occasion. If I had bothered looking at a map, I would have seen that three Missouri counties border each other and that Great-grandpa had lived at the intersection of all three. Some of his records were in one county, and some in another! If I had looked at a map, I would have saved myself years (and yes, I mean *years*) of searching.

On another occasion, when I was young and uneducated in the way of research, I kept trying to find a 1790 record in Kentucky. When I consulted an early map I realized Kentucky wasn't even a state until 1792. Prior to that time, Kentucky was a territory, part of Virginia—and so that's where I'd find that record. Duh.

But beyond my own research gaffes, it's important to understand that being able to place the family in a specific place during a specific time opens a huge door to other research possibilities. Once you know when and where the family lived, you can start pouring over land, birth, death, marriage, and tax records.

Before we dig into Ancestry.com's Maps, Atlases & Gazetteers subcategory, you'll need to know these key terms:

- A *map* is a graphical representation of a place.

- An *atlas* is a compilation of many maps (think a road atlas of the United States).

- A *gazetteer* is a blend of maps, as well as a geographic dictionary of sorts. Modern gazetteers include basic information about a place, including recreation, gardening, tidal times, wildlife, and things to see.

Once again, head to the Card Catalog to get to this category. Use the Filter by Collection option, then choose Maps, Atlases & Gazetteers. The Maps & Atlases subcategory has about fifty collections, and the Gazetteers category has more than 150. Let's look at both subcategories.

Maps & Atlases

This subcategory contains early land maps dating from the late 1700s. In particular, this is where you'll find those oh-so-valuable plat maps. A plat map (image **E**) is a map that shows the divisions of an area of land. In some cases, a plat map may reference the original patent or tract. Plat maps are among my favorite maps because they show exactly where

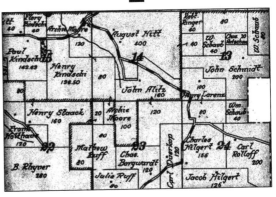

Plat maps show divisions of land, often including the landowner's name.

the family owned land and the names of all of the neighbors. A plat map also can show roads, railroad lines, creeks, cemeteries, and schools.

Additionally, you'll find maps of English counties, German topography, an 1817 atlas of London, early maps of Massachusetts and Ohio, and (another favorite) the *Emigration Atlas of 1862* (image **F**). This is a slim volume—only eighteen pages—and is comprised only of images.

According to Ancestry.com, the *Emigration Atlas* had basic information for people emigrating from Great Britain, including maps of Canada, the United States, Mexico, South America, and other countries. Write-ups on each destination provide brief descriptions of the country, cost of passage, length of journey, type of workers each destination needed, wages, cost of living, and more.

Gazetteers

Ancestry.com has so many gazetteers that I'd advise filtering by location. (Unless, of course, you just want to spend a lovely afternoon combing through old maps!) One gazetteer collection you may want to spend some time with is the "U.S. Gazetteer, 1854." This volume was created using data from the 1850 census. It includes information about the population of states, counties, and townships, as well as agricultural and other statistics of the counties. If you're looking for a place that no longer exists, search this collection first.

F

There are three great routes from Europe to California :—

1st, By sea-voyage direct to New York (or some other of the Atlantic ports of America), and thence overland through the United States, passing along the upper part of the valley of the Missouri, and crossing the chain of the Rocky Mountains. The overland journey occupies about three months, and a great portion of it is through a country destitute of roads, and presenting almost insurmountable difficulties to the traveller.

2d, By sea-voyage to the port of Chagres, on the Isthmus of Panama (either direct, or by way of New York), thence overland across the isthmus to the coast of the Pacific, and afterwards by steamer to San Francisco. The distance from New York to Chagres is 2,300 miles, the time occupied from twelve to fifteen days ; from Chagres to Panama, on the opposite side of the isthmus, a distance of 50 miles, occupies between two and three days ; from Panama to San Francisco, 3,500 miles, occupying about twenty days.

3d, By a direct sea-voyage round Cape Horn (the southern extremity of the American continent) to San Francisco, a distance of 17,000 miles, and of about five months in duration.

The *Emigration Atlas of 1862,* available in Ancestry.com's Maps & Atlases category detailed three different ways of getting from Europe to California.

> The town of Rothesay was originally a village in connection with the castle; and in its more matured, as well as in its infant state, it necessarily shared the castle's fortunes,—at times basking in the favour of the powerful and eventually royal family who owned it, and at other times suffering capture and plunder from the Norwegians, the Islesmen, the English, and the conflicting parties in civil wars. At an early period, it was made a burgh-of-barony; and in 1400, it received from Robert III. a charter erecting it into a royal burgh, and conferring upon it a considerable quantity of landed property. In 1584, a charter of confirmation and novodamus was given by James VI. The town seems to have grown slowly but steadily in prosperity; and it gradually became a very great mart for the Lowlanders exchanging commodities with the Highlanders and Islesmen. About the

Gazetteers contain detailed information about specific places. Here, the *Scotland Gazetteer* discusses the town of Rothesay.

Gazetteers also include information about businesses, so if your ancestor had any kind of business you may find a mention in one of the state publications such as the "Iowa Gazetteer and Business Directory, 1884–1885."

If you're searching for non-US places, you can choose from dozens of European gazetteers and more than a dozen from Canada. If you know the county in which your UK ancestors lived, you may luck out and find an ancestor in a publication such as the "Dorset, England Tithe Apportion and Maps, 1835–1850." And of course the *Scotland Gazetteer* (image **G**) is a must-search for anyone with Scottish ancestry, as it contains detailed history of many Scottish towns and villages.

As you search the gazetteers, you'll notice almost all of them are printed books that have been scanned and indexed.

REFERENCE, DICTIONARY & ALMANACS

Many of the items in this category are indexes to journal articles or scanned books, so you may not be able to read a full-text version of some findings. In other instances, as with *Virginia Colonial Abstracts*, you'll find fascinating abstracts of county records, from depositions to accusations of cheating, to orders for one party to make payment to another.

To access this collection go to the Card Catalog, filter by Collection, then select Reference, Dictionary & Almanacs. As you can see, this subcategory has four subsets, comprising more than seventeen hundred collections:

1. General Reference Materials

2. Research Guides & Finding Aids

3. Dictionaries & Encyclopedias

4. Almanacs, Country Studies, & Gazetteers

This collection is so varied—not only across topics but also across geography—that unless you want to take the time to skim through all of the collections, you might

Filter Titles

⊗ Reference, Dictionaries & Almanacs

Filter By Collection

General Reference Materials   526

Research Guides & Finding Aids   840

Dictionaries & Encyclopedias   142

Almanacs, Country Studies & Gazetteers   293

The Reference, Dictionary & Almanacs subcategory is large and varied, so you'll likely want to filter by subcategory.

Card Catalog
Searchable listing of all record collections

Title
compendium american genealo

Keyword(s)

SEARCH   or   Clear All

Filter By Collection

Stories, Memories & Histories   7

Reference, Dictionaries & Almanacs   2

Filter By Location

USA   7

Results 1-7 of 7   Sort By Popularity ▼

Title	Collection	Records	Activity
The Compendium of American Genealogy, Vol. IV	Stories, Memories & Histories	695	
The Compendium of American Genealogy, Vol. VII	Stories, Memories & Histories	795	
The Compendium of American Genealogy, Vol. VI	Stories, Memories & Histories	748	
The Compendium of American Genealogy, Vol. I	Stories, Memories & Histories	1,144	
The Compendium of American Genealogy, Vol. III	Stories, Memories & Histories	606	
The Compendium of American Genealogy, Vol. V	Stories, Memories & Histories	752	
The Compendium of American Genealogy, Vol. II	Stories, Memories & Histories	394	

1

The Compendium of American Genealogy, a collection of published genealogies, contains seven volumes, each of which is a collection on Ancestry.com.

benefit from doing a search across all of the categories, then using multiple filters (location, date, collection, keyword) to narrow your search depending on what you're trying to find (image **H**). To search the entire collection, click the Search Entire Reference, Dictionaries & Almanacs category link.

If you're interested in learning the history of a location, either filter down to almanacs, use the keyword filter to enter a location, or search by title for something like *geographic* or *geography*. I wanted to know what collections might pertain to my home state of Missouri. By entering *Missouri* as a keyword, I got more than a hundred hits, among them the "Missouri History Encyclopedia, 1901" and the "Missouri State Gazetteer and Business Directory, 1881." In the history, I found a wonderful account of the founding of Lone Jack, the place my ancestors settled in 1836.

If you're searching Jewish ancestors, don't miss the "Jewish Given Name Variations" collections, which will allow you to view alternate spellings for your ancestors' names. When searching for the given name *Herschel*, results returned a list of name variations including Hersh, Hershl, Hirsh, Herschan, Herschl, Hercel, Hersel, and Hershel.

If you've been hoping to find a genealogy already written about your family, don't miss doing a search of *The Compendium of American Genealogy*. The seven-volume set lists 345,000 names in more than forty-five thousand lineages. Enter the collection name in the Title box on the Card Catalog page, then search each of the volumes for your surname (image **I**).

A search for the surname *Dimmitt* found hits in Volumes I and IV, but none in the others. One of the hits in IV was listed in a lineage, with the place of marriage in Baltimore. Yet one more clue to tracking down this family line.

SEARCH STRATEGIES

Let's take a closer look at strategies to aid your search.

Searching a Category

Follow along with me as I do a category-wide search. I want to learn more about the Dimmitt line in Texas, so I decided to do an all-category search of the Maps, Atlases & Gazetteers category. The only thing I entered in the search box was the surname and keyword *Texas* (image **J**). This gave me twenty-two hits, with the three most relevant results in *A Gazetteer of Texas* (image **K**).

I learned that Dimmit was the county seat of Castro County, but also that there is a Dimmit County. I wondered who the Dimmit(t) was that these places were named for. A quick Google search found the county named for Philip Dimmitt for his "outstanding service" to the Republic of Texas. Apparently Dimmitt had been at the Alamo but was sent out on a scouting mission and was gone during the attack. What interested me was that Dimmitt was originally from Kentucky, yet one more clue for research.

Searching a Collection

Let's do a sample search of a collection. In this case, I decided to search for the obituary of any Hendrickson who lived in Cass County, Missouri. In the Card Catalog, I selected the Newspapers & Publications category, then entered the keyword *Cass*. Next, I selected the collection "Web: Cass County, Missouri, Obituary Index, 1870–2011." Note: Collections with the prefix of "Web" take you off the Ancestry.com site to view search results.

After searching for the surname *Hendrickson* and birth year of *1888* +/- 10 years, I found an obituary for Arthur Harry Hendrickson. Instead of showing me the entire obit, the page (image **L**) displays a Go to website link on the right side of the results. When I clicked this, it took me to the website of the Cass County Historical Society, where I could order (for a small fee) a copy of the obituary.

J

Use keywords in conjunction with last names or place names to help narrow your search.

K

Dimmit; a southern county, with an area of 1,164 square miles. The population was 1,106; the county seat, Carrizo Springs. The mean magnetic declination in 1900 was 8° 30′. The mean annual rainfall is 25 inches, and the mean annual temperature 70°.

The *A Gazetteer of Texas* collection gives this detailed description of Dimmitt County, Texas.

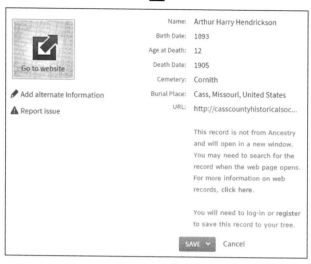

Name:	Arthur Harry Hendrickson
Birth Date:	1893
Age at Death:	12
Death Date:	1905
Cemetery:	Cornith
Burial Place:	Cass, Missouri, United States
URL:	http://casscountyhistoricalsoc...

This record is not from Ancestry and will open in a new window. You may need to search for the record when the web page opens. For more information on web records, click here.

You will need to log-in or register to save this record to your tree.

SAVE ⌄   Cancel

The Go to website icon and link indicates you'll need to leave Ancestry.com to view the record.

Browsing a Scanned Book

Scenario: Let's say Ancestry.com found a mention of your relative in a scanned book. When you click the link it goes to page 705 (an index), with the notation that your ancestor's information is on pages 105 and 347. How do you easily go from page 705 to the earlier pages, without back-clicking through the entire book? This happened to me when searching *Virginia Colonial Abstracts* for the surname Ballard.

Here's how to make quick work of navigating a scanned book: Click on the text on the top of the page, under the title of the collection. A dropdown menu will pop up and show you the various sections in the book. From here, click the section that you *think* is about in the correct page range. Once you're close, it's easy to use Ancestry.com's back-and-forth arrows at the bottom of the document for navigation.

With two clicks I found the page I wanted—much better than the three hundred or so clicks it would have taken me to page back using the back-and-forth arrows. In this instance, I learned that ancestor Thomas Ballard owed an estate for his bill of thirty yards of buckram. A search of Wikipedia **<www.wikipedia.org>** told me that buckram was a fabric made of cotton or linen.

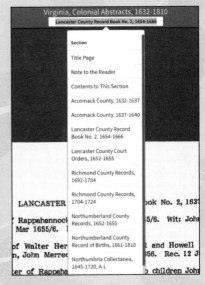

Ancestry.com gives you access to tables of contents for collections that were originally published in book format, allowing you to more easily move between sections.

9

SEARCHING STORIES, MEMORIES, HISTORIES, AND PICTURES

Like most family historians, I love collecting stories about my family or the places they lived. In fact, it was stories that first launched my interest in genealogy back when I was about eight years old. One grandmother recounted stories about her Civil War grandfather—a story that (when I was a bit older) led me to my first request for military information from the National Archives. My other grandmother told one of the family's favorite stories about how her father was born in a field during the Civil War when William Quantrill's raiders burned down the family farmhouse. With stories like that, you can see why I have always been drawn to genealogy!

Family stories are the closest we'll get to knowing the real people behind the names and dates. Stories tell us about personality, character, events, and beliefs. Many stories, like the one you'll read later in this chapter, have been documented in a published work—and if you're lucky, you'll find those stories on Ancestry.com. Other stories may not be in a published book, but it's possible you'll find them uploaded in Ancestry.com users' family trees. In fact, users have uploaded more than nineteen million such stories.

In chapter 2, you learned about the value of uploading a public family tree to Ancestry.com. In addition, I covered how to upload your own images and stories to a family tree. Hopefully by now, you've uploaded pictures and tales about your own family—and if you're like me, you'll see (in the Member Connect module on your home page) that your uploads have been saved in other trees within days of you uploading a story or photo. It's this spirit of sharing that has always been a hallmark of the genealogy hobby.

But this chapter isn't only about family stories and memories. It's about finding histories of the places your family lived. Again, these may be well documented in a published book, such as a county or state history, or they may be user-generated. Local histories are among my favorite tools because they place my family in historical context, which then helps me when researching when they may have arrived or when they may have left for greener pastures.

There is a caveat, of course. In chapter 1, I wrote about not trusting everything you see in print. That goes for both user-uploaded stories and printed books. When writing a county history, for example, the author likely didn't include some of the negative traits about a person in his biography, and it's likely he may have exaggerated the better qualities. In one county history, I found a biography of my great-great-grandfather that extolled his Civil War service and his booming post-war sawmill business. What it didn't mention (not surprisingly) was the fact that he deserted one Civil War regiment and later joined another. 'Nuff said.

In this chapter, we'll explore two categories of Ancestry.com's records collections that can provide these rich stories and photos: the Stories, Memories, & Histories category, and the Historical Pictures category. Given that Ancestry.com has thousands of collections between these two categories, I'm hoping you'll find at least one family and more than a few mentions of the places they lived. Included in the collection are both family and local histories, place histories, interviews, military histories, histories of societies and organizations.

THE STORIES, MEMORIES & HISTORIES CATEGORY

To begin, we'll use Ancestry.com's Card Catalog filters to do several searches, all of which should give you insight into the value of putting your family into historical context, understanding the events that impacted their lives, and—perhaps the best—learning more about who your ancestors really were. (We'll delve into Pictures later in this chapter.)

Start at the Card Catalog and choose the Stories, Memories & Histories category. From here, you could do a global search of the entire twenty thousand-plus collections—but before you do, let's discuss the many subcategories and types of records available.

Family Histories, Journals & Biographies

Who wouldn't like to discover a journal kept by a distant ancestor? Sadly, that discovery isn't going to be in my future because, based on census and other information, I don't think many people in the family could read or write. However, that doesn't mean your family was the same.

This subcategory includes the more than nineteen million stories uploaded by Ancestry.com users, as well as from publications and compilations such as:

- *Annals of Southwest Virginia, 1769–1800*
- *Burke's Family Records*
- *U.S. Family Photo Collection, c. 1850–2000*
- *Dictionary of National Biography*
- *Early Settlers of New York State*
- *Settlers of Maryland, 1679–1783*
- *Irish Relatives and Friends*
- *The Loyalists in Ontario*
- *Who's Who in Australia, 1921–1950*

Can you see the depth and breadth of this subcategory?

For example, I had once read that one group of ancestors (the Snow family) lived on Fisher's River. In the Card Catalog with the Stories, Memories, & Histories category selected, I filtered the location for USA and North Carolina, and added *Fisher's River* as a keyword. (Note: If you're searching and don't know if a body of water was named a river or creek, just use the proper name only as a keyword, such as *fisher's*.) My search got only two hits. The first, *History of the Fisher's River Primitive Baptist Association*, was a bust. However, the second was what genealogy dreams are made of.

The second hit, *Fisher's River Scenes and Characters*, was written based on stories "enacted and told between 1820 and 1829." I didn't learn that much about John, but the jewel in the crown was the story about John's father, Frost. There was a fabulous physical description:

> He was of small stature with a triune countenance—the sad, the quizzical, and the cheerful, the cheerful preponderating—ever ready for a loud, hearty laugh.

The author went on to tell how Frost loved using "rustic" language instead of sounding like the educated man that he was (image **A**). There's also a scene in which Frost relates threatening his "Negro boy" Anderson for using a better vocabulary word than Frost, himself; however, as I kept reading, it was clear that it was all a joke to Frost. I also found one of the best insults I've ever read, when Frost calls Anderson a "lamper-jawed, cat-hamed puke." That's a new one for me.

Remember that, in chapter 3, we discussed you can view by Records or Categories when viewing search results. Use the tabs at the top of the results column to select Records (this

> He was raised in "Albermarle, Fudgin-ny," and didn't care "a durn whether he b'longed to one on the fust famblys uv Fud-ginny ur not." He certainly came from a section where rustic literature had attained to perfection; and he clung to the language

Biographies can give you insight into an ancestor's personality. This excerpt from Fisher's River Scenes and Characters talks about my ancestor Frost Snow's speech patterns.

Oral Histories & Interviews

With only twenty-one collections, this subcategory may not have your family in it, but you may find information about a specific time, place, or event relevant to your ancestors. For example, the collection "Interviews With Former Slaves, 1936–1938" is a chilling look at the way many slaves were treated as objects, rather than people (image). If you're researching African-American ancestors, use the Browse This Collection feature and select the state in which your ancestor lived. The records you see may give you a fairly good sense of what it was like to be a slave in that location.

In this subcategory, you'll also find collections such as the "New York City, Ellis Island Oral Histories, 1882–1976," a

shows all of the results for your search) or Categories (shows the category in which your search appears).

> De white folks house wuz big, wid porches, an flowers all aroun', an sweet locust trees in de do'' yard. Dis wuz up in Perry County, a few miles fum Seventy Six Landing.
>
> When Ole Mastuh died, dat wuz de fathuh ob young Mastuh Joe--he war sick a long time. Dar he lay fum openin' o' spring, 'bout de time flies cum, 'til wheat-sowin' time in de fall. An' its de God's trufe, all dat time he made me stan' side o' his bed--keepin' de flies offen him, I wuz jes seben year ole but dere I had tuh stan, day en night, night en' day. Co'se I'd sleep sumtimes wen he wuz sleepin'. Sumtimes when I'd doze, my bresh ud fall on he's face, den he'd take he's stick an' whack me a few across de haid an' he'd say, "Now I dare you to cry." I cried, but he didden see me do it.

A former slave shares his experiences in his own words in this transcription of an oral interview, available in the "Interviews With Former Slaves, 1936–1938" collection on Ancestry.com.

Collection Highlight:
American Genealogical-Biographical Index

One of the most important biographical collections on Ancestry.com is the "American Genealogical-Biographical Index" (AGBI), which includes the names of millions of people who have appeared in published genealogical records.

According to Ancestry.com, sources in this collection are largely from the nineteenth century, and each entry contains the person's complete name, year of the biography's publication, the person's state of birth (if known), abbreviated biographical data, and a reference to the original book and page number. Also included in the collection is the 1790 US federal census, with a listing for all heads-of-household.

If you are doing US research, be sure to search this valuable collection.

must-search if you had ancestors come through Ellis Island. (See chapter 7 for more on researching immigration records on Ancestry.com.)

Social & Place Histories

Place histories (a.k.a. local histories) typically detail the history, topography, people, crops, weather, and industry of a specific geographic region, such as a county or town. Many also include brief biographies of prominent townspeople or early settlers. If you want to get a sense of what it was like to live in a place during a specific time frame, start searching for a place history.

Ancestry.com has more than twenty thousand social and place history collections that cover much of the world. The Canadian group of records, for example, contains millions of public family tree stories, early settlers in Ontario, a dominion directory, and a history of provinces. Interestingly, I discovered an illustrated history of Southern California (including San Diego) tucked into the grouping of Mexican collections. And with roughly two thousand collections, the Europe filter includes information on many Old World countries (some of which are in German or French).

I wanted to learn more about the history of Highland County, Ohio, as it was the birthplace of my third great-grandfather, Joseph Knox. In Ancestry.com's Card Catalog, I selected the Stories, Memories & Histories category, then the Social & Place Histories subcategory. I typed *Ohio* in the Title box and *Highland* in the Keyword box. The search returned four hits.

One of the hits was exactly what I'd hoped to find: "The History of the County of Highland in the State of Ohio: From Its First Creation and Organization, to July 4th, 1876." Although the publication made no mention of Joseph Knox, I did find an abundance of information on the county's creation, the value of property, and the politics, legal, and religious history. I had better luck in the collection "General Business Review of Highland County, Ohio," another of my four hits. There, I learned that Joseph was the first wheelwright in the county—but, according to the review, the man who succeeded him was more skilled!

Society & Organization Histories

With more than twenty-six hundred collections, this is an eclectic subcategory if there ever was one! From orphan asylum records to professional baseball players to the Old Dutch Church of Sleepy Hollow, this subcategory has plenty of interesting information to browse. The good news is that if your ancestor belonged to any kind of professional organization or society, you might find him listed here. You'll also find lineages of various genealogical societies like Colonial Dames, Sons and Daughters of Pilgrims, and the "elite family directory." If your ancestor belonged to a particular religion, also check out the many church histories.

In this subcategory, you'll want to make good use of filters when focusing in on the best collections to search, but also be creative in how you're searching. For example, the Seattle Genealogical Society published a collection of five-generation ancestral lineages for its membership; however, Seattle doesn't appear anywhere in the collection title. The collection only appears in search results when *Seattle* is used as a keyword.

Military Histories

This subcategory encompasses military histories spanning centuries. The largest single collection is the "Official Records of the Union and Confederate Armies, 1861–1865." In this collection, you'll find official correspondences, orders, and reports from both armies. It's possible your ancestor is named in one of the documents (and, if not by name, certainly by regiment or name of battle).

If you're searching for information on a specific war or conflict, I'd suggest filtering by decade, otherwise you're likely to get a lot of irrelevant hits. For example, when I filtered by the date of 1860s, almost all of the hits were relative to the Civil War. Filtering by the 1600s brought up Colonial military records, along with a sprinkling of French military histories.

One of the collections, "Soldiers in King Philip's War," is about a war fought during 1675 to 1678 (although the book traces conflicts from 1620 to 1677). Also known as the First Indian War, this conflict pitted English colonists in New England against Native Americans. Even if you didn't have ancestors in America as early as this war, it's still a fascinating read about early Colonial America.

If you filter by the 1700s, you'll find close to two hundred collections, including those of Colonial militia, Revolutionary War soldiers and loyalists, and burial sites of those fighting for independence. Several of the Revolutionary War documents relate to specific states, so the Location filter is another tool you might employ. You can filter by USA, then by the state name. For example, filtering for Alabama returns a collection called "Revolutionary Soldiers in Alabama," and filtering for New Jersey returns a collection called "New Jersey Volunteers (Loyalists) in the Revolutionary War."

If your searches turn up less than you expected, be creative in adding or deleting sets of filters. And, of course, use the Title and Keyword search boxes.

Findings vary by collection, but oftentimes you can find more than just a name in one of those histories. For example, "Early Dublin: A List of the Revolutionary Soldiers of Dublin, N.H." contains short biographies about the men listed.

```
                    FIRST TROOP OF GEORGIA RANGERS

Pay Bill, First Troop of Georgia Rangers, Captain John Milledge,
Commander, 18 May 1759 to 18 Aug 1759

Nr  Rank        Name                    Remarks
1   Captain     Milledge, John          comm. 18 Aug 1757
1   1st Lieut   Parker, Thom:           died 18 Jun 1759, 34 days
1   2d Lieut    Baily, Robert           comm. 4 Nov 1757
2   "   "       Rivers, Moses Nunes     "     4 Jul 1759
1   Qtr-Mstr    Farmer, John            "     "  "    "
1   Cadet       Milledge, Thomas        "     18 May 1759
2   "           Campbell, John          "     28 Sept 1758
1   Corporal    Fraking, Conrad         enl.  26 Sept 1758
2   "           Fox, John               "     3 Nov 1758
3   "           Daniel, John            "     11 Feb 1758
1   Drummer     Gray, Thomas            "     26 Sept 1758
```

Military histories can provide more than just narratives about regiment activities. "Colonial Soldiers of the South, 1732–1774" includes this list of the First Troop of Georgia Rangers.

Conversely, another collection, "Colonial Soldiers of the South, 1732–1774," has records that Ancestry.com describes as "chiefly muster rolls and payrolls of the militias of Maryland, Virginia, North and South Carolina, and Georgia, and they identify about fifty-five thousand soldiers by name, rank, date, militia company, and district." Within this collection is a list of First Troop of Georgia Rangers, which includes the names—not biographies (image C).

Royalty, Nobility & Heraldry

As you might imagine, less than a dozen of the collections in this subcategory relate to the United States, with the majority pertaining to Europe. That means if your family stories tell of royal blood—perhaps you're a descendant of an English king or a French queen—then you'll enjoy digging through "A Chronicle of Kingship, 1066–1937" or even the "Annals of the House of Hanover." Note that many of these collections are in French, Italian, German, or other foreign languages.

The "Peerage of the British Empire" collection provides a fascinating look at the high-born in 1848, describing the family history of five classes of nobility (Duke, Marquess, Earl, Viscount, and Baron), plus their coats of arms. Likewise, the "Tudor Roll of the Blood Royal" (which traces the descendants of Edward IV and Henry VII, Kings of England, and James III, King of Scotland) lists descendants of specific royalty (image D).

If you're unsure which country your royal heritage originates, pull up the "Dictionary of Royal Lineage of Europe and Other Countries From the Earliest Period to the Present

62. Descendants of VICTORIA, Queen of the United Kingdom of Great Britain and Ireland, Empress of India, 1819–1901. (See Table VIII.)		
6040	859	⊽ Edward VII., of the United Kingdom of Great Britain and Ireland, and of the British Dominions beyond the Seas, King, Defender of the Faith, Emperor of India, 1841. } Eldest son.
6041	860	⊽ George, Prince of Wales, 1865. York Lodge, St. James's Palace. } Grandson. Only son of No. 6040.
6042	861	⊽ Prince Edward of Wales, 1894.
6043	862	⊽ Prince Albert of Wales, 1895.
6044	863	⊽ Prince Henry of Wales, 1900. } Great-grandchildren. Children of No. 6041.
6045	864	⊽ Prince George of Wales, 1902.
6046	865	⊽ Princess Victoria Alexandra of Wales, 1897.
6047	866	⊽ Louise, Princess Royal, Duchess of Fife, 1867. 15 Portman Square, W. } Granddaughter. Eldest daughter of No. 6040.

Those with royal ancestors should check out Ancestry.com's Royalty, Nobility, & Heraldry category. This is a partial list of Queen Victoria's descendants, found in the "Tudor Roll of the Blood Royal" collection.

Date" collection. The book was published in 1902, so you won't find modern-day royalty listed. But you will find genealogies of descendants of various royal families.

Did you know that some American families were entitled to bear a coat of arms? The collection "Virginia Heraldica" is a registry of such Virginia families. Use this collection to read about the coat of arms given to the Tarrant family of Essex County, Virginia. (If all of the heraldry vocabulary is Greek to you, look for the collection "Bolton's American Armory" to learn what all of the terms mean.)

SEARCHING STORIES, MEMORIES & HISTORIES

The most logical approach to searching records is often to globally search an entire category. This is especially true when the information you have about a person is scant, but *not* when the information is scant *and* you're searching for a very common surname. That's why, in this section, we'll discuss how to search both the entire category and individual collections.

Searching the Entire Category

I chose to do a global search of this category for the surname Dimmitt. I know the family was in Maryland, Texas, Iowa, North Carolina, and Indiana, but other than that, I don't have a lot of solid information. The surname is uncommon enough to try this type of search.

In Ancestry.com's Card Catalog, I chose the Stories, Memories & Histories category, then clicked on the link near the top of the page to search the entire category. This opened a search page where I could fill in as much as I knew about an individual. However, in this case, I only typed in the surname *Dimmitt* because I wasn't looking for a specific individual, but rather references to the family. I also changed the Collection Focus to be the United States.

This search returned several thousand hits, many of them from "Public Member Stories." Among them was a document of Dimmitt descendants of William Dimmett, born 1650 in Baltimore. What a find! Other documents included wills, land records, marriages, and letters.

But why stop here? Because I knew the family was in Iowa at some point in time, I went back to the search box, entered the surname, and entered *Iowa* in the Lived In box. A whole new set of results came back, with the most interesting in a collection called "History of Wapello County, Iowa." What to search next? I needed to search the specific collections I found.

Searching within a Collection

Because I knew there were several hits within the "History of Wapello County, Iowa" collection, I went back to the Card Catalog and searched for it by title. Interestingly, two collections share the title, so I decided to search both of them.

To search each collection, I clicked on the name of each, which opened a search form. After searching, I found a mention of several family members, a reference to their previous residence (Indiana), and a little about their children and their occupations. That's much more than I knew at the beginning of the search.

As you can see, it's effective to do a global search when your knowledge about a family line is sketchy. Then, once you find relevant hits in the global search, do more focused searches of individual collections that you find.

THE HISTORICAL PICTURES CATEGORY

Finding an ancestral photo is like discovering a gateway to who we really are. We scan old pictures, looking for similarities in the set of the jawline or the shape of the mouth. What a delight to see an old picture and say, "Hey, that's where Uncle Jim got his high cheekbones!" Thanks to photos, we make connections.

Some families are blessed with an abundance of old family photos; others, like mine, are not. That's why having a place like Ancestry.com to search for pictures of family members, a hometown, or even a military regiment is so valuable. Not only can you search the Ancestry.com collections for images, you also can find them in user-submitted public family trees. In fact, were it not for another researcher, I would never have known what my great-great-grandparents looked like (image **E**).

Millions of photos are online at Ancestry.com and on free websites. While it's possible you may find an ancestor's photo online, it's more likely that you'll find a picture of a group of people, images of an ancestral hometown or places your ancestors might have traveled, military uniforms/period clothing, types of houses, and other depictions of daily life.

After you find a photo—assuming the photos are copyright-free and/or you have permission from the copyright holder—you can use them in your genealogy software program, your website, your online family tree, or your family history book.

Access Ancestry.com's picture collections by going to the Card Catalog and filtering by category. While North America and Europe have the largest number of photo collections, the site has a few from around the globe. In terms of record numbers, the two largest collections in the Pictures category are the "U.S. School Yearbooks, 1880–2013" (more than 372 million) and "Public Member Photos and Scanned Documents" (more than 220 million) collections. Coming in third is the collection "Private Member Photos," with more than seventy-five million. Let's look at the top two collections, then discuss how best to use the remainder of this category.

E

Thanks to Ancestry.com's Pictures category, I was able to find another user's picture of my great-great-grandparents—the first image I've ever seen of them.

The U.S. School Yearbooks Collection

This collection includes middle school, junior high, high school, and college yearbooks from across the United States. If you find a family member, you'll probably find a photo, or brief blurb about his or her activities, and a history of either the school and/or the town. If a student went by a nickname, the nickname is often shown along with his or her legal name.

Once you've found a family member, take some time to browse through the entire yearbook. If your yearbook was like mine, you'll appear in several places like sports teams and activities. Also look through other grades to see if photos of siblings appear. If your direct ancestor was a senior, you may find a sibling—or even a future spouse—as a junior or sophomore in the same yearbook.

Many yearbooks included more information about (and larger photos for) seniors than for other grades, including post-graduation plans. I remember my senior yearbook told which people were going into the military and who was going on to college. You also can find the names and members of clubs and sports teams, both of which vary greatly throughout the decades.

There are two ways to search this collection: by using the search form or by browsing the collection.

USING THE SEARCH FORM

If you use the search form, fill in the usual information (name, date of birth, where the ancestor lived). Additionally you can specify the name of the school and the name of the yearbook. Knowing the name of the yearbook will help you narrow your results. However, you need to check the Exact box next to the name of the yearbook to force the system to only return results from that specific yearbook.

Search results will take you to a page with all of the hits that Ancestry.com thinks are relevant. From there, click to view the image.

BROWSING THE COLLECTION

If you decide to use the browse function, you'll find it in the right-side column—Browse This Collection. Using the dropdown box you can specify state, city, name of high school, and year (image **F**). Doing this will take you directly to a scanned image of the yearbook you specified.

"The Wakitan" yearbook from St. Joseph, Missouri, has a history of the town, the school, and wonderful interior photos of the halls, auditorium, lunchroom, and office (image **G**). Little did I know that my dad was a horseshoe champion until I found his listing in the yearbook (image **H**).

F

Browse this collection

To browse this image set, select from the options below.

State

Missouri ▼

City

St Joseph ▼

School Name

Central High School ▼

Year

1918

1923

1924

1926

1927

1928

1929

1930

1931

1932

Use the Browse this collection function to view what schools have had their yearbooks digitized (and for what years) in the "U.S. School Yearbooks, 1880–2013" collection.

G

THE

WAKITAN

CENTRAL HIGH SCHOOL

SAINT JOSEPH, MISSOURI

1936

When viewing yearbooks in the "U.S. School Yearbooks, 1880–2013" collection, be sure to browse through the full yearbook to look for other pictures of your ancestor.

H

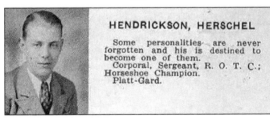

HENDRICKSON, HERSCHEL

Some personalities are never forgotten and his is destined to become one of them.
Corporal, Sergeant, R. O. T. C.; Horseshoe Champion. Platt-Gard.

This yearbook entry for my dad, Herschel Hendrickson, features his favorite quote as well as some notes about his accomplishments and affiliations while at school.

Results 1–50 of 87			
Member Photo	Photo Info	Description	Attached To
	(Other)		Miles Dimmitt (born 1815)

Other Ancestry.com users uploaded dozens of photos potentially related to Miles Dimmitt, and I found them by searching the "Public Member Photos and Scanned Documents Database" collection in the Pictures category.

PUBLIC MEMBER PHOTOS AND SCANNED DOCUMENTS

In this collection, you'll find photos of people and images of documents that users have scanned, such as wills, and military, birth, and death records. The search form for this collection has fewer options than you're used to seeing. If you get too many hits, experiment with using the Exact box. If you get too few results, eliminate keywords. In a search for my third great-grandfather, Miles Dimmitt, I used all of the boxes except the keyword. I mistakenly added his place of birth as Iowa, when it should be Indiana—fortunately the system found him anyway.

Among the results were two images of particular interest: one was a picture of Miles Dimmitt's tombstone, and the other was a photo of Miles himself—the first I've ever seen (image).

The photo of Miles is in several trees. However, without contacting the original image holder, I have no way of verifying whether this really is a picture of Miles. But of course, I hope it is.

Note that, because all of the images are user-generated, Ancestry.com cannot verify the accuracy of the information attached to each image. If you recall from chapter 2, when you upload an image you can include:

- title
- notes or comments
- locality (which may include city, state, and/or country)
- names of people photographed
- date of photo

Private Member Photos

What about the Private Member Photos collection? Although I'm not able to view the photos, I could see the name of the person to whom the photo was attached. In this way, I could at least skim through a list, looking for links to my family. If I found any of interest, I could contact the owner of the image to see if I could get access. But was there anything else I could discover without seeing the photos? Yes.

In going through the list of private photos during my Hatton search, I discovered a passenger arrival list into Charleston, South Carolina, for a Marion Hatton who was born in 1796. Could this be the family? I don't know (my Hatton research hasn't gone back further than Wiley), but, again, it gives me another place to begin searching.

My suggestion is to attach as much information to an uploaded image as possible—this way other users have more options to verify accuracy—and to actually find your image. And if you do find an image for your family, contact the person who uploaded it—there's a good chance he or she is a distant relative, so reach out to them via Ancestry.com's messaging system.

SEARCHING THE PICTURES CATEGORY

The remainder of the Ancestry.com Pictures category is so varied that, unless you're fairly certain you'll find family-related images in a specific collection, you may want to search the entire group globally.

Feel free to subdivide the category in whatever way you like, but I've found it most useful to think of them as belonging to four subcategories, each focusing on a different kind of subject: Places (e.g., "Australia, Sydney Harbour Bridge Construction, 1922–1933" and "U.S. Historical Postcards"), People (e.g., "U.S. School Yearbooks" and "California WWI Soldier Photographs, 1917–1918"), Ships (e.g., "Passenger Ships and Images"), and Things (e.g., "Historic Catalogs of Sears, Roebuck and Co., 1896–1993").

Each collection—even those you might not think of as being useful—can contain interesting images. The Sears, Roebuck, and Co. catalogs, for example, are an excellent source

TRY, TRY, TRY AGAIN

Successful searches can require trial and error when entering search terms and phrases, so keep trying different combinations of terms and filters if your search is fruitless but you're confident relevant records exist.

LADIES' AND MISSES' BATHING SUITS.

32 to 42 Bust Measure.

No. 38C1301 Ladies' Bathing Suit with attached bloomers, made of good quality alpaca. Large sailor collar trimmed with three rows of soutache down the front and detachable skirt trimmed around waistband and bottom with three rows of soutache to match, wide hem. Colors, black or navy blue. Price..... **$2.25**
If by mail, postage extra, 17 cents.

Always give bust measure.

No. 38C1303 Girls' or Misses' Bathing Suits, ages from 8 to 16 years. Same style as No. 38C1301, with attached bloomers and detachable skirt. Color, navy blue with white trimmings. State age desired.

Price.................**$1.69**
If by mail, postage extra, 15 cents.

Curious about what bathing suits your ancestors were wearing? The Sears, Roebuck, and Co. catalog (searchable on Ancestry.com) can answer this and other questions about your ancestors' everyday life.

for discovering the everyday things your family used, from watches to microscopes to silverware. The Browse This Collection feature (right-side column) lets you specify which year to search. If your 1905 ancestor went swimming, she may have worn the swimsuit shown in image **J**.

Searching the Entire Category

If you're not searching for a specific person, but rather for any images relating to your surname or a location where the family lived, try doing a global search of the millions of records in the Pictures category. Before starting, though, pick one of your more unique surnames; doing a search through millions of records for *John Smith* isn't likely to locate anyone in your Smith family.

For example, I decided to work with two of my more unique surnames: Faulkenberry and Hatton (also spelled Hatten). Going into this search I knew:

- the earliest Faulkenberrys were in South Carolina and Georgia

- the Hattons were in Virginia and then Indiana

I went to the Ancestry.com Card Catalog and chose Pictures from the list of collections and clicked the Search Entire Pictures Category link. The "all pictures" search form gave the options to include:

- name

- birth date

- birth location

- lived in location

- any event date and location

- keyword

- collection focus

K

Pictures

- Public Member Photos &   4366
  Scanned Documents
- U.S., School Yearbooks, 1880-   2539
  2012
- Private Member Photos   928
- Lockport Area, Illinois, Church,   45
  Cemetery, and Other Records,
  1811-1995
- California, WWI Soldier   4
  Photographs, 1917-1918
- Selected U.S. Headstone   4
  Photos

Filtering your search results by collection is particularly important in the Pictures category, which has a wide variety of sources.

L

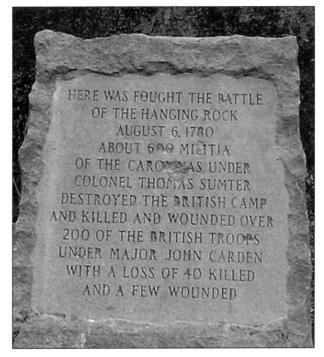

HERE WAS FOUGHT THE BATTLE
OF THE HANGING ROCK
AUGUST 6. 1780
ABOUT 600 MILITIA
OF THE CAROLINAS UNDER
COLONEL THOMAS SUMTER
DESTROYED THE BRITISH CAMP
AND KILLED AND WOUNDED OVER
200 OF THE BRITISH TROOPS
UNDER MAJOR JOHN CARDEN
WITH A LOSS OF 40 KILLED
AND A FEW WOUNDED

Among the records I found in my search for David Faulkenberry photos is this image of a monument commemorating a battle he fought in.

The only box I filled in was Last Name box: *Faulkenberry*. The search returned nearly eight thousand results. The left column showed the collections within which the results fell.

As you can see, the majority of hits came from the Public Member Photos subcategory. However, because there were only four results in the "Selected U.S. Headstone Photos" collection (image **K**), I did a quick check there but found no one directly related to my family. Because I wanted to find as early an image as possible for this family, I didn't search through the yearbook hits because I knew the family was in America prior to the Revolutionary War, and yearbooks would be too recent of a collection.

That left me with the Public Member Photos and Private Member Photos subcategories, each with thousands of hits. Clearly, too many to search through. But before returning to the search form and adding more filters, I quickly skimmed through the first few pages of search results, which turned up some amazing finds:

1. a transcription of David Faulkenberry's Revolutionary War pension statement

2. a photo of a monument at Hanging Rock, a battle in which David participated (image **L**)

This map, from the Pictures category on Ancestry.com, shows where my Faulkenberry family owned land in Fort Parker, Texas.

3. a page from the South Carolina Revolutionary War militia roster, which included a brief biography of David's service

4. a photo of Fort Parker (in Texas) where David's son moved in the 1830s

5. a photo of the Faulkenberry Cemetery in Texas

6. a photo of a monument commemorating the battle, including a list of those who fought at Fort Parker (including the Faulkenberrys)

7. a map showing where the Faulkenberrys owned land just south of Fort Parker (image **M**)

And these were just from the first few pages of results. I wondered if I would fare as well with the Hatton global search. I typed *Hatton* into the Last Name box and *Shelbyville, Shelby, Indiana* into the Lived In Location box of the search form. Even adding the place filters, I still got more than eighty thousand hits.

Again, I ignored the yearbook photos, as well as images from the Australian collections. Although I had no information on any Hatton serving in the Civil War, I first checked the one result in the "New York Cartes-de-visite, 1860–1865" collection. (A Cartes-de-visite is a small photograph that was very popular among Civil War soldiers.) The result in this collection brought up a John Hatton from New York. Because I have discovered no New York connection, I ignored it, but I made a note of it in my software just in case I make a connection later.

Continuing the search, I had no luck in the "U.S. Family Photo Collection, c. 1850–2000," "Selected U.S. Headstone Photos," or "Member and Institutional Collections" collections. That left me, again, with the "Public and Private Member Photos" collection. Unlike the Faulkenberry search, though, these results were far too broad for me to hope to find anything about my family, so I went back to the search form. This time I added the earliest Hatton I

1. Marriage Bond 13 December 1819- Washington County, Kentucky
   Wiley Hatton and Smith Gregory- marriage shortly intended
   between the above bound Wiley Hatton and Miss Nancy Gregory,
   daughter of the above bound Smith Gregory.

This marriage bond between Wiley Hatton and Nancy Gregory that I found on Ancestry.com was a turning point in my research.

had found: Wiley Hatton, born in 1797. Although Wiley was born in Virginia, he lived in Shelbyville, Indiana, so I kept that as my Lived In Location.

Now this was more like it! Among the findings relating to the family:

1. a marriage bond between Wiley and Nancy Gregory (image **N**)

2. a photo of Wiley's tombstone, as well as for his wife, Nancy

Although I didn't find as many documents for my Hattons as I did for the Faulkenberrys, what I did find clearly points me to English roots. In fact, there were so many England references to Hatton that I'm fairly certain this is where I'll start searching next.

Before leaving this search, did we forget any clues? Yes, Nancy Gregory's father—Smith Gregory—was named in the marriage bond document. I went back to the global Picture search, looking for Smith Gregory in Virginia. Again, I found treasures!

1. A full-page typewritten biography of Smith Gregory and his wife Martha (or Patsy) Vaughn (another name to investigate). The biography included the dates of Smith and Martha's marriage, the names of their children and their children's spouses, where the family cemetery is located, the name of goods sold after Smith's death, the location of the courthouse where his will was filed, and the early records on which his name is found.

2. An inventory of Smith Gregory's estate, including two guns, six slaves, one lot of books, one shovel, one lot of earthenware, and one deck of cards. Given the lot of books, I'm assuming someone in the family could read.

Once I found the scanned image of the Smith Gregory biography, I knew the many clues would lead me far back into this family line, even though I had just begun the search with the Hattons. You never know where a search will take you! Remember, this search started because Smith Gregory was mentioned as the bride's father in the marriage bond.

Searching a Collection

Now that you've seen where a global Pictures collection search can lead, let's see if a single collection can yield results just as valuable. Because I'm interested in collecting images

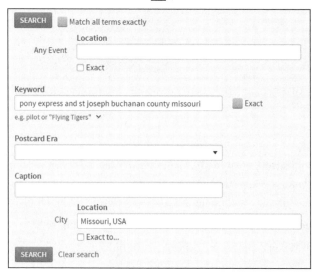

Refining your search, particularly in the Pictures category, can help you better find relevant images. Here, I'm refining my search to focus on the Pony Express in St. Joseph, Missouri.

of places my family lived. I decided to focus on the "U.S. Historical Postcards" collection. Specifically, I want to focus on ten towns and villages in the Midwest and South.

The search form for this postcards collection is different than you're used to seeing— there are no boxes for names. You can enter year, location, keyword, (optionally) postcard era, caption, and city.

I began this search with the place I knew I would find, my hometown of St. Joseph, Missouri. Because it was the jumping-off place for the Pony Express (as well as the Oregon Trail), I knew I'd find lots of postcards related to the Pony Express. For this search I entered *St. Joseph* as the Location and *Pony Express* as the Keyword. Because I didn't check the Exact box, the search returned many results that weren't related to my search.

Going back to the search form, I checked the Exact box for the keyword and location. Guess what? No results! This tells me I need to be more creative with search terms I enter into each search box. After several trials (one of which yielded several thousand hits), I finally found the one that gave me the desired results.

By entering the location as *Missouri*, caption as *Pony Express*, and *St. Joseph, Buchanan, Missouri* as the keywords (image 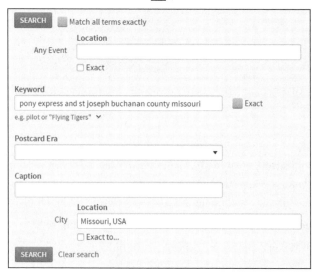), the system returned several hits, including a historic Pony Express Stables postcard.

A Note About Copyright Laws

According to US copyright law, works published before January 1, 1923, are in the public domain, meaning anyone can use, adapt, or copy them freely. However, be aware of some odd twists and turns. Before you assume an image you find is copyright-free, read Sharon DeBartolo Carmack's excellent guide to "Copyright for Genealogists" **<www.familytreemagazine.com/premium/copyright-for-genealogists>**.

Images taken by the federal government don't fall under copyright law; in essence, they are the property of "we the people." However, you may find images on a government site that are owned by a library or archive, and you'll need to get permission or pay a licensing fee for use. Copyright statements are usually obvious on a site.

If you're on a government site (which will have .gov in the domain name), you'll almost always find a link to copyright information indicating how to credit an image. For example, the image of a 1902 Nebraska farmer requests this credit line: *Nebraska State Historical Society, [Digital ID, nbhips 12448]*

Some images on Ancestry.com may fall into the public domain, while others may be copyrighted. When in doubt about copyright status, ask the original poster of the image (whether it's Ancestry.com or an Ancestry.com user), and be sure to consult Ancestry.com's Terms and Conditions to learn how you're permitted to use content from the site.

Now, onto other locations. My search for Milan, Missouri, turned up only a couple of finds. However, Shelbyville, Indiana's hits included postcards of main streets, churches, libraries, hospitals, and courthouses. Searching for Groesbeck, Texas, was a bust, but a search in Springfield, Kentucky, yielded something I didn't realize—near Springfield stands the home of Abraham Lincoln's grandmother, Bathsheba. As Smith Gregory lived in Springfield at the same time as Bathsheba Lincoln, I had to wonder if they knew one another. Searches for Rich Square and Lincoln were fruitless. Lima, Ohio, where my third great-grandparents were married, had some interesting postcards, but most were too modern for what I wanted to save.

My last search—for Williamsburg, Virginia—was one I knew would come up roses. I had family living there as early as the late 1600s, and many of Williamsburg's historic buildings are still standing, including Bruton Parish Church where my ancestor Thomas Ballard is buried. A simple search for the city *Williamsburg* returned thousands of hits—far too many to browse through. But among the search results were a lot of historic buildings in the lot, such as:

- George Wythe's house
- Governor's Palace

P

TO THE GLORY OF GOD AND IN MEMORY OF
THE VESTRY OF 1674-1683 · WHO ERECTED THE
FIRST BRICK CHURCH UPON THIS FOUNDATION

THE HONORABLE COL · DANIEL PARKE
ROWLAND JONES · MINISTER
JOHN PAGE · JAMES BESOUTH
MAJOR OTHO THORPE · ROBERT COBB · JAMES BRAY
CAPT · PHILIP CHESLEY AND WILLIAM AYLETT
CHURCH WARDENS.
GEORGE POYNDEXTER · GEORGE MARTIN
SAMUEL TIMSON · HON · THOMAS BALLARD
CAPT · FRANCIS PAGE · TREASURER · ALEXANDER
BONYMAN · CLERK · AND JOHN OWENS · SIDESMAN
ATTORNEY OF THE VESTRY · MAJOR ROBERT BEVERLEY

Another Ancestry.com user uploaded this plaque inside Bruton Parish
Church in Williamsburg, Virginia.

Q

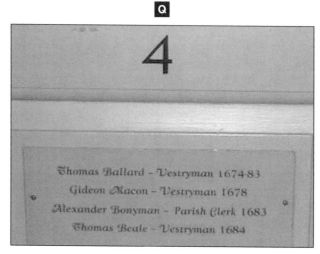

Thomas Ballard – Vestryman 1674-83

Gideon Macon – Vestryman 1678

Alexander Bonyman – Parish Clerk 1683

Thomas Beale – Vestryman 1684

The Bruton Parish Church features this plaque, which marks the pew
where Thomas Ballard regularly sat.

- Wren Building
- Magazine and Guard House
- College of William and Mary
- Bruton Parish Church

Because my family lived in Williamsburg at the time the buildings above would have been in use, I wanted to save them all. I knew they would have been places my ancestors knew well. Seeing a picture is *almost* as good as visiting there myself, but not quite.

I found so many postcards for Bruton Parish Church in this search that I used the Postcard Era section of the search form to find the earliest postcard possible. I selected the Divided Back Era, 1907–1915. Using the Postcard Era option, I also found postcards of the church in the Linen Era, c. 1930–1945 (my favorite) and Photochrome Era, c. 1939–present. However, as much as I wanted a postcard of the church interior or the cemetery, I couldn't find one in this collection. At that point, I went ahead and saved postcards of the other historic buildings, all of which I'll add to my Ballard family tree.

I still wanted those interior shots of the church and the cemetery, so I went back to the Card Catalog, chose the Pictures category, and did a category-wide search. I didn't type in any names in the search box, only *Bruton Parish Church Cemetery* in the Keyword box. I was thrilled to find many photos of the cemetery in the "Public Member Photos" collection, including one we history-junkies would appreciate: the tombstone for Daniel Parke Custis, Martha Washington's first husband. As for interior shots: Another member posted a plaque inside the church that named Thomas Ballard (image **P**). Score!

But that's not all: In doing the global search for *Bruton Parish Church Cemetery*, I also had several hits in the "Library of Congress Photo Collection, 1840–2000." One search result was an engraving of the church as it looked during the time period of Lord Dunmore (1770s). My family was still in Williamsburg during this time, and this was the church they would have known, so I saved this image, too. Of all of the found images, I think my favorite was image **Q**, of the pew in which Thomas Ballard sat (#4). (By the way, George Washington had pew #16, Thomas Jefferson #17, and Patrick Henry #18.)

10

MAKING THE MOST OF SCHOOLS, DIRECTORIES, AND CHURCH HISTORIES

While genealogists tend to focus on researching census returns and vital records, the truth is, our ancestors' lives encompassed so much more. Like us, they joined organizations, were listed in directories, went to school, and probably attended church.

It's hard to conceive of the many publications or directories you might find an ancestor in until you begin thinking about your life. For example, I know for certain that you can find me listed in the following places, and who knows where else:

- Internet searches on search engines and on Amazon.com **<www.amazon.com>**
- Western Writers of America membership list
- Association of Ghostwriters membership list
- high school yearbook (San Diego High, if you're interested!)
- list of college alumni
- Fort Phil Kearny/Bozeman Trail Association membership list
- San Diego Genealogical Society membership list
- North Dakota State Historical Society membership list
- Friends of the Little Bighorn membership list

Before reading further, take a minute and jot down all the places your name can be found, both online and off. Does looking at your list give you an idea of the types of records, publications, or other documents where you might find your ancestors on Ancestry.com?

We may assume that our ancestors didn't have the opportunity to join as many organizations as we do today, but is that really true? Who knows what organizations existed 150 years ago but are now defunct. A quick search of the Internet turned up the Lincoln Suffrage Association, the Radical Reform Christian Association, the Prohibition Club, and the Farmer's Alliance—all organizations that at one time thrived in Lincoln County, Kansas. I'm betting none exist today. Even in more-recent years, we can find evidence of fraternities and sororities that no longer exist. Don't discount finding your ancestor in at least one directory, no matter how unlikely it may seem.

Ancestry.com currently has more than 4,500 collections in its School, Directories & Church Histories category, with millions of records. In this chapter, I'll show you the five main record groups, what they contain, how best to search them, and what you can expect to find. Then, I'll do a few sample searches so you can follow along.

To begin, go to Ancestry.com's Card Catalog and from the left column select the collection of Schools, Directories & Church Histories. Filter to this category to see the five subcategories:

- City & Area Directories
- Professional & Organizational Directories
- Church Histories & Records
- School Lists & Yearbooks
- Telephone Directories

Let's start by going through each of the subcategories.

CITY & AREA DIRECTORIES

This group comprises more than one thousand collections that primarily cover North America and Europe, with the remainder from Oceania, Australia, Mexico, Africa, and Asia. When filtering, you'll find that Oceania and Australia share some of the same collections. The largest collections in this group is the "U.S. City Directories, 1821–1995," weighing in at more than a whopping 1.5 billion records. You'll also find directories for every state.

In case you've never worked with city directories, here's a summary: A city directory is an alphabetical listing of all of the people who lived in the town, listed by head-of-household, address, and occupation. Some directories can include the name of a spouse (read: wife), names of businessmen, and even a death date for someone who had been previously listed in the directory.

Beyond the names of people, city directories also provide insight into the community because the directories often include information on churches, hospitals, clergy, clubs, businesses, and local organizations. It's likely you'll also find ads (that's a sure bet), a map of the area, and a history of the town or community. When searching a city directory, be alert to people with the same surname, as they could easily be a family member or an in-law.

If you're not sure where your family lived—and you're not searching for an ultra-common surname—use Ancestry.com's search form to search the entire "U.S. City Directories" collection. If you know the state in which your family lived, after you search, use the Browse This Collection function (right column) to pre-select the state, city, year, and/or title of the directory.

In my experience, you'll usually get the most relevant results when changing the Use Default Settings option to Restrict To This Place Exactly in the Location box. But, as always, experiment.

Information will vary by year. For example, when using the Browse This Collection function, I searched for Albert Einstein in Princeton, New Jersey, and found the scientist in the 1942 directory listed under a category of Professors, Preceptors, and Teachers. In 1934, however, he's listed as a professor at the Institute for Advanced Study, while in 1954 he's a professor emeritus (image **A**). If someone in your family lived in the same town for a number of years, you can see how easy it might be to trace his career path (or change in occupation).

A search of the 1860 Nashville, Tennessee, directory (which I located using the Browse This Collection function, then by selecting the state, city, and year) is interesting in that it shows the person's occupation as well as his address, including whether he's a boarder at a hotel (see L.T. Hardy in image **B**) or lives in the country (P.F. Hardcastle).

Something I didn't expect to find was that the listing in the 1951 St. Joseph, Missouri, directory for my grandmother stated she was a saleswoman and the widow of Hershel. This little gem sent me calling my mom, who told me Grandma worked for a while selling cleaning products. I think the real surprise was that, although my grandfather died in 1948, Grandma is still listed as his widow in 1951. That same directory listed, not only my mom along with my dad, but also my dad's place of work and home address.

Are you beginning to see how valuable a city directory can be?

A second valuable collection to investigate is the "U.S. Public Records Index" (look for volumes 1 and 2). With more than one billion records, the volumes are a compilation of public records in all fifty states dating from 1950 to 1993. Here, you'll find an interesting blend of records taken from:

- white pages
- directory assistance records

A

> # Princeton Fuel Oil Co.
> ### Heating Oil — Gasoline — Motor Oil
> #### OIL BURNERS — SALES and SERVICE
> 216 Alexander   Tel. 1-1100
>
> Einolf Margt F Mrs sec to pres Prin Theo Sem r100 Stockton
> —Wm L (Margt F) instr r100 Stockton
> Einstein Albert prof emeritus h112 Mercer
> —Margot artist r112 Mercer
> Eisen Fred H asst to prof PU h263 Harrison

You can use multiple city directories to track someone's growth over the years. For example, Albert Einstein was listed as a professor in 1934 but had retired and become a professor emeritus by 1954.

B

> Hardcastle, P. F., firm of Rhea, Hardcastle & Co., residence country.
> Hardenstein, F. L., watch-maker, 25, Public-Square, residence Edgefield.
> Hardy, Bro's., auction and commission, 42, Public-Square.
> Hardy, L. T., above firm, boards at Commercial Hotel.
> Hardy, C. E., as above.
> Hardy, Wm., Sr., cabinet-maker, residence 93, south College st.
> Hardy, Wm., firm of Barker & Hardy, saloon, College st., near Broad st.
> Hardy, John, varnisher, boards south Nashville.
> Hardy, Miss M., millinery, 30, Union st., up-stairs.
> Hardin, Wm. S., fireman, at N. & C. Railroad, residence College st., above
>   Mulberry st.
> Hardin, Robert, car-painter, at N. & C. Railroad, residence as above.
> Hardin, John, residence 85, Church st.
> Hare, S. E., proprietor of Commercial Hotel.
> Harford, B., dry-good store, Harding's pike.
> Harford, H. B., dry-goods and groceries, corner Franklin pike and south
>   Union sts.

City directories can provide great details about people in a town, such as occupation, address, and even if he or she was a boarder.

- marketing lists
- postal change-of-address forms
- public record filings
- historical residential records

Because this collection only begins in 1950, you won't find individuals who lived several generations ago. But the collection can still help you track down a family member you may have lost. In searching for my own family members, I found some addresses were

C

Era Street,

51 *Hope road.*
(No thoroughfare.)

North side.

1 Steen Charles, motor driver
3 Whitehead Harry, fitter
3a, Whitelegg Ernst. platelayer
5 Fleming William, motor mech
7 Parish Thos. police constable
9 Burgess Miss Sarah
11 Bracegirdle Mrs. Elizh. E.
13 Dean Samuel, joiner

South side.

2 Wright Wilfred, steam roller
driver
4 Stone John Henry, fireman

This 1929 directory from Manchester, England, lists residents by street.

fairly current, and some were from several residences ago. However, if you want to contact someone this will give you a starting place.

Another large collection in this group is the "U.K., City and County Directories, 1766–1946," which is truly a boon to those of you doing UK research. With more than forty-two million records, the data is taken from street, commercial, trade, court, and post office directories. Information varies by directory type, but may include listings of residents, businesses, or tradesmen by street address; alphabetical listings of tradesmen or businesses; business owners' private residences; lists of wealthy residents or government officials; or lists of homeowners' names and addresses.

According to Ancestry.com, "The original purpose of directories was to provide information about towns and localities for travellers and other visitors. A directory would include a general description of the town or area and then include details on local transportation, churches, schools, government offices, shops, and businesses ... Later directories began to include sections on private residents."

In this collection, use the Browse This Collection function to select the country and county of interest in the dropdown lists.

This 1929 directory of Manchester, England, lists residents by street, including their names and occupations (image **C**). What I thought was interesting was the number of occupations that I didn't recognize. If your family lived in the area during this time period, think of all that could be added to your software or a family history book—and think of how daily conversation might have gone between a pavior (someone who paves) and his neighbor, the marble polisher!

As you skim down the list of the many directories included in the City & Area Directories subcategory, you'll see many specific to a location or to a location and date. For example, the "Brooklyn, New York, Directories,

GENERAL ABBREVIATIONS

acct	accountant	drsmkr	dressmaker	mfg	manufacturing	s or S .... South
adj	adjuster	e or E	East	mfr	manufacturer	san .... sanitary
admn	administrator or administration	educ	education	mgr	manager	Sav .... Savings
adv	advertising	elec	electrical or electric	mkr	maker	sch .... school
agcy	agency	electn	electrician	mkt	market	se .... southeast
agrl	agriculture	electro	electrotyper	mldr	molder	sec .... secretary
agt	agent	elev	elevator	mlnr	milliner	serv .... service
al	alley	emp	employee	mn	man	ship .... shipping
Am	American	eng	engineer	mono	monotype	sht mtl .... sheet metal
appr	apprentice	engr	engraver	mngr	messenger	sls .... sales
apts	apartments	equip	equipment	mstr	master	smstrs .... seamstress
archt	architect	es	east side	mtce	maintenance	soc .... society
asmblr	assembler	exam	examiner	mtge	mortgage	solr .... solicitor
assoc	associate	exch	exchange	mtr	motorman or motor	spl .... special
asst	assistant	exp	express	mus	music	sq .... square
atndt	attendant			mut	mutual	srtr .... sorter
				n or N	North	ss .... south side

Look for a list of abbreviations used in city directories, as that shorthand can help you decipher valuable details about your ancestors and their communities.

1888–1890," or "San Francisco, California Directories, 1889–1891" collections cover those specific areas during those specific time periods. Because of this, you may want to employ a few filters such as state and date to be sure you've covered all of your search possibilities. If you want to find directories that also include maps, be sure to use the term map in the Keyword search box.

After you find a directory, keep in mind that city directories often used abbreviations in the listings (image **D**). You can usually find a guide near the front of the directory. Common abbreviations include:

- *r* for resides
- *slswn* for saleswoman
- *n* for near
- *w* for widow
- *wldr* for welder

PROFESSIONAL & ORGANIZATIONAL DIRECTORIES

This subcategory is so eclectic that your best strategy is to search globally across all collections or make judicious use of location filters and keywords. It's also a subcategory that researchers with German ancestry will love, because many of the collections pertain to Germany.

This subcategory also has more than 750 US collections, with the highest concentration from Michigan, New York, Pennsylvania, and Colorado. I suggest filtering first by location

NASHUA, ACTON & BOSTON DIVISION.

Trains leave North Acton for Concord Junct. and Boston at 8.00, 8.35 A.M.
From Ellsworth Station, 8.10, 8.39 A.M.
Trains leave Ellsworth Station for Nashua at 2.52 and 5.33 P.M. From No.
Acton at 2.57 and 5.43 P.M.

The Professional & Organizational Directories subcategory
has an eclectic mix of records, including a railroad timetable in
a directory about the town of Acton.

BOUCHERVILLE,

A VILLAGE situated in the Seigniory of Boucherville, .County of Chambly, C. E.—distant ¦
treal, 9 miles—steamboat fare, 10d.

ALPHABETICAL LIST OF PROFESSIONS, TRADES, &c.

LACOSTE, LOUIS, notary public.
NORMANDIN, LOUIS, notary public.

Aubertin, Toussaint, shoemaker.
Berthiaume, Joseph, wheelwright.
Birtz, J. B., wheelwright.
Bourdon, Joseph, shoemaker.
Bouvier, Solomon, wheelwright.
Carrière, Adolphe, blacksmith.
Dagenais, Rev. Thomas E., Roman Catholic.
Guimond, Charles, blacksmith.
Favreau, Henry, wheelwright.
Lefebvre, Charles, shoemaker.
Lefebvre, Hypolite, shoemaker.
Loiseau, Magloire, shoemaker.

Latour, Dr. Théophile H.
Marchessault, Léon, blacksmith.
Monarque, Pierre, storekeeper.
Pépin, Rev. Thomas, Roman Catholic.
Riendeau, Jean B., sen., storekeeper.
Riendeau, J. B., jun., storekeeper.
Robert, Antoine, shoemaker.
Roy, Eusèbe, blacksmith.
Roy, Maurice, wheelwright.
Sénécal, Pierre, shoemaker.
Weilbrenner, Dr. Rémi C.
Weilbrenner, Joseph, land surveyor.

Ancestry.com holds some collections of foreign directories,
including this one from Boucherville, Quebec, Canada.

```
WILSON
1840, 5,27. James Smith & w, Hanneh, & Louisa
    Wilson, a niece, minor, gct Haddonfield
    MM
1840, 7, 1. Richard Harlem, minor, gct Woodbury
    MM
1848, 9,27. Sarah C. gct Spruce St. MM, Phila.
1858, 3,31. Sarah C. rocf Spruce St. MM, Phila.,
    dtd 1858,1,22
1859, 2, 2. Wm. dis mcd
```

The "Encyclopedia of American Quaker Genealogy" is among
the most useful collections in the Church Histories & Records
subcategory, detailing marriages and the names of people
disowned from the church.

and date; if you get too many results, add
a keyword. For example, if you had an
ancestor who worked on the railroad, you
can search all of the railroad directories,
but, because railroad companies merged
over time, you may not be looking in the
right directory. You could put *railroad* in
the Keyword box, then search all of the collections that include that keyword.

As always, you can never be certain of
what you'll find in the search results. For
example, when I typed in *railroad* to the
Keyword box, one of the collections was
the "Acton Directory" (image). If I had
just been skimming through the collection
names, this one would never have caught
my eye because it doesn't include *railroad*
anywhere in the title. When I opened the
collection, I found it was a scanned book
about the town of Acton. Why did it appear
in railroad search results? Because included
in the book was a railroad timetable.

Almost all of the results for keyword
railroad were collections of businesses
along specific railroad routes—a great find
if your ancestor happened to live along the
route of a railroad.

Curious as to what else this group of
records held, I removed the *railroad* keyword and changed the location filter to USA,
then District of Columbia. The collections
for this search are another blend so varied
you'd really have to skim through all of the
titles to see if any of them would be worth

searching (or, return to no filters and search the entire subcategory). Here's a small sampling of D.C.-related collections:

- "Motion Picture Studio Directories, 1919 and 1921"
- "Register of the Society of Mayflower Descendants in the District of Columbia, 1970"
- "Presbyterian Ministerial Directory 1898"
- "Handy Book of American Authors, 1907"
- "The New-York Annual Register for the Year of Our Lord 1834"

If you have Canadian ancestors, an interesting find is the collection "The Canada Directory." This collection contains the names of professionals and businessmen in the principal locations of Canada, along with information on population, trade, and a variety of statistics (image **F**). What a find if your ancestor is listed in this directory!

CHURCH HISTORIES & RECORDS

This subcategory of the Schools, Directories & Church Histories group pertains to churches. With more than two thousand collections, the majority of which are from the United States, these records give you a good chance of finding an ancestor if he had a church membership or was a founding member of a church.

The shining crown of this group is the "Encyclopedia of American Quaker Genealogy" (volumes I through VI). The volumes contain meeting notes, where you'll find mentions of everything from marriages to people who were disowned from the church (image **G**). If you look back to chapter 5, you'll learn more about how to use these records in your research.

In each volume, you'll find a list of abbreviations such as:

- *MM* for monthly meeting
- *gct* for granted certificate to
- *rocf* for received on certificate from
- *dis* for disowned
- *mcd* for married contrary to discipline

If you're searching for references to a specific religion in the Church Histories & Records subcategory, include the name of the religion in either the Title or Keyword search box. You may still need to filter by state only (rather than using a keyword or title) to get the best search results.

Date.	Names of Parties.	Residence.	Place of Birth.
June 6 1871	William Morrow	Philadelphia	Ireland
	Eliza J. Begley	"	"
" 8 "	John Wilson	Chester Co. Pa.	Delaware
	Elizabeth W. Pierson	" "	Chester Co. Pa.

Church histories and records include marriage registers, like this one from the Scott Methodist Episcopal Church in Philadelphia.

For example, there's a collection titled "Connecticut, Church Record Abstracts, 1630–1920." Open this collection, and you'll find a scanned copy of a multivolume book. Each volume is a history of the Congregational church in the area. However, if you filter by location for USA and Connecticut, and then add *congregational* to either the Title or the Keyword box, this particular collection does not appear in the search results.

When searching this subcategory, in addition to church histories or memberships, you'll also find birth, marriage, and death records. The "Pennsylvania and New Jersey, Church and Town Records, 1708–1985," for example, includes records from various churches. In a marriage record from the Scott Methodist Episcopal Church in Philadelphia, information from the church book included the ages of the bride and groom and the groom's occupation (image **H**).

Although I did find family in the Quaker records, I couldn't find a mention in any of the other collections. What I did find—and for me this is just as good—was the history of two churches that my family attended. Hopefully by reading about the history and beliefs, I will gain some insight into my ancestors' religious life.

SCHOOL LISTS & YEARBOOKS

This subcategory has more than 270 collections, with the largest being the "U.S. School Yearbooks" collections of more than 372 million records. We covered quite a bit about school yearbooks in chapter 9, so now I will guide you to some other collections where you're most likely to find family or possibly a history of a school.

The first is a collection you may have overlooked: the "U.S. School Catalogs, 1765–1935." The title (at least to me) suggests classes offered by various schools. In a way that's true, but there's much more to discover. The collection lists names of students, faculty, alumni, and others associated with US colleges and universities, seminaries and theological institutes, normal schools, medical schools, academies, and military schools. It also has listings of individuals from various fraternities, societies, and associations. It includes data from

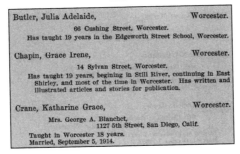

This catalog from the 1914 Massachusetts State
Normal School includes biographical information
about students.

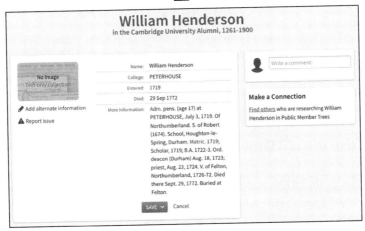

Some schools kept tabs on their alumni and collected it into publications, such as
this "Cambridge University Alumni, 1261–1900" collection.

forty-three states, with the majority from the nineteenth century. Some catalogs, like
the one from the 1914 Massachusetts State Normal School (image **I**), may include brief
biographical information and the graduate's address, while other directories simply list
the student's name.

The thirty-plus UK collections have records as early as the 1200s (see "Cambridge
University Alumni, 1261–1900"). While this collection doesn't have images of original
records, it does provide a transcription with plenty of clues for further research, such as the
student's name, college, date entered, and death date, plus burial information (image **J**).

> BARWICK, Hugh Atkinson; 61 Chestnut Park Rd., Toronto. "B; '98-'07; S. of Walter Barwick, Barrister, 151 St. George St., Toronto; Miss Moodie's Private Sch.; Age 9-1"; Clk., Trusts and Guarantee Co. Ltd., Toronto; Lieut., "F" Co., 48th Highlanders, and 15th Bn., 1st C.E.F.; reported missing after Langemarck; prisoner of war, Apr. 23, 1915, at Bischofswerda, Saxony, Germany.

"The Roll of Pupils of Upper Canada College, Toronto, January 1830 to June 1916" contains biographical information about each of its students.

The Canadian collections cover several provinces. Like the Normal School directory, "The Roll of Pupils of Upper Canada College, Toronto, January 1830 to June 1916" list also contains biographical data (image K). These are the listings we family tree climbers live for!

To find this Toronto collection, conduct a global search of the School Lists & Yearbooks subcategory. In Ancestry.com's Card Catalog, filter by the Schools, Directories & Church Histories category, then by School Lists & Yearbooks. Click the link to search the entire subcategory. Remember: When using the search form, use the Collection Focus option to narrow results. In this case, select Canada as the Collection Focus.

TELEPHONE DIRECTORIES

The final subcategory in this group covers a couple dozen collections of telephone directories. You'll only find a handful of collections covering the United States here, but those few collections comprise over one billion records, with three of them covering the entire United States beginning in 1950.

Telephone directories are the logical evolution of city directories. They're an excellent research choice when trying to place a twentieth-century family member in a specific time and place. Sadly, unlike city directories, they won't tell you a thing about the person's occupation, spouse, or children. But if you've found someone in a city directory, you have a good starting point for relocating him in a telephone directory, assuming he stayed in the same area.

The "U.S. Phone and Address Directories, 1993–2002" collection has a nifty feature that you'll appreciate. Not only does it give you the phone number and the year(s) the person had that number, but it also provides a link to view their neighbors that you can click on. If other family members lived nearby, this is a way to track them down.

The Telephone Directories subcategory includes a smattering of collections from Canada ("Canadian Phone and Address Directories, 1995–2002"), the United Kingdom, and Germany (almost all of them in German). The "British Phone Books, 1880–1984," requires you to enter a name and country in order to do your search. The best strategy may be to use the Browse This Collection function (in the right sidebar) to select the year range.

SEARCHING FOR RECORDS

Now that we've reviewed the kinds of records available in this category (and how they're broken up into subcategories), let's look at some search strategies for this group of records and documents.

Searching the Whole Category

Let's do a search of the entire Schools, Directories & Church Histories category to see what we can find on Franklin D. Roosevelt. He's not an ancestor (sadly), but I want to get an idea in how many sources in which an individual could possibly appear.

Start by going to the Ancestry.com Card Catalog and selecting the Schools, Directories & Church Histories category. Click on the link at the top of the page to search the entire category. Enter FDR's name and birth date (January 30, 1882). I don't want to limit search results to the United States, so don't select any collection focus.

Not surprisingly, FDR comes up in Harvard University school yearbooks—in some he's listed as a student, but in later yearbooks (after his election to the presidency) he's mentioned by several alumni.

The results show several subcategories he may appear in (image). In the Professional & Organizational Directories subcategory, for example, we find FDR listed as a member of the Holland Society of New York, a member of the Navy Department, as well as a listing in *Who's Who*. He's also in a 1933 City Directory of New York along with his wife Eleanor, living at 49 E. 65th Street (image).

L	
Schools, Directories & Church Histories	
– City & Area Directories	+5,000
– Professional & Organizational Directories	162
– Church Histories & Records	87
– School Lists & Yearbooks	1,060
– Telephone Directories	1,036

Search results for Franklin D. Roosevelt show numerous possibilities for places he's listed.

M

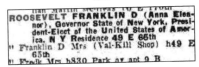

Even famous people are included in city directories. Franklin and Eleanor Roosevelt are listed in this 1933 New York City directory.

Professional & Organizational Directories	
– U.S., Register of Civil, Military, and Naval Service, 1863-1959	78
– New York, Holland Society Yearbook, 1896	34
– New York, Holland Society Yearbook, 1915	15
– Leavenworth, Kansas Who's Who, 1941-43	8
– Biographical Directory of the United States Congress, 1774-2005	5

We see fewer results for Franklin D. Roosevelt in the Professional & Organizational Directories subcategory.

Hendrickson Albert lab r235 N Chandler
—Alice student r124 N Knox av
—Doris E ofc wkr r1019 Topeka blvd
—Ellsworth M (Bertha J) janitor New England
    Bldg h2135 Madison
—Gloria ofc wkr r1019 Topeka blvd
—Harley (Ludie) washer Capital City Lndry
    & Dry Clng Co h831 Jefferson
—Helen r124 N Knox av
—Herschel (Bessie) heat supt h124 N Knox av
—Hershel (Marjorie) lab r220 Taylor

I was surprised to find a whole host of Hendricksons living in Topeka in a 1942 city directory.

If you type in the address on Google Maps <maps.google.com>, you can see a street view of what the residence looks like.

Remember, when you do a global search, you'll see a list of the individual collections the system pulled for you and the number of records in each under each category in the left column. For example, under the category Professional & Organizational Directories, you'll see a sampling of collections, with FDR results in each (image **N**).

Granted, your search for an ancestor (unless he was famous) won't yield as many results as the FDR search, but using the global search will give you a fairly good idea of what you can expect to find.

Now that we've searched for the famous, let's do a global search for a regular person, my grandfather Herschel B. Hendrickson. Using the search form, I typed in his name and birth date, and then selected United States from the Collection Focus dropdown menu. Although there were many results, I knew only a handful would be relevant.

I found my grandfather in a St. Joseph, Missouri, city directory (not a surprise), but what did surprise me was finding him and my grandmother in a 1942 city directory for Topeka, Kansas (image **O**). I knew that my mom and dad lived in Topeka for a year while my dad worked at a military base. What I didn't know was that my grandfather worked at the base during that year as well. Imagine my surprise to find my parents, grandparents, and two aunts in Topeka.

While searching the city directories, I also found my folks in 1943 in Jacksonville, Florida, where dad was doing work at a Navy base. The cool thing about this was it gave their address, which my mom couldn't remember. Now we can use Google Earth <earth.google.com> to fly over and see where they lived.

Unfortunately, I couldn't find my grandfather in any of the listings for the next four subcategories. This wasn't a surprise because the directories begin in 1950 and my grandfather died in 1948.

Searching a Single Collection

To search for John Chapman, my eighth great-grandfather, I took a different approach: searching in a single collection. I knew John was born about 1634 in England and died about 1695 in Bucks County, Pennsylvania. I also knew he was a Quaker, had been imprisoned in York, and then took his family to Pennsylvania, and I'm hoping to find out more about this branch of the family in one of the church histories.

Using the Ancestry.com Card Catalog filters, I filtered down the category to a reasonable number of collections by selecting the Church Histories subcategory, filtering by location, and adding the keyword *Quaker*. In this case, the filters resulted in eighteen different collections. I could also have added Bucks County as the location, but I wasn't sure the family lived there a long time.

I realized, after the fact, that while these filters would bring up collections with the keyword *Quaker*, it may not catch any with the keyword *friends*, so I went back to the drawing board. This time the results with the *friends* keyword came back with more than twenty collections—plenty for me to search.

The first collection that caught my eye was "Early Friends Families of Upper Bucks." Using the collection search form I typed in *Chapman* as the surname, but left all of the other search boxes empty. This search alone returned thirty-two hits, most of which related to my Chapman line. One was a lengthy biography of the Chapman family, beginning with my direct ancestors John and Jane (Sadler) Chapman. The first paragraph contained so much information that I'll be spending a considerable period of time doing English research. In part, it read:

> The pioneer ancestors of the Chapman family of Bucks County was John Chapman, a native of Stanghah, in the Parish of Skelton, Yorkshire, England, who, with his wife Jane and their five children, came to Pennsylvania in 1684. Having sailed in the Ship Shield from New Castle on the River Tyne, they arrived in Maryland on September 15, 1684, from which point they migrated overland to Bucks County, in the latter part of October. John Chapman was born at Stanghah in 1626 and, as early as 1656, was a convert to the principles and faith of Friends, suffering imprisonment and other persecutions for his religious principles. In 1660 he was confined in York Castle for eight weeks,

for refusing to take a prescribed oath and at several times thereafter had goods seized for the payment of fines imposed for attending non-conformist meetings. He married, first, on 10 mo. 14, 1665, and had one daughter Ann, who died in childhood. His wife died 8 mo. 2, 1668 and he married, second, 4 mo 12, 1670, Jane Sadler of Langenby, Yorkshire. To this marriage were born seven children, five at Stanghah, and two in Bucks County.

The information on the family in this one collection stretches down through a few generations and includes names and birth dates of spouses and children—what a find!

Although I searched for my family in the other collections, the only one that had family information was the "Encyclopedia of American Quaker Genealogy, Vol. II" (New Jersey and Pennsylvania monthly meetings).

At this point, I couldn't resist digging a little deeper. Using Google, I searched for information on places mentioned in the collection entry. I discovered that the ship the *Shield* left from Stockton, England, with a master named Daniel Towers (or Towle or Toes). Using Google Maps <maps.google.com> I discovered that today you can drive from York to Newcastle on Tyne in about an hour and a half. Of course, I wondered how long it would have taken the Chapmans to cover the ninety miles in 1684.

If you remember, in chapters 7 and 9, I wrote about the collection of ship images, so I went back to the Card Catalog to find that collection, in hopes of finding the *Shield* or at least a ship like it. No luck. Next, I tried the collection "Passengers and Ships Prior to 1684." This time I got lucky—not with an image, but with mentions of the ship in the following articles in this collection:

- "The Lyon of Liverpool in the Chester Port Books, 1682"
- "Early Shipping to the Jersey Shore of the Delaware"
- "Index of Vessels"
- "The Philadelphia and Bucks County Register of Arrivals"

The last book on the list contained this:

John Chapman aged about 58 yeares and Jane his wife about 42 yeares Came from Stangnah in the parish of Skelton in the County of York yeoman Came in the Ship the Shield of Stockton the master Daniel Toes arived in mary land in the beginning of the 8th month 1684 & from thence in this River the latter end of the Same month - Children: marah born the 12th 2 mo 1671, Ann born the 18th 3 mo 1676. John born ye 9th of the 11th mo 16__ [sic]. Jane his daughter Came at Same time & dyed at Sea.

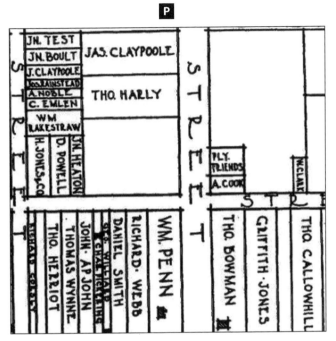

This street map shows Philadelphia "as William Penn knew it" in 1864, found in "Philadelphia and Bucks County Register of Arrivals."

What this search taught me was not to concentrate only on the name of the person. If you can find the name of his or her ship, use it in the search form.

By the way, on pages 175–176 of the article "Philadelphia and Bucks County Register of Arrivals" you'll find a fabulous street map of 1684 Philadelphia, "as William Penn knew it," a portion of it shown in image P.

11

USING THE WILLS, PROBATES, LAND, TAX & CRIMINAL CATEGORY

'm hoping that, as you've explored the Ancestry.com Card Catalog, you've had more than one surprise discovery. In making your way through previous chapters on school directories, church histories, military records, vital records, pictures, censuses, immigration records, newspapers, and family stories, you've found a multitude of ways to approach research problems. In this chapter, you'll learn another: how to use tax records, criminal records, land records, and wills to learn more about who your ancestor was and how he conducted daily life.

The more than eleven hundred collections in this category are organized into these subcategories:

- Land Records

- Tax Lists

- Court, Governmental & Criminal Records

- Wills, Probate, Estates & Guardian Records

- Bank & Insurance Records

There are more than nine hundred collections for the United States; the United Kingdom has more than two hundred. Of the five subcategories, you'll find the largest number of collections in the Court, Governmental & Criminal Records subcategory and the least under Bank & Insurance Records.

What can you expect to find in this category? This chapter will explore each of the five subcategories, then invite you to follow along with step-by-step searches.

LAND RECORDS

With hundreds of collections to explore, this category hopefully holds information about where and when your ancestors owned land. But first, let's go over a few basics in case you've never worked with land records.

Because land has always been a valuable asset, landowners and governments took great care in documenting ownership. Land records are generally far older than vital records (birth, death, marriage) and have been kept in the United States since the days of early colonization. Land records can show exactly where and when your ancestors lived, thus giving you a starting place for locating other official records.

Types of Land Records

You may encounter four main types of land records:

1. **Deeds**: A deed is the official record of land ownership. The most common terms you'll find in a deed are *grantee* (the buyer) and *grantor* (the seller). Deed indexes are exactly what you'd imagine—an index of land transactions. You won't find details about the transaction in an index, but you will find the date of the transaction and the names of grantors and grantees. In the United States, most deeds were recorded at the county level.

2. **Bounty Land Warrants**: Bounty land was used as an incentive for military service during the Revolutionary War, the War of 1812, the Mexican-American War, and Indian wars between 1775 and 1855. Bounty land was carved out of the federal public domain, although Virginia, New York, and Pennsylvania also set aside bounty land for veterans of the Revolutionary War. Warrants may contain information similar to military pension files. Typically you can find the name and rank of the soldier, the state from which he served, and the names of his heirs.

3. **Homestead Records**: In 1862, Congress passed the Homestead Act, giving settlers up to 160 acres of land, free of charge. The only stipulation to the free land was that it had to be improved over the following five years. This deal left behind documents: Title papers include the legal description of the land, name of landowner, the number of acres, and details about the office from which the title was issued.

4. **Land Grants**: Land grants were gifts given by a county, king, or government. For example, Mexico gave land grants (*ranchos*) in early California, while Spain offered land to those settling in its Florida colony. You might find the name of the grantee, the date of the grant, and description and location of the acreage in the land grant.

Land Surveys

When searching land records, you'll find two different survey methods: the public land survey system, and the state land survey system

The public land survey system was used in all of states except the original thirteen Colonies, Kentucky, Tennessee, Texas, Vermont, West Virginia, Maine, and Hawaii. In public land states, a land transaction was done via a patent or grant. Surveys were done using a rectangular survey system. Lands were divided into townships containing six square miles, and each township was subdivided into thirty-six, 640-acre sections (image **A**). Each section was further subdivided into halves and quarters, repeatedly, until the parcel of land was accurately described.

Public land was distributed by acts of Congress, either through sale, homesteads, or military warrants. As you might imagine, the US government promoted public land sales as a way of encouraging people to settle the West.

State land surveys for the original thirteen Colonies and the seven other states listed earlier were done using a system known as metes and bounds. This system used geographical and man-made landmarks (creeks, trees, fences) to describe a property's boundaries. In this method, boundaries were described by citing the length of each "course" along some line, such as "along a fence" or "ten paces north from the large oak tree."

Searching Ancestry.com's Land Records Collections

Ancestry.com's Land Records subcategory is a fabulous collection of land records, ranging from the Colonial era to recent years. "London, England, Land Tax Records, 1692-1932" and the "U.S., Indexed County Land Ownership Maps, 1860–1918" have the largest records collections. The latter collection contains approximately twelve hundred US county land ownership atlases, which can include the names of landowners.

To search this collection, use either the search form (name, location, year, keyword) or the Browse This Collection option (located in the right sidebar) where you can select a state, county, and year. Then, you'll see a scanned copy of the atlas itself.

Interestingly, another large collection of US records in this subcategory is the "Georgia, Property Tax Digests, 1793–1892," which I'll cover in more depth in the Tax section of this chapter.

Another record-heavy collection is "U.S. General Land Office Records, 1796–1907," with more than two million records. These records are primarily homestead and cash transactions from a handful of states, including Alabama, Florida, Indiana, Michigan, Ohio, and Wisconsin.

The records in this collection will help you map exactly where your ancestors' land was located, because each entry includes a legal land description: state, county, township, range, meridian, section, aliquot parts, block, and survey number. If all of these terms are Greek to you, see the Bureau of Land Management's glossary at **<www.glorecords.blm.gov/reference/default .aspx#id=05_Appendices|01_Glossary>**.

Because I knew that Hendricksons had land in Indiana, I did a quick search using the search form, filling in only *Hendrickson* as the surname and *Indiana* as the location. After getting more than three hundred hits, I knew I had to make better use of filters! After restricting to Shelby County only, the number of hits dropped to twelve, all with members of my family (image **B**).

Once you find a record in this collection, you can view a copy of the original document, which includes a legal description

A

Township Line

6	5	4	3	2	1
7	8	9	10	11	12
18	17	16	15	14	13
19	20	21	22	23	24
30	29	28	27	26	25
31	32	33	34	35	36

Range Line

In public land states, land surveys divided land into rectangular plots. Townships were six square miles and divided into thirty-six sections, each with 640 acres.

County land atlases, like this one from Shelby County, Indiana, contain original records.

The land record for Thomas Hendrickson, found on Ancestry.com, contains detailed information about the land he purchased.

of the land. In one case, Thomas Hendrickson bought eighty acres of land (image **C**), described as being:

> The west half of the southeast quarter of section eighteen in Township eleven north of Range Eight East in the District of lands subject to sale at Indianapolis Indiana

The Land Records subcategory is extensive, not only geographically, but also through time. I recommend either filtering down to where your family lived or taking the time to skim through the titles to make sure you don't miss a potential collection.

TAX LISTS

Tax lists can be dandy census substitutes because they place a person in a specific place and time. You'll find a large number of US records (over 130 million) in the "U.S., Social Security Applications and Claims Index, 1936–2007." The "U.S. IRS Tax Assessment Lists, 1862–1918," is another large collection (with more than eight million records), while the "Georgia, Property Tax Digests, 1793–1892" has nearly five million records.

Hitt John H.	Brookville		Income	519	5	2595
Haile M. H.	"		"	338	"	1690
Hendrickson Wm H.	"		"	1261	"	6305
Hackmann A.	Oldenburg		"	300	"	15
Hinckley Fudah	Springfield		"	113	"	565
Howell Elias	Bath		"	270	"	1350
Howell Isaac C.	"		"	214	"	1070
Hansel David	"		"	114	"	570

Tax lists can be quite detailed, providing the name of the person at the residence, its value, and the amount of taxes due (if you can read the handwriting in them).

The Social Security collection is considered an extension of the Social Security Death Index (SSDI). Information you may find in this collection includes:

- applicant's full name
- Social Security Number (SSN)
- date and place of birth
- citizenship
- sex
- father's name
- mother's maiden name
- race/ethnic description

The IRS (originally known as the Bureau of Internal Revenue) was formed in 1862 and was created to help pay for the enormous expenses created by the Civil War (1861–1865). The lists in the IRS collection were organized alphabetically by surname and recorded the value, assessment, or enumeration of taxable income or items and the amount of tax due.

Like the land collections, you can search the IRS records either by using the search form or the Browse This Collection function by state and roll title (e.g., Annual and Monthly Lists; 1866). Once you find a person, you can view the original image as well as note the title of the roll and the National Archives and Record Administration (NARA) series and roll on which the record appears.

Some of the original images are quite good; others may prove difficult to read—so thank the transcriptionists for helping us overcome this! The records give the name of the person's residence, his valuation, and the taxes due (far right column). In the record in image **D**, William Hendrickson (third name from the top) was valued at $1,261, with a 5-percent tax equaling $63.05 owed.

The surprisingly large "Georgia, Property Tax Digests, 1793–1892" collection features a lot of information in each record, including values for real estate and possessions.

The "Georgia Property Tax Digests, 1793–1892" collection lists the names of taxpayers and assessments of property and asset values. Records should include all men age twenty-one and over and women who owned property, including African-American freemen by name. Compare these handwritten records from 1838 to the census-like forms of the IRS collection, and you'll see quite a difference.

Later, Georgia records added more columns for free persons-of-color, slaves, dentists, Daguerreian artists, and number of persons subject to military duty. Interestingly, land was categorized by type (pine) and quality (1st, 2nd, 3rd), while personal estate values included money, merchandise, number and value of slaves, investments, and household goods (image **E**). All in all, an immense amount of information for a genealogist!

Another valuable collection is the "Pennsylvania, Tax and Exoneration, 1768–1801." Primarily a resource for eighteenth-century Pennsylvanians, the lists contain a variety of information such as:

- name
- residence
- occupation
- land owned
- slaves owned
- tax rate
- whether a man was a single freeman

You'll find curious taxes like those on billiard tables and carriages, and you'll also run into supply and eighteen-penny taxes. According to Ancestry.com, "supply taxes were levied to help pay debts from the Revolutionary War, while the eighteen-penny tax included both a poll tax on freemen and property taxes assessed to back issuances of paper money." It may just be the record I found on my own family, but even with high magnification, the handwriting on these records was a challenge to decipher.

COURT, GOVERNMENTAL & CRIMINAL RECORDS

Aha! The category everyone's anxious to search. Was Great-great-grandpa a criminal, or was that just a family legend? (I did find several Hendricksons in the federal penitentiary at Leavenworth, Kansas, but none were mine!) With hundreds of collections to choose from, you can find:

- probate records
- criminal lists
- gaol entrance books
- divorce records
- criminal case files
- court records

There's much more to find here, so you may want to skim the list yourself to see what's available. As always, consider using filters to refine search collections or the Browse This Collection function to focus in on the part of the collection with the highest likelihood of success.

Top-ranking collections in this subset include "Quebec, Canada, Notarial Records, 1626–1935" and "London, England, Land Tax Records, 1692–1932." One of the more interesting collections is the "U.S. Patent and Trademark Office Patents, 1790–1909," which contains invention patents granted by the government. If your ancestor was the inventive type, search for him by name or keyword. Even if your ancestor never filed a patent, it's fascinating to see the patents that were filed over several hundred years, including those for:

- waterproof fabric
- hydrant
- inkstand
- bridle rein
- electric arc lamp

Several state-specific collections are in this subcategory, with records from states that include Oregon, New York, Pennsylvania, Ohio, and North Carolina.

Ancestry.com's Court, Governmental & Criminal Records subcategory contains information on your law-breaking ancestors, such as this record for Belle Starr, a famed outlaw.

As for convict records, you'll have plenty to search. In perusing records, the thing that struck me—surprised me, really—was the list of women convicted of murder in the "Alabama, Convict Records, 1886–1952" collection. The convicts (most of them African-American) had unusually harsh sentences (e.g., a forty-three-year-old woman was convicted to serve seventy-five years, while a man, age twenty-five, was sentenced to forty years for the same crime). Of course, we can't know for sure what was afoot without seeing more records.

Speaking of criminals, just for a little historical fun look through the "Fort Smith, Arkansas, Criminal Case Files, 1866–1900" collection. Fort Smith was the court of the famous "Hanging" Judge Parker. The descriptions in the collection provide the first and last name of the defendant, the type of crime, the year, and even the jacket number, along with other information. In twenty-one years on the bench, Parker tried over thirteen thousand cases. Among them was one against Wyatt Earp for stealing horses, and another was on outlaw queen Belle Starr for larceny (image **F**).

WILLS, PROBATE, ESTATES & GUARDIAN RECORDS

You never know what family secret you'll discover in a will, guardianship record, or probate file. I remember one will in which the father left all of his children (male and female) an equal amount of money. However, the money for one of his daughters was to be administered by her brother, not her husband. Hmmmm.

When a person dies, his property is distributed as per his will or trust, and any claims filed against the estate are resolved (e.g., payment of a debt). The process of resolving an

G

BARNWELL COUNTY.

Name	Vol.	Date	Section	Page
Abney, Nathaniel	1	1787–1826	Bk. I	2
Absten, John	2	1826–1856	C	4
Adams, Francis	2	1826–1856	D	28
Adams, Wm.	1	1787–1826	A	71
Afhley, Nathaniel	1	1787–1826	A	4
Afhley, Nathaniel	1	1787–1826	A	180
Alexander, Raine	1	1787–1826	A	13
Alexander, Wm. H.	1	1787–1826	B	89
Allen, John M.	2	1826–1856	D	257
Allen, Sarah	2	1826–1856	D	275
Anderson, Wm.	1	1787–1826	B	95
Armstrong, William	2	1826–1856	D	242
Ashe, R.C.	2	1826–1856	C	127
Ashley, Nathaniel, see	– – – – – – – – – – – – – – – – – – –		Afley, Nathaniel	

You may find a will index among Ancestry.com's records. This won't provide you with an image of an original record, but it will give you reference material that makes it easier for you to find actual records.

estate in court is called probate. During probate, the executor follows the directions given in the will. If you've ever done (or want to do) courthouse research, you'll find all of the court papers relating to the person's death and disposition of property in a probate file.

If someone dies without a will, he is said to be intestate (as opposed to testate, in which the deceased had a will). Whether a person died with or without a will, court records are created pertaining to the distribution of the estate.

Probate records can generate many types of documents, from inventories of possessions (cows, dishes, hay, and unfortunately slaves) to bonds and petitions. Wills and probate records can be filled with genealogical clues, such as the names of a spouse, witnesses, children, and in-laws. They can also have information about guardianship if children were minors at the time of their parents' death.

Probate records and wills truly do put flesh on an ancestor. Reading these records will show you how much or how little he owned, his heirs, witnesses, and debts owed to him or by him. Probate records are especially valuable because, in some locales, they were kept years before state-mandated birth and death records.

And luckily, Ancestry.com now has an even more robust collection of more than three hundred collections of wills, intestate records, guardianship applications, and inventories from all fifty states. Uploaded in 2015, these records are organized into collections by state and go back as far as 1668 for some areas.

In some of the Ancestry.com collections, you'll find an abstract of a will, in others a will index. Some records list the names of individuals mentioned in the will. A will index (image **G**) lists the names; volume, section, and page number where the record can be found; and the date.

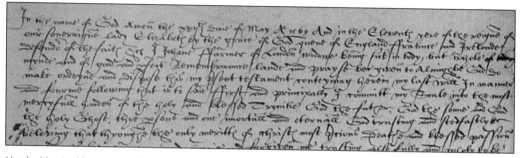

Handwriting in older records—like in this UK record from "London, England, Wills and Probate, 1507–1858"—can be hard to read, but they can contain valuable information if you're lucky enough to decipher or find a transcription.

When searching Ancestry.com for probate records, you're likely to find an abstract (summary) of the record. An abstract is more than an index, but less than a full transcript. An abstract is a detailed summary of the document.

If you're searching for UK records, collections like "London, England, Wills and Probate, 1507–1858" have images of the original books, like the one in image **H**. (Good luck with reading that handwriting from 1569! By 1857, however, the handwriting was much easier to read.) If the collection you're using does not include images, you'll probably need to view the microfilm in person once you find probate records or a will.

When searching individual collections, remember to check out the Browse This Collection function. In the case of the London wills and probate, Browse This Collection allows you to filter by year and by surname.

BANK & INSURANCE RECORDS

With only a couple dozen collections, this is the smallest group within the Tax, Criminal, Land & Wills category. The "U.S., Freedmen Bureau Records of Field Offices, 1863–1878" collection has the largest number of US records, as do the New York Emigrant Savings Bank, Philadelphia Bank, and Freedman's Bank—the final three are a boon if you're doing emigrant or African-American research.

The Freedmen's Bureau was established in 1865 and was responsible for overseeing freedmen, refugees, and land that was abandoned or captured during the Civil War. This collection contains records pertaining to many of the Confederate states as well as Kansas and Washington, D.C. The Browse This Collection function allows you to search by state as well as record type.

Former slave Allen Brown proved his military service with this document, found in "U.S., Freedmen Bureau Records of Field Offices, 1863–1878."

Additionally, African-American researchers can find some interesting information in the Freedmen's Bureau collection on its Confidential List of Claimants. For example, one list gives the Union Army history of a former slave, Allen Brown, who joined the 83rd Regiment of United States Colored Troops (image **I**). The form gives his physical description, where he enlisted, birthplace, age, occupation, enlisting officer, and muster-out date—a bounty of information.

You can find records such as Brown's by using the filters under the Browse This Collection function.

Here are some other records you can find in this subcategory:

- bank records of thousands of Irish immigrants (New York)
- Jewish immigrant bank records (Philadelphia)
- bank records of former slaves (Freedman's Bank)

You'll find a sprinkling of other collections in this group, but the three above are the aces of this subcategory.

The "New York Emigrant Savings Bank, 1850–1883" collection records comprise four books:

1. Index Book
2. Test Books
3. Transfer, Signature, and Test Books
4. Deposit-Account Ledger

This portion of a test book gives the date and place of birth, plus any of the individual's relatives.

The test books (image **J**) include the name and residence of the individual, as well as birthplace, occupation, and "relations" (i.e., the person to whom they're related).

The records within the collection titled "Philadelphia Bank Immigrant Passage Records, 1890–1949" can include the name and US address of the person who paid for tickets to America, the port of entry, and final destination. The information is scant, but it can give you an opening to learn more about your Jewish ancestors.

The amount of family information may be overwhelming, including name of applicant, parents' names, names of children, birthplace, residence, and occupation. What doorways these records open to further research!

SEARCHING FOR RECORDS

Now that you know what types of records you can expect to find in the Tax, Probate, Criminal, Land & Wills category, let's do some searching. As in previous chapters, we'll start by searching the entire category, then examine how to search in a specific collection.

Searching the Whole Category

In the last chapter, we did some sleuthing about Franklin Roosevelt, so let's see what we can find about the other Roosevelt president—Theodore. In the Ancestry.com Card Catalog, click the Wills, Probates, Land, Tax & Criminal category link. At the top of the collections list, click the "Search entire 'Wills, Probates, Land, Tax & Criminal' Category" link. Type in the first name and surname, the date of birth (1858), and date of death (1919). My search returned more than 650 hits.

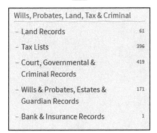

The left column of your whole-category search results will show how many results are from each subcategory.

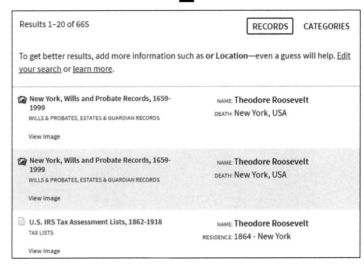

I searched the Tax, Criminal, Land & Wills category for Theodore Roosevelt. Unfortunately, many of the results aren't what I'm looking for.

Note that, while the main column of search results names each of the records found, the left column of search results (image **K**) gives you the number of results by subcategory. What difference does this make? If I search all records, I know that several of the results (image **L**) won't really relate to what I'm trying to find. However, if I look at the left column, I can easily see the subcategories where records appear, making it easier to focus in on the best results.

As I scrolled through Teddy's records, I see that the Roosevelts owned a considerable portion of the land by Oyster Bay, New York, including Teddy's home at Sagamore Hill (image **M**). Because I had visited Roosevelt's cabin in North Dakota, I hoped to find a mention in these records, but no such luck.

Why do a category-wide search in the first place? Unless I'm working with a very common name, I like to employ this strategy to see how many different subcategories of results might be available. For instance, it may not occur to me to search a tax list or a court record, so when I do this kind of search I have the opportunity to pick up results I wouldn't have looked for had I been searching only individual collections.

Let's do another search. Next, I employed a category-wide search for my great-great-grandfather, John Hendrickson, who was born in 1822 in Kentucky and died in 1906 in Missouri. Among the best finds was the discovery of land he owned in Cass County,

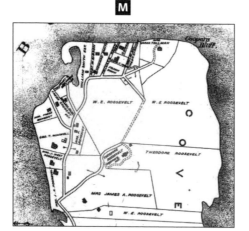

My search results for Theodore Roosevelt include this map of his property in Oyster Bay, New York.

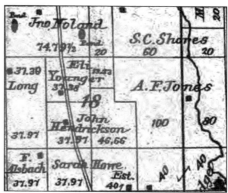

John Hendrickson resided in Cass County, Missouri, and this plat map shows part of his township.

Missouri, in 1895. Search results provided a plat image of the township where John resided (image **N**).

Two things of interest popped out when I looked at the map: First, there's a Shore family close by, and John's son married into the Shore family. Second, next to John's land is that of Eli Younger, and I know that the outlaw Cole Younger was from the same area. Family connection? I'm not sure.

Searching a Specific Collection

To discover more about John S. Strange, a Kentuckian who married two Hendrickson sisters (one in 1849, and the second after the first sister's death in 1862), I'm going to search a specific collection. John Strange and his family lived in Lincoln County, Kansas, following the Civil War. I've always wanted to know more about him and his family because my own second great-grandfather (John, the man we discussed earlier) lived in Lincoln for a time as well.

To search a specific collection, I again went to the Ancestry.com Card Catalog and chose the Wills, Probates, Land, Tax & Criminal category. I then filtered by Land Records subcategory, then by location (USA, then Kansas) and date (1800s). This filtered down to twenty-one collections. After browsing the collection options, I chose two that I wanted to search. The first was "U.S., Indexed County Land Ownership Maps, 1860–1918," and the second was "Kansas Settlers, 1854–1879."

I started with the Kansas settlers collection, which was a bust. Next, I launched the search form for the land ownership maps collection. I searched for John by name, and the

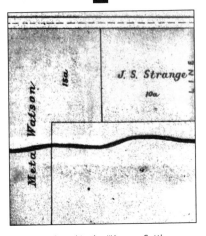

collection quickly found him with a ten-acre lot in Lincoln, Lincoln County, Kansas (image 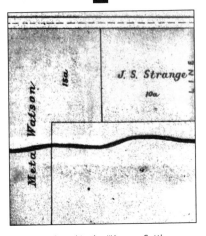). Upon looking at the map more thoroughly, I realized John lived in town, not out in some rural area (despite Ancestry.com's census records listing John as a farmer). Hmm? I investigated further. A search for his grave revealed he's listed as a pioneer minister and his tombstone refers to him as "Rev." I continued to investigate.

Next, I checked the Tax Lists subcategory. In the Card Catalog, I filtered this subcategory by location (USA, and then Kansas). The only collection that seemed to have any potential for answering my questions was "U.S. IRS Tax Assessment Lists, 1862–1918." Again, no luck there, nor in the Bank & Insurance subcategory. For now, it looks like finding John's land may be the best I can do in this particular category.

This map, found in the "Kansas Settlers, 1854–1879" collection, shows John S. Strange's ten-acre lot in Lincoln County, Kansas.

Instead of giving up, though, I decided to take one more approach. After selecting the Wills, Probates, Land, Tax & Criminal category, I filtered *first* by location (instead of by subcategory). I chose USA and then Kansas. After that, I selected the Court, Governmental & Criminal Records subcategory.

After clicking the link to search the entire category, I typed in *John Strange* in the name fields, and entered his year of birth (1831).

Guess what? I discovered that John was appointed Postmaster of Lincoln Centre, Kansas. Something I had never heard among all the family stories.

If you've followed along with these searches, I think you'll now have a really good idea of why it's so important to tackle a research problem from as many directions as you can think of. Honestly, I would never have looked in the collection for US postmasters because it would have seemed like a waste of time. Lesson learned for me.

PART 3

UNCOVERING ANCESTORS WITH
ANCESTRYDNA

12

INTERPRETING YOUR DNA RESULTS

When DNA testing first hit the genealogy scene, genetics had limited utility for family history research. Tests were expensive, and the tests at the time allowed you to discover information about just one of two of your ancestral lines. Y-chromosomal DNA (Y-DNA) tests could give you information about your strictly paternal line (your father's father's father, etc.), while mitochondrial-DNA (mtDNA) tests could tell you about your strictly maternal line (your mother' mother's mother, etc.). And even if you were lucky enough to get a match in those early days, the info wasn't much help—the mtDNA and Y-DNA tests didn't reveal information about relatively recent generations, focusing instead on "deep ancestry."

This created several problems for genealogists, particularly for women. Only men could take a Y-DNA test, meaning Y-DNA tests were pretty much useless for women who didn't have a father, brother, or paternal uncle to test. And since so few women signed up for DNA tests, a woman's chances of finding a female mtDNA match in a predominantly male database were slim.

Fortunately, today's advanced AncestryDNA testing **<dna.ancestry.com>** has much greater research benefits. An AncestryDNA test can provide you with information about recent ancestors in all your ancestral lines, and a woman can find male matches just as easily as she can find female matches.

All of this is possible thanks to autosomal DNA testing. Instead of Y-DNA or mtDNA, the AncestryDNA test analyzes autosomal DNA—the twenty-two pairs of chromosomes that all people (male or female) have. These chromosomes contain genetic information from *both* of your parents, who in turn received their DNA from both of their parents, and so on. The results can be astonishing.

If you were among the early adopters of genetic genealogy, it's likely that you went years without finding a close match. Thanks to autosomal testing, those days are over. Welcome to the wide and wonderful world of modern-day genetic genealogy!

Wondering how likely it is to make a DNA match? At the time of this book's publication, AncestryDNA had five million customers in its DNA database. This makes AncestryDNA the largest consumer genetic testing company in the world—and it continues to grow rapidly. And as the database grows, so too does your chance of finding a match.

In this chapter, we're going to take a look at DNA as a genealogical tool, including the testing procedure, and show you how to navigate the DNA portion of the Ancestry.com site.

THE BENEFITS OF DNA TESTING

Those who have been doing genealogy for many years might be skeptical about what DNA can offer their research. After all, when DNA tests were first introduced, finding family tree matches was difficult because of a few critical factors:

- The number of participants was relatively small (resulting in less chance for a match).

- Testing was expensive.

- Potential matches were often more "anthropological" than genealogical. While your DNA may have matched another person's in a database, your common ancestor likely lived thousands of years ago. This made real-life genealogical research breakthroughs more difficult.

- Genetic ethnicity estimates were limited to large geographic areas (Western Europe instead of more specific ethnicities, for instance).

However, technological advancements have allowed modern DNA testing to overcome these difficulties. As we've already discussed, your chances of finding a match increases as AncestryDNA adds hundreds of thousands of test-takers each month, and the availability of new technology has allowed testing companies to drop the price of their tests, usually to one hundred dollars or less. Because Ancestry.com's test uses autosomal DNA rather than Y-DNA or mtDNA, you can use your results to solve genealogical problems in even the last couple of generations. Even the ethnicity estimates (once just a loose approximation of what part of the world your DNA comes from) have become more specific, now identifying specific countries and even immigrant communities.

This means you have a higher chance of breaking through previous roadblocks. For example, while you may be stuck at a fourth-generation ancestral line, a DNA cousin may take your research (and source) back two more generations by giving you genetic relatives

America	1%
⊖ Low Confidence Region	
⚬ Native American	1%
Pacific Islander	**< 1%**
⊖ Low Confidence Region	
● Polynesia ›	< 1%

Your ethnicity estimate breaks down what percentage of your DNA comes from each region of the world. You may find, for example, that you have traces of DNA from Polynesia. Note: All ethnicities with predicted percentages of less than 4.5 percent appear as low confidence regions.

to research. Or, if your DNA shows a surprising (and previously unknown) ancestry, it may help you make the leap over the pond to regions such as Ireland, Scandinavia, the Iberian Peninsula, Eastern Europe, or Africa. You may even find you have some surprising ancestry, such as Native American or Polynesian heritage (image **A**). In some instances, DNA can solve a problem in a heartbeat; in others, DNA offers clues for further research.

Testing through Ancestry.com specifically has benefits as well. In addition to having access to Ancestry.com's database of more than five million users, you can also sync your results up to your Ancestry.com family tree, making it easier to find genetic relatives amongst the site's users.

Ancestry.com also presents various tools such as DNA Circles, New Ancestor Discoveries, and Migrations (all of which we'll discuss later in this chapter and in chapters 13 and/or 14).

ABOUT THE TEST

Before we dig into results, let's discuss the actual testing process. The test takes a sample of your saliva and runs a series of tests on it, comparing it to all the other samples in its database as well as tests from certain sample populations from around the world. You can purchase a kit online at **<dna.ancestry.com>** or (usually) from the company's booth at genealogy conferences. The cost of the AncestryDNA test, including tax and shipping, is usually a little over one hundred dollars, though during certain holiday periods the costs can drop twenty dollars or so.

Once you get your kit (and *before you send in your sample*), you need to activate it and connect it to your Ancestry.com account **<ancestry.com/dna/activate>**. You'll be prompted to enter the activation code that's printed on the side of the saliva-collecting tube. You'll then be asked to fill in a form, including your name, birth date, gender, and whether you want your ethnicity estimates to be available to your DNA matches in the database. You'll need to read and agree to terms and conditions, then click to activate your test.

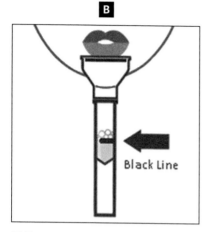

DNA tests require a saliva sample. You'll receive instructions on how to complete the sample (which requires you to spit into a tube up to a certain line) along with your test.

Now it's time to actually do the test. The kit includes instructions on use, but in brief: Deposit saliva into the provided tube up to a certain line (image **B**), then mix your saliva with a special preservation solution and put the result in the collection bag. The bag then goes into the pre-paid mailing box, which is shipped away. Note: Do not eat, drink, smoke, or chew gum or tobacco for thirty minutes prior to the test, as these activities could throw off your results.

After mailing in your test, you'll receive an e-mail when the sample is received and another when processing begins. A third e-mail will alert you when results are available, usually six to eight weeks after Ancestry.com receives the sample.

While You're Waiting for Test Results

If you haven't already uploaded a family tree to Ancestry.com, your six- to eight-week waiting period is a good time to do so. While AncestryDNA does not take your pedigree chart into account when generating DNA matches, having a family tree does help when trying to determine relationships with your matches. If your family tree is uploaded and made public, DNA cousins can more easily look through your surnames to find your common family line. If your tree is not public or you don't have one at all, anyone who is a DNA match will have to e-mail you to get information about the family. This can become a slow process, particularly if you or your new cousin is only online once every few months. By keeping your tree marked as Private, you'll miss out on several different opportunities to network with other family researchers.

CHECK BACK FOR THE UNKNOWN
According to Ancestry.com, if your ethnicity returns as "uncertain" it means that small traces of a specific genetic population have been found in your DNA, but the levels were too insignificant to pinpoint a specific ethnicity. Over time, it's likely that Ancestry.com will be able to update the uncertain percentage listed on your results, so be sure to check back regularly for any changes.

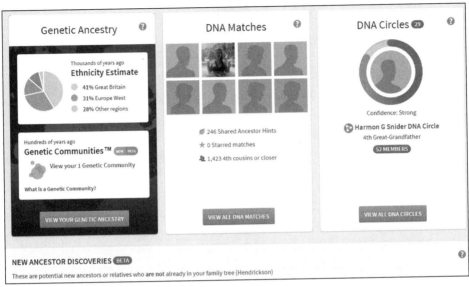

From your DNA home page, you can access AncestryDNA's most useful tools, including ethnicity estimates and DNA matches.

In addition, having both your public tree and your DNA results online allows you to access some pretty nifty Ancestry.com features: DNA Circles (where you can receive New Ancestor Discoveries, a clue to other relatives to research) and shared ancestor hints (people in your tree who also appear in the tree of your DNA matches).

If you originally uploaded a family tree and marked it private, you can go back and change the settings to public. Here's how to do it: Click Trees in the top menu, then Create & Manage Trees in the dropdown menu. Select the appropriate tree (if you have more than one), then click Manage Tree. On the next page, choose Privacy Settings. Click the Public Tree button to change from a Private Tree. (Remember: Ancestry.com automatically masks information about living people.)

NAVIGATING YOUR DNA HOME PAGE

To view your DNA home page, click the DNA tab from the Ancestry.com main menu. On the dropdown menu, you'll have the choice of going to your Last Viewed Match or Your DNA Results Summary. (You can also purchase another test). For now, click on the DNA Results Summary menu item; this takes you to your DNA home page (image **C**).

The first things you'll notice are three columns across the top: DNA Story (formerly Genetic Ancestry), DNA Matches, and DNA Circles, and one on the bottom (New Ancestor

Discoveries). Note that at the top of each column is a question mark. Click on each to learn more about each how each group of matches is calculated. For example, the question mark at the top of the DNA Story column has items to help you understand how things like ethnicity and trace regions are determined.

Under DNA Story, you'll see your ethnicity estimates, a summary breakdown of your genetic ancestry. You'll only see the top two to three regions in this box. I'll show you how to drill down to more regions later in this chapter. Within your ethnicity estimates, you'll also find a section called Migrations. In brief, it shows communities of AncestryDNA members who are genetically connected, probably because they descend from a population of ancestors who traveled together.

The middle column of your DNA home page displays thumbnails of several of the people whose DNA matches your own. Beneath the thumbnail images are the number of shared ancestor hints, the number of starred matches (these are matches you've starred as being more important to you), and the number of fourth-cousin matches (or closer).

The right column shows your DNA Circles. A DNA Circle is a group of individuals who share DNA and have the same ancestor in their trees. Here you'll see the number of Circles you've been placed in, as well as a most recent DNA Circle along with the confidence level. (Note: It's possible to not have been put in a Circle.) DNA Circles can change over time as new information makes the connection stronger or weaker.

At the bottom of your DNA home page, you'll find a section called New Ancestor Discoveries. These are people who you match via DNA but are not currently in your public member tree. As with DNA Circles, it's possible you don't have any New Ancestor Discoveries.

Let's take a look at each of these tools.

Ethnicity Estimate

This is the section everyone goes to first because, after watching all of those exciting television ads, who doesn't want to see what surprises are in store? As noted, the DNA home page only shows the top few ethnicities. To see your complete range of estimates, click the Discover Your DNA Story button at the bottom of the left column. On the following page, view a more complete breakdown of your Ethnicity Estimate regions, along with a map (image **D**).

Ancestry.com determines your ethnicity estimates by comparing your DNA to the DNA of people who are considered native to that region (called reference populations). Note that these are merely estimates—the average percentage of your DNA that overlaps with

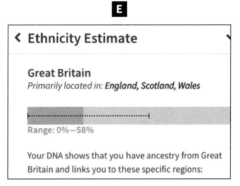

You can view your complete ethnicity results by clicking Discover Your DNA Story. Note the Migrations Group Germany & the Midwestern United States.

AncestryDNA allows you to compare your DNA percentage with that of a native population.

each reference population—so take them with a grain of salt. As AncestryDNA grows in size (and the science improves), your DNA results will change.

Click an ethnicity to learn more about it, plus to view the confidence range that you have ancestry of this ethnicity (image **E**). Note that confidence ranges can vary dramatically—again, take your ethnicity estimates with a grain of salt. You can learn more about the history and genetic diversity of each ethnicity by reading the text under Overview and clicking "Continue reading." Don't skip the history, as it's where you'll learn about the original inhabitants of the area as well as the migrations into and out of the region. By learning the history of a region, you'll have a much better sense of how, where, and when your ancestor lived.

Migrations

One of Ancestry.com's newest additions to its DNA arsenal is called Migrations (formerly called Genetic Communities). Your ethnicity estimate may include one genetic community or many—and (like many aspects of DNA test results) your communities may vary from those of your siblings. The Migrations feature shows where your family probably lived at sometime in the recent past (up to a few hundred years ago). These communities are made up of people who share common DNA. The supposition is that those of us in a genetic community are all descended from a population of common ancestors who lived in a specific area. For example, my sister's genetic community is that of Early Settlers of

What If Your Ethnicity Results Differ From Your Research?

Ethnicity and research can be strange bedfellows. In my own family, legend has it that the Hendrickson line (my dad's family) was Scandinavian in origin. I've yet to find any genealogical evidence of that being true. However, my own DNA testing shows 26-percent Scandinavian. My Danish friend tells me she sees a lot of Hendricksons while doing Danish research. Could it be the family is Danish? Or is it more likely that Hendrickson began life as a British *Henricks*?

By checking Ancestry.com's name origins, I see that Hendrickson is an Anglicized spelling of the Dutch Hendriksen, as well as the Scottish and English patronymic from *Hendrick*. Can DNA solve the mystery? Not until I get more close matches. But I definitely know more about possible areas of research than I did before.

Here's another scenario: Let's say you've traced your family tree to England, but your ethnicity shows only a small percentage of Western Europe DNA with the larger percentage coming from Scandinavia. A possible reason for this finding is that the Vikings (from Scandinavia) settled in England as early as 876 AD and controlled a third of Britain for nearly eighty years.

Discrepancies between estimates and your actual heritage could also be caused by inheritance patterns. As a post on Ancestry.com Support Center notes, "You received exactly 50% of your genes from each of your parents, but the percentages of DNA you received from ancestors at the grandparent level and further back are not necessarily neatly divided in two with each generation. . . At seven generations back, less than 1% of your DNA is likely to come from any given ancestor."

Unfortunately, we inherit DNA in random chunks rather than a neatly organized bundle! For example, one great-grandparent may have passed 10-percent of his DNA to you, but another great-grandparent may have only given you 3 percent. This is also why one sibling may show 12 percent of a specific ethnicity while you may show 40 percent of that same ethnicity. In fact, you may not have one of your sibling's ethnicities at all! A great example of this in my own family is that my brother and I both show Jewish heritage while my sister does not. Likewise, my sister shows 41 percent Great Britain while my DNA only shows 19 percent.

Lastly, if you're wondering how you came up with Scandinavian DNA when you've never run into any Scandinavian family line, note that the Vikings traveled and plundered all over northern Europe from 793 to 1066 AD. Those guys got around!

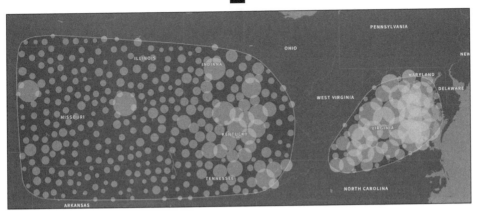

F

Migrations can help you visualize how your ancestor fits into wider trends. This screenshot shows birthplaces in a particular genetic community.

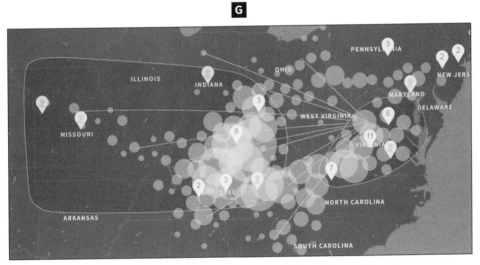

G

You can view where members of your family tree were born in relation to other members of Migrations groups

the Lower Midwest and Virginia. Clicking on that community launches a map as well as an historical timeline (image **F**). Click each timeline to show ancestral birthplaces from both your tree and other member trees, and click on the inverted teardrop icons to see a list of who in your family was born in the place marked on the map (image **G**).

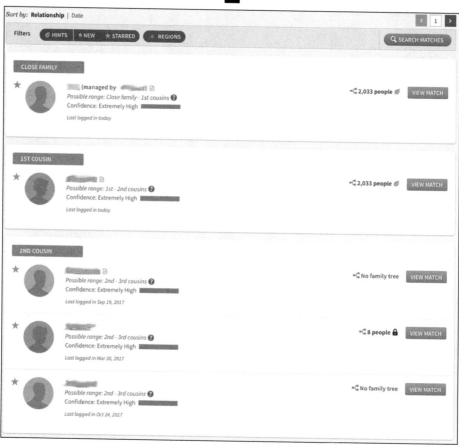

Your DNA results page will provide you with a summary of your match, including what AncestryDNA predicts your relationship to be.

Be sure to click the names of your Migrations group, then the i icon. Here, you'll see an estimate of how likely it is that you're connected to this community. With a rating of "Very Likely," AncestryDNA can say with 95-percent confidence that you share recent ancestors with others in the community. By comparison, a rating of "Possible" indicates only a 20-percent confidence level of being connected. Click Learn More to read Ancestry. com's "white paper," which explains the test's methodology in more detail.

One more thing: When viewing details about a Migration group, scroll down past the Overview and check out the section titled AncestryDNA Members. Click the number to discover which of your DNA matches have also been placed in this Migration group.

Filter and sort your DNA matches by whether you have shared hints, whether you've viewed the match before, or whether you've flagged/starred the match.

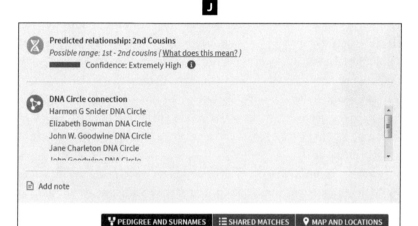

Click on a DNA match to view details about your predicted relationship, including what degree of cousinhood and information about your DNA Circles.

DNA Matches

The middle column on your DNA home page shows your DNA Matches. By comparing everyone in the AncestryDNA database, the system determines how closely you're related and assigns a suggested relationship: siblings, first cousins, second cousins, etc. Beneath the thumbnail icons of six or eight matches, you'll find the number of shared ancestor hints, the number of starred matches, and the number of fourth cousins or closer. A shared hint is an ancestor who appears in the trees of people who share DNA. In other words, you'll only receive a shared hint if you and another person have the same ancestor in your trees and you share DNA.

Click on Shared Hints (or View All DNA Matches) to open the AncestryDNA results page (image ■). At the top of the page, you can organize the page by relationship or by date. If you sort by relationship, the results are sorted from closest to furthest relationships. You can also sort results by how recently test-takers entered the database, useful when you check back with your results later.

Keep in mind that, while relationship results are close, they may not be exact. Because multiple degrees of relatives can share similar amounts of DNA, the test sometimes struggles to distinguish between these family relationships. For example, when you see someone listed as "Possible range: Close family—1st cousins," this person could be your cousin, niece, or nephew, as all three kinds of relationships share similar amounts of DNA.

In addition to sorting capabilities, you can also filter results by Hints, New, or Starred (image **I**). Filtering by Hints will sort your matches by the people whose tree has a shared ancestor hint. Filtering by New will show you the newest matches. Starred are those connections you've favorited or short-listed by marking them with a star.

If one of the members who has matched your DNA has also uploaded a public family tree, you can view the user's tree to see where you're a likely match by clicking View Match. Once you click on a DNA match's tree, you'll see the relationship as well as the DNA Circles that you share (image **J**).

Below the Circle connections, you can also sort matches by pedigree/surnames, shared matches, and maps/locations (image **K**). If you sort by Surnames, you'll see a list of surnames shared by both you and your match. Maps and Locations will show you the locations that the two of you share. Shared Matches will display of list of other Ancestry.com DNA members you share.

DNA Circles

The third (right) column on your DNA home page is for DNA Circles. A Circle represents a group of individuals who share DNA as well as a person in their family trees (which is essentially the same criteria as that for a Shared Ancestor Hint). You may be in several circles or just a few. Your DNA Circles page (image **L**) will list all of your circles, the ancestor who is shared by everyone in the circle, and the number of circle members.

Click on any circle, and you'll find a brief biographical summary of the shared ancestor as well as circle members. Circles can be viewed either graphically or by a list. If you're viewing by relationships (graphically) the thickness of the orange lines tell you the strength of the connection. I think it's easier to view the circle as a list (image **M**) because connections are written out; that way I don't have to guess about the thickness of an orange line!

The more people who belong to a circle, the more evidence you have of the original connection.

Katie Hendrickson
Member since 2017, last logged in Aug 11, 2017

SEND MESSAGE

Ethnicity

Regions: Great Britain, Ireland, Scandinavia, Europe West

Predicted relationship: Close Family
Possible range: Close family - 1st cousins (What does this mean?)
■■■■■ Confidence: Extremely High ⓘ

Trace Regions: Italy/Greece, European Jewish, Iberian Peninsula

Add note

♈ PEDIGREE AND SURNAMES | ≡ SHARED MATCHES | ♀ MAP AND LOCATIONS

When evaluating a DNA match, you can view what family members/surnames, matches, and locations you share.

Wiley C. Hatton DNA Circle
3rd Great-Grandfather
(1797-1872)
22 MEMBERS

Nancy Caroline Gregory DNA Circle
3rd Great-Grandmother
(1797-1895)
22 MEMBERS

Aaron Hendrickson DNA Circle
3rd Great-Grandfather
(1793-1870)
39 MEMBERS

James Goodwine DNA Circle
3rd Great-Grandfather
(1780-1851)
14 MEMBERS

DNA Circles show a group of individuals who share DNA with a person in their family trees. Access DNA Circles from your DNA home page.

22 DESCENDANTS	CIRCLE MEMBERSHIP CONFIDENCE	RELATIONSHIP TO VICKI FITE	RELATIONSHIP TO WILEY C. HATTON
Vicki Fite	Good		
C.G. (administered by mgroves02) Ray Jessie Groves Family Group	Strong	✖ DNA MATCH ⌄	◂⁍ VIEW RELATIONSHIP

You can also view DNA Circle members as a list.

5 DNA Myths Busted

The biggest genealogy myth prior to the popularity of DNA was that an ancestor was an American Indian (often, Cherokee) princess. In fact, that myth was so prevalent that many novice genealogists hoped to find the princess by delving into Native American genealogy. Fortunately, over the years, that myth has been pretty much relegated to the genealogy junk pile. However, in its place came new myths—most of them related to DNA. Let's look at five of the most prominent.

MYTH 1: IF I HAVE NATIVE AMERICAN DNA, I CAN JOIN A TRIBE.

This age-old myth has carried over to the DNA era. Each tribe is a sovereign nation, and each determines its own criteria for membership. If you don't know who in your family was Native American, you won't be able to prove the lineage. In addition, DNA isn't advanced enough to identify individual tribes.

MYTH 2: MY DNA WILL BE USED FOR NEFARIOUS PURPOSES.

Most, if not all, genetic genealogy testing services have clear privacy policies. You can find AncestryDNA's privacy policy by clicking AncestryDNA Privacy Statement at the bottom of any page. Although you're encouraged to read the entire policy, you can rest assured that you own your DNA and Ancestry.com cannot share identifiable genetic data without your consent.

MYTH 3: YOU HAVE TO GIVE A BLOOD OR HAIR SAMPLE IN ORDER TO GET YOUR DNA TESTED.

While hair and blood are used by scientists for forensic testing, genetic genealogy services only require either a cheek swab or a saliva sample, both painless and simple.

MYTH 4: ONLY MALE DNA IS USEFUL FOR GENEALOGY RESEARCH.

Back in the day, you had two options for DNA testing: Y-DNA (which traces the patrilineal male line) or mtDNA (which traces the female line). Because Y-DNA is passed along on the Y-chromosome (which only males have), only men could take both tests. However, popular modern genetic genealogy tests sample a third category of genetic material called autosomal DNA that appears in both males and females and can give you information about relatives of any gender. This means if a woman takes an autosomal test, it will show both her patrilineal and matrilineal lines—the same as if a man took the autosomal test.

MYTH 5: ONCE I GET MY DNA RESULTS I'LL KNOW MY ENTIRE FAMILY TREE.

Sorry. I wish this one were true! DNA does not show you specific individuals. However, used in connection with family trees and DNA matches with other people, it can help point the way to individuals in your tree or answer specific questions about your heritage.

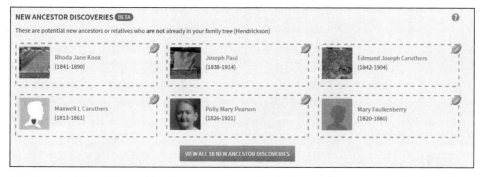

New Ancestor Discoveries are other Ancestry.com users who don't currently appear in your family tree that the site believes are your ancestors based on DNA.

New Ancestor Discoveries

At the bottom of your DNA home page, you'll find the section on New Ancestor Discoveries (image N). These are people that Ancestry.com thinks are your ancestors based on your DNA but don't appear in your family tree.

Often, the people who appear here are siblings of your direct ancestors who you haven't yet added to your tree. Finding such a person in New Ancestor Discoveries is a quick and easy way to add them to your tree.

Click on any of the New Ancestors to read a brief biography and see what other people are included in the ancestor's DNA Circle. Knowing about a DNA connection makes it a lot easier for you to have a degree of certitude about the discovery. As you can see, the more you dig into your AncestryDNA information, the higher the likelihood you're going to find proven matches.

HOW USEFUL IS DNA TESTING?

The truth is, DNA will not "name names." By that, I mean a DNA test will not pinpoint your relationship to a specific individual. However, your AncestryDNA test can do two things that may aid in your research: give you an estimate of your genetic ethnicity and provide research leads in the form of DNA matches.

Let's start with the first. You may think that ethnicity estimates, while cool, are not very useful for genealogy research. And, for the most part, you'd be right—ethnicity estimates are not gospel truth, and they're really most useful for cocktail party banter. Sample populations can be inaccurate, and the ethnicity estimate regions aren't specific enough to be useful. (They can't help you pinpoint an ancestor's town or county, for example.)

However, under the right circumstances, ethnicity estimates can provide a clue to your ancestors' heritage and lend evidence to support other research claims. For example, if I suspect that my ancestor with an Irish-sounding surname is from Ireland and my DNA suggests I have a large percentage of Irish DNA, then I might a little more confident in turning my attention to Irish records. I could be wrong, but it's a clue worth following.

You should focus most of your time on the second key takeaway from AncestryDNA: DNA matches. Although DNA itself cannot pinpoint an exact relationship, AncestryDNA has built so many features into how it uses your results that you have a good chance of making a research breakthrough. By viewing the amount of DNA you share with other users, you can hopefully find genetic relatives amongst the site's massive database of test-takers—some of whom you've never even heard of. And even if you can't find specific relatives, you'll likely find other researchers who are investigating the same genetic lines. This will allow you to reach out to other users and collaborate on breaking down brick walls in your research. This potential for teamwork is tempered somewhat by Ancestry.com's policy allowing test-takers to opt out of DNA matches, but you'll still likely find more DNA matches than you'll know what to do with.

Testing with AncestryDNA will also open you up to performing more intricate dives into your genetic ancestry. You can download your raw data results from AncestryDNA, then reupload them to other services that provide you with even more detailed results and tools. Uploading your results to other services will also allow you to compare your DNA to test-takers from other companies like Family Tree DNA <www.familytreedna.com> and 23andMe <www.23andme.com>, some of whom may not have tested with AncestryDNA. We'll discuss three of these services (DNA.land <dna.land>, GEDmatch <www.gedmatch.com>, and DNAGedcom <www.dnagedcom.com>) in chapter 14.

13

CONNECTING WITH OTHERS

n chapter 12, you learned about the many elements of your Ancestry.com DNA home page. In this chapter, I'm going to dive more deeply into how to use your DNA results to connect with other researchers. You'll learn the best ways to interpret and infer relationships using AncestryDNA's various tools and features.

DNA MATCHES

Once you receive your DNA results, log into Ancestry.com and head to the DNA summary page. Once you've gone through the Ethnicity Estimates—after all, isn't this the "cool" part?—move on to your DNA Matches. Under thumbnail images of matches, you'll probably see a list of the number of Shared Ancestor Hints and fourth cousins or closer. Remember, you'll only see Shared Ancestor Hints if you've uploaded your own tree; the hints relate to the people in your tree who also appear in the tree of your DNA matches.

First, click on any person's image to see his or her profile and his or her predicted relationship to you. The predicted relationship range may be close or (in the case of image **A**) distant, meaning fifth to eighth cousins.

You'll also see a "confidence meter," telling you how confident Ancestry.com is about this match. Confidence levels are determined by the amount of DNA two people share. Your match's ethnicity is displayed on the right of their profile, along with a link for you to send them an e-mail within the Ancestry.com system.

At this point, do you e-mail the potential cousin? It depends on the current status of your genealogy research. If you're just starting out, this isn't a relationship I'd encourage you to pursue at this time. A fifth cousin means you share a great-great-great-great-grandparent.

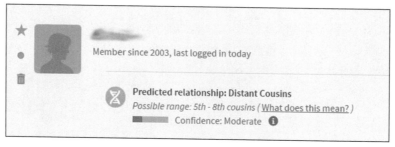

DNA Matches comes with a confidence rating, indicating how likely it is that you and the other user are connected in the predicted relationship. This match has a low confidence rating and a predicted relationship of "Distant Cousins." As a result, this match probably isn't worth pursuing. Note: The user's name has been blurred for privacy.

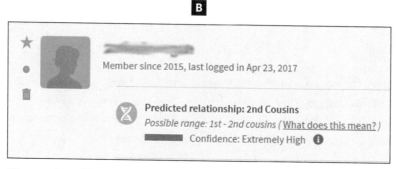

Other matches will be predicted as closer relatives, such as second cousins. This match also has an extremely high confidence rating, so I'll probably want to put it on my "short list" by clicking the star in the upper left of this image to favorite it.

For many new researchers, the chances of even knowing the identity of that fourth great-grandparent is small. (Go back to an eighth cousin, and you're now even further up the ancestor tree!) However, if you've been working on your genealogy for years, you may be at a juncture where you've picked all the low-hanging fruit and now need helping going after the tougher lines. In this case, connecting with a fourth or fifth cousin could prove productive.

Because DNA ethnic regions are so generic at this time (e.g., Western Europe, Iberian Peninsula), trying to make a match by looking at the ethnicity list to the right of the match's profile is only minimally helpful. However, as you move further back into your research and manage to get your family tree to another continent, then those ethnicity matches could very well be helpful.

For example, AncestryDNA is somewhat specific when it comes to African roots, identifying several different regions. If you or the person you're researching has a family that's been in the United States for generations, it's almost certain the country will lie on Africa's "Slave Coast." And once you've identified your ancestor's African country of origin, you can quickly check the Ancestry.com-provided map to see where the country is located. But before you go too deeply into researching the African country, read Ancestry's overview of the region to better understand the history of the people who live(d) there. In the case of Benin, for example, you'll find that several ethnic groups live in the modern country, including the Fon, Adja, Yoruba, and Bariba. As Ancestry.com notes, the ethnic ties are the results of "long-standing kingdoms that flourished before European colonists created new borders," creating more research knots to untangle.

What if the relationship is much closer, like the one shown in image **B**? As you know, a first cousin is a non-sibling who shares a grandparent with you (usually a child of one of your aunts or uncles), while a second cousin is a non-first cousin who shares a great-grandparent with you (usually a grandchild of one of your grandparent's siblings). That's a close relationship, and most of us probably have known people in our family who meet those criteria. As a result, it's probably worth pursuing that connection so you can swap genealogical notes.

If you look beneath the match, you'll see their family tree (or a partial tree) along with the common surnames in both trees (yours and your match's). Skimming down through surnames is a quick way to identify your possible connection (image **C**).

I hope you're now beginning to see the value of uploading a public family tree. Without a public tree it's much more difficult to make connections. If you have a public tree, the Ancestry.com system actually does a lot of

C

Surnames (10 generation pedigree)

> Franklin

> Johnson

> Mc Grew

> McGrew

> Yarbourough

When reviewing DNA matches, look at the list of surnames to see if you and your match have any overlapping surnames.

the work for you. Note, too, that you and other users have the ability to opt out of DNA matches, though I would discourage you from taking this option. At the time of this book's publication, users receive DNA matches by default and have the ability to turn off this capability—but this would close you off to the great research opportunities afforded by DNA matches.

What if the surname list shows surnames common to both you and another user, but you don't recognize anyone in the match's tree? In this case, you should send a message through the Ancestry.com system to your DNA match and learn more. To do this, click the green Send Message button to the right of the match's profile picture (or person icon if no picture). This will launch a pop-up e-mail box that is automatically populated with your name and the username of your Match. Begin by introducing yourself by name and letting the person know you're a DNA match. If you can't identify anyone in the match's tree, give the other member your tree name and let them know that you're trying to understand which ancestor you have in common.

If you want to share your full DNA results with another user, select the Settings button from your Ancestry.com DNA home page, and scroll down to DNA Result Access. Enter a user's e-mail address or username and select a permissions role: Viewer (view test results), Collaborator (view results, add notes, and favorite matches) or Manager (view and modify test results, message users). I would use this option selectively, as it gives another person total access to your DNA results. (See chapter 14 for info on when to make this choice.) This is especially important when working with someone else who has agreed to test their DNA, as AncestryDNA now requires each test-taker to have a separate Ancestry.com account (i.e., you can't manage multiple DNA tests from your account). If you wish to work with someone else's test, you'll need them to share their DNA results with you and make you a Collaborator or Manager.

One of the more maddening DNA Match results is when Ancestry.com shows a fairly close connection, yet the match has no tree or a private tree. This makes it almost impossible to know how you're related unless you contact the person. If someone has a private tree and you click to view the match, a box will pop-up letting you know this is a private tree and you'll need to contact the tree owner. If the person has no tree, simply send a message explaining that you're a DNA match but (because they don't have a tree) you can't determine the relationship. Ask them politely if they'll share their family tree with you.

Underneath the DNA Match person's profile are three choices: Pedigree and Surname, Shared Matches, and Maps and Location. By default, you'll automatically see your shared surnames and a partial pedigree chart. Click on Shared Matches to see the other Ancestry. com members with whom your "cousin" shares DNA. Maps and Locations launches a really

Maps and Locations in your DNA match profile shows birthplaces your ancestors share with your match's ancestors.

cool map (image) that pinpoints birth locations of people in your tree and your match's tree. Because so many birthplaces can be clumped together on the map, be sure to use the zoom function (+) to better see the places. Click on a shared birthplace (inverted teardrops are green and show two-people icons) to see where the two trees have matching birthplaces (image **E**).

If you're wondering what to do after you find a match and the two of you share e-mails, share research that you've both done, as well as documents and family photos. By sharing what each party has already discovered, you and your match will expand your family knowledge, hopefully getting you both back another generation or two.

Click on any of the inverted teardrop markers to see which family members were born at that location.

One last note: What if you have a lot of family information and your match has just begun researching? In this instance, you'll probably have far more photos and documents to share with the other person. Hopefully you won't look at this as a quid pro quo situation and instead freely share what you've learned, continuing the time-honored tradition of genealogists sharing without expectation of return. (Of course, that's just my opinion!)

DNA CIRCLES

As we discussed in chapter 12, DNA Circles are groups of individuals who share the same ancestor in their tree *and* DNA. As a result, I can say with high confidence that I have ancestors in common with those in my DNA Circles, making them valuable tools in uncovering information about my family history.

Circles are created around a particular ancestor, and everyone in a circle has DNA evidence that links them to you or someone else in the group. To summarize, Ancestry. com requires that members of a DNA Circle:

- share DNA with at least one other DNA Circle member
- have public family trees attached to their DNA tests
- share a common ancestor (according to their trees)

More specifically, DNA Circles revolve around people who are already in your family tree, including both direct and peripheral family lines. For example, if you are genetically related to members of your great-great-grandaunt's DNA Circle and she is in your tree, you will be included in that specific DNA Circle.

Note that DNA Circles can change over time as new information makes the connection stronger or weaker.

Ancestry.com kindly adds a short biography of the ancestor that heads the circle. You can click the bio to view the shared ancestor's profile page. In my case, all the members of one of my DNA Circles share Harmon G. Snider as an ancestor. The page provides a summary of Snider's life:

> Harmon G Snider was born in 1756 in Kassel, Hesse, Germany, the son of Elizabeth and Mattheus. He then married Elizabeth Bowman and they had 12 children together. He also had two sons and two daughters from another relationship. He died in May 1822 in Spencer, Kentucky, at the age of 66, and was buried in Owenton, Kentucky.

One of the most important things to understand about DNA Circles is that not all members of a DNA Circle are genetic matches, but each Circle member matches DNA with at least one other Circle member. In other words, Ancestry.com might find a cousin of your cousin, rather than your cousin.

How can you be in the same Circle (i.e., share a common ancestor) but not share DNA? Remember that you only inherit small chunks of DNA from each of your ancestors, and this amount of DNA varies from parent to child and sibling to sibling. That means that (despite sharing a common grandparent or great-grandparent) you may have inherited a different chunk of DNA than your first or second cousin did.

If you look at the list of people in a DNA Circle, you'll note that the DNA matches are in orange and the non-DNA matches are in blue. Click a blue link to see an explanatory box of why the person is in the circle but doesn't necessarily match your DNA.

When genetic genealogy took off, I felt that it would be most useful in proving relationships. It's no secret that many researchers probably have illegitimate members in the family tree. I've reached a point where I take no relationship for granted unless a) I have a DNA match to the ancestor or b) there's such a strong physical family resemblance that the relationship can't be denied. While I would love to absorb another person's research that shows my relationship to Thomas Jefferson, I want proof.

DNA Circles is one way of giving me that proof. DNA Circles provides evidence of relationships. For example, if you and several people have the same ancestor in your tree along with matching DNA, the chances of you all being related and you all being descended from a common ancestor are high. This helps me establish the relationship between shared ancestors and matching DNA, providing evidence that the connections in my family are what I believe them to be.

Once you've identified a member of a DNA Circle who you'd like to collaborate with, contact them using the message button and ask for help researching your shared ancestor. You might also consider asking a family member (especially a sibling or parent) to get tested, as he or she (with a different set of DNA) might match the other person even though you didn't, allowing you to triangulate the relationship among the three of you.

MIGRATIONS

As you do genealogy research, you'll find time and again that families tended to intermarry and to move from one location to another together. In my own family, I've found the Hendricksons often marry, live next to, and travel near the Shirleys, Moores, and Hattons. For example, it's not uncommon for me to find two Hendrickson brothers marrying two Hatton sisters. As a result, I can fairly easily trace their movements from Kentucky to Indiana and Missouri.

Migrations (formerly Genetic Communities), the newest addition to the AncestryDNA toolbox, is designed to help you identify these kinds of relationships. A Migrations group is a collection of AncestryDNA members who likely descend from an historical population of common ancestors. Migrations groups, which appear as part of your Ethnicity Estimate, will show you information about populations that lived in the same place and probably descended from the same group of ancestors. Ancestry.com finds groups of people in its DNA network "who have more matches to each other than to people in other parts of the network and set that group apart as a genetic community." Then Ancestry.com looks for linked family trees to identify people who were in the same area at the same time.

Note that the connections are ranked in order of confidence. My own DNA results show a higher likelihood of my Settlers of the Lower Midwest than Early Settlers of Tennessee & the Deep South.

Once you select a Migrations group from your Ethnicity Estimates, read the Overview. This will provide historical context for the Migrations group, including when they migrated and where they came from. For Settlers of the Lower Midwest and Virginia, it reads:

Kentucky fever lured one-time English, German, and Scots-Irish immigrants and their descendants further west looking for land. Roads, steamboats, and canals helped transform the frontier into settled farms, thriving towns, and even major cities in a matter of decades. The Civil War hit hard, dividing states and sometimes families. The years that followed saw the steady march of generations leaving the land for jobs in manufacturing and oil but taking their roots with them.

Once I begin going down the provided timeline, I find that the area was settled as early as 1700. By reading on, I discover that early settlers were farmers or wealthy landowners, the latter of whom also brought African-American slaves. Just that small amount of information provides clues for future research, including countries of origin and occupations.

Add to that the fact that Ancestry.com lists the people in your tree who fit into that Migrations group, and you'll be well prepared to begin your search. How? On the details page for your Migrations group, click the link under AncestryDNA members to find a list of your DNA matches who also belong to your community.

As you did with DNA matches, take the opportunity to send e-mails to matches who you feel can best further your own research. And, while Migrations groups are a great jumping-off place for discovering your family origins, they won't identify your ancestor's next-door neighbor—at least, not yet.

NEW ANCESTOR DISCOVERIES

Of all of Ancestry.com advances in genetic genealogy, New Ancestor Discoveries are (in my opinion) among the most useful for actually adding names to your family tree. That's because Ancestry.com uses your DNA to find potential new ancestors or relatives who are not already in your family tree. Once you click on any of your New Ancestor Discoveries, a box will pop up explaining why Ancestry.com believes you're descended from this person (image **F**).

How can you best use New Ancestor Discoveries, since the individuals named are not in your tree—and ostensibly not in your research? Do some digging to either confirm or deny a person's presence in your tree. For example, the system suggested a relationship to Allen Carmack—a surname I've never heard associated with any family line. The only hint in the description that the site provided is a reference to Sullivan County, Missouri—a place where my Knox family lived. Clicking the Learn More About Allen Carmack link on the pop-up box mentioned above, I found a new page detailing Allen's life, with facts and documents compiled from "393 family trees." The overview, which included the name of his spouse and children as well as the places he had lived, didn't help much.

F

Are you related to Edmund Joseph Caruthers?

DNA evidence suggests that you're related to a group of Edmund Joseph Caruthers descendants. And because your DNA matches people in the group, there's a good chance you're also related to Edmund Joseph Caruthers.

Edmund Joseph Caruthers
(1842 - 1904)

DNA CIRCLE: Edmund Joseph Caruthers's descendants
14 members · 6 matches

When Edmund Joseph Caruthers was born in October 1842 in Cannon, Tennessee, his father, Maxwell, was 29 and his mother, Mary, was 22. He was married four times and had nine sons and ten daughters. He died on December 2, 1904, in Oxford, Arkansas, at the age of 62, and was buried there.

Using DNA evidence and family trees, we've created a DNA Circle of probable descendants of **Edmund Joseph Caruthers.** You match 6 of 14 members.

SEE YOUR CONNECTION

LEARN ABOUT EDMUND JOSEPH CARUTHERS

Ancestry.com's New Ancestor Discovery feature suggests ancestors who may be related to people in your tree, based on how your tree matches with other users' as well as how you relate to members of a DNA Circle.

Next, I clicked on Facts to see a list of all of the Ancestry.com documents associated with Allen. Because Allen lived in Sullivan County (the same as my ancestors) in 1860, I clicked on the link to the 1860 census but couldn't find him living anywhere near my family. Ditto with the other census records, Find A Grave <www.findagrave.com>, and military records. I then went back to the DNA Circle because Ancestry.com noted that I matched four of the Circle's members. I clicked into each of the members' pedigree charts and discovered that in the early 1800s, a Carmack married a Goodwin (one known line of my family)—finally making the connection clear.

Sometimes—often, actually—you'll see New Ancestor Discoveries that are foreign to you. (After all, if you knew about them, they'd already be in your family tree!) Using the facts about the ancestor, as well as their profile and the link to their DNA Circle, you have plenty of options to discover exactly how this person fits into your family tree. By the way: The person you match may not be a direct ancestor, but rather a sibling of your direct ancestor.

14

APPLYING DNA TO YOUR RESEARCH

You've gotten your DNA results, cherry-picked the most obvious matches, and started to work your way through DNA Circles, New Ancestor Discoveries, and Migrations. What can you do next?

Before we explore this question, I'll give you a quick reminder to upload a Public Member Tree and link your DNA results to it. If you don't remember how to connect DNA results, here's a brief reminder:

1. Go to your DNA Results Summary page

2. Click Link to Tree

3. Choose your tree from the pulldown menu

4. Click Link to DNA

Once you've linked up your DNA results to your family tree, Ancestry.com will begin populating your DNA pages with even more information. If you haven't yet linked DNA and a tree, stop now and make the link-up.

Now it's time to see how to put all of your findings together.

SOLVING OLD MYSTERIES

As much as we'd like to think genealogical DNA testing is "just for us," we couldn't be more wrong. Advances in technology have helped historians solve lingering mysteries—some of them centuries old. In 2012, testing (combined with good old-fashioned research) helped identify skeletal remains buried under an English parking lot as those of Richard III, the last of the Plantagenet kings. Richard—known for his twisted back (scoliosis of the spine)—died at Bosworth on August 22, 1485, the last English king to fall in battle.

After the skeleton with a twisted spine was discovered at the site where priests were said to have buried the king, genealogists went to work tracking down a direct descendant of Richard's sister, Anne of York, for DNA testing. Researchers made a positive identification thanks to a combination of radiocarbon dating, contemporary reports of Richard's appearance, and (important for the purposes of this chapter) a mitochondrial DNA match with Anne's descendant, a Canadian named Michael Ibsen.

Irish researchers will like this one: DNA helped solve a long-held question about the Irish Potato Famine. Using DNA sequencing of plant specimens dating from the mid-nineteenth century, scientists identified the pathogen that caused the death of nearly one million people and the mass emigration of another two million from Ireland by 1855. In a strange twist, the culprit was found to be a previously unknown strain of *Phytophthora infestans* (or *P. infestans*) that originated in the Americas. The strain, known as HERB-1, devastated crops in America before making its way across the Atlantic sometime in 1844. Within two years, three-quarters of Ireland's potato crop was infected. Thanks to DNA testing, we can now identify what caused this great devastation and (hopefully) prevent it from happening again.

Not a day goes by that I don't read a new study showing how DNA solved old mysteries or helps understand our ancient roots. National Geographic's Genographic Project <genographic.nationalgeographic.com> uses DNA to help understand all of human migration out of Africa, while AncestryDNA tells us the story of British DNA. It might surprise some to learn that the British are not as "British" as some might think. According to the study, "The genetic make-up of the nation has been revealed, with Yorkshire proven to be the most 'British' region in the United Kingdom, while London is the most ethnically diverse and the East Midlands the most Scandinavian region." Interestingly, "Scottish residents have the highest amount of Finnish/Northwest Russian (1.31%) heritage, which is explained by their geographic proximity. Welsh residents have the highest proportion of ancestry from the Iberian Peninsula (Spain/Portugal) in the UK (3%)."

Bottom line: DNA can definitely shake up long-held beliefs about our origins.

DISCOVERING ETHNIC HERITAGE

While finding another family researcher can open up previously unknown branches, identifying specific ethnic origins can be just as helpful. In this section, we'll look at a couple of research problems and how DNA might be useful in solving them.

A person I've worked with can trace her family tree back to an African-American family working in Arkansas a few years after the Civil War. According to her ethnicity estimate, she has ancestry on Africa's "Slave Coast," a fairly strong indication that her family came to America as slaves. Because she doesn't know the time frame of the first arrivals, her first step in research might be to track down historical information on when slaves began coming from those regions, as well as when the slave trade from Africa stopped.

According to Wikipedia **<www.wikipedia.org>**, the so-called Slave Coast became one of the most important export centers for the Atlantic Slave Trade from the early sixteenth century to the nineteenth century—too wide a time frame to help with research. However, a federal law prohibited new slaves from being imported into the United States beginning in 1808. The law was not strictly enforced, but this fact does narrow the possible time that her ancestors came to America. But where, other than Arkansas, might she focus more research?

According to the FamilySearch Wiki **<familysearch.org/learn/wiki/en/Main_Page>** on Arkansas emigration/immigration, many slaveholding Virginians of Scottish, Scots-Irish, and English descent moved south and west into southern states of Tennessee, Mississippi, and Missouri. I concluded that perhaps this ancestor with African descent was one of the slaves brought along with these travelers, opening up new research opportunities.

Now this is where Ancestry.com's Migrations groups can come in handy. Ancestry.com places my friend in the "African Americans in the Deep South" Genetic Community. According to Ancestry.com, "Most African Americans in this Genetic Community can trace their ancestry back to West Africa. Over a hundred years many were enslaved and brought to Virginia to work on tobacco farms." From there, slavery spread across the south.

Using the information provided in the group's timeline, I determined most members of the community stayed in the "Black Belt" after the war, with many going to Arkansas and East Texas. Although the Migrations group doesn't pinpoint a modern location, it does guide me to research Arkansas and trails leading there. In addition, I've found ancestors living in Oklahoma in the late nineteenth century. According to the Oklahoma History Center, the history of black Oklahomans is closely linked to the westward movement and the desire for land. Is it possible that land or marriage records for this family can be found in Oklahoma?

In addition to helping you confirm or deny heritage you already knew about, ethnicity estimates can flag new areas for you to research. For example, I discovered I'm 25-percent Irish. What does that mean for my research? Because I had only a hunch of which ancestor might have been from Ireland, I decided to take a fairly simple approach—let Ancestry.com help me nail down surname origins.

Going to the Ancestry.com page to search for surname histories <www.ancestry.com /learn/facts>, I started adding surnames—not just willy-nilly, though. I picked the names that clearly appeared several times in my DNA results, either in DNA Circles or New Ancestor Discoveries. After poking through names for a period of time, "McClelland" seemed to be the most possible. According to Ancestry.com, McClelland/Mcclelland means "northern Irish" and can be a variant of the name "McClellan."

With that information in hand, I went back to DNA Circle based around my McClelland ancestor. Before contacting other people in the Circle, I first clicked on each and examined their family tree. One by one I searched trees, looking for the McClelland surname. If you don't remember how to access another person's tree, click through to their Ancestry.com profile page. Here, you'll find a list of their Public Member Trees. This process could take some time, depending on the number of Public Member Trees the Ancestry.com member has created.

This approached worked well for me. After working through multiple trees, I found a mention of Robert McClelland, my fifth great-grandfather, being born in 1760 Northern Ireland. Since I know next to nothing about this family (other than that my third great-grandfather was named Robert McClelland Hume; image **A**), I poked around the Internet, looking for collections of Irish surname distribution. Although this isn't a definitive answer, I did find that the surname was most often found in County Antrim, so I'll feel a little more confident in following a piece of data if it's from County Antrim. As Robert McClelland's wife was born in Pennsylvania, this gave me one more target to search in terms of both immigration and marriage. And, because I knew one of his children was born in Kentucky, I added that state to my search list.

Due to Robert's age (born in 1760), he could have been of military age during the American Revolution (assuming he was in America at that time). However, at fifty-two years old, he would have been too old for the War of 1812—again, one more clue to research. In fact, a quick peek into the "Kentucky Soldiers of the War of 1812" collection revealed several McClellands listed. Even though my direct-line ancestor was probably too old, it doesn't mean he didn't have a child of the right age (image **B**).

Before leaving this DNA Circles-prompted search, I went to the 1850 US federal census. According to the Public Member Tree information, both Robert and his wife Margaret should be alive in 1850. I did find Margaret, an eighty-two-year-old living with her son, but no Robert. Among the clues were the fact that her son had been born in Ohio in 1808. I did take a gamble to see if Robert might be on a mortality schedule, but no luck. However, what a mass of clues I've now accrued.

RESEARCHING NEW ANCESTORS

As we've already discussed, one of AncestryDNA's most useful functions is partnering you with other researchers and even distant cousins. But more importantly, you can use AncestryDNA's matching feature (along with traditional research methods) to find relatives that other users have been researching.

When you click on DNA Matches from your DNA Summary Page, you'll note that matches are categorized by "nearness," beginning with immediate family members, then close family, followed by second, third, and fourth cousins (and beyond). Next to each match, you'll find a star; click it to add the match to your favorites. If you see a blue dot, the match is new or you haven't yet reviewed it. A leaf represents a shared ancestor hint between your tree and your match's tree. As time goes by (and more and more people take the AncestryDNA test), your number of DNA matches will increase. If you have hundreds or even thousands of fourth-cousin or closer matches, you'll never run out of kin with whom to share research.

First, how do you choose a match? Finding and sharing information is fairly simple when it comes to close family or first cousins. But after that, finding your common link can be more challenging. Let's look at an example to see how the system works and how you can best drill down into those DNA matches.

If you choose a match with whom you have shared ancestor hints, you'll have a much easier time finding your common ancestor than choosing a match without any

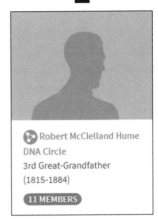

 Robert McClelland Hume
DNA Circle
3rd Great-Grandfather
(1815-1884)
11 MEMBERS

Don't overlook DNA Circles when working with DNA matches.

McClelland, Benjamin	119
McClelland, James	226, 324
McClelland, John	164
McClelland, John G.	170
McClelland, Joseph	27
McClelland, Joseph G.	167
McClelland, Mastin	51
McClelland, Michael	332
McClelland, Richard	226
McClelland, Robert	175
McClelland, Thomas	349
McClellen, Robert	107

DNA Circles led me to this list of Kentucky soldiers in the War of 1812, some of which could be my ancestors.

CHECK MORTALITY SCHEDULES

If you think your ancestor would have been alive in a census year but can't find them, be sure to check Ancestry.com's "U.S. Federal Census Mortality Schedules, 1850–1885." These schedules enumerate the people who died in the twelve months prior to the census being taken. Although deaths were generally under-reported, this collection is still worth taking the time to investigate.

shared hints. This was my approach. I took a few hours to look through matches, searching for ones that had Public Member Trees and a shared surname. One tree took me back a generation beyond my own research to William Vaugh (b. 1702 in Prince George County, Virginia, d. 1786 in Mecklenburg County, Virginia), married to Julia Green.

Armed with this information, I could now move into full search mode, using the tips and techniques we discussed in chapter 3. But before that, I did what I typically do on every new person/place research: I stopped and went to both Wikipedia and the FamilySearch.org Wiki to find out what was happening in that place during the time my ancestor lived there. That meant I gathered background information on both Prince George and Mecklenburg Counties.

Why take this extra step? I think you've gathered by now that genealogy goes hand-in-hand with history. If you don't know anything about your ancestor's times, you're missing out on a fascinating part of their own life journey. Plus, you may find something that changes exactly where you look for records. In this case, William Vaughn is reported to have been born in Prince George County in 1702. However, that county wasn't formed until 1703; originally it was part of Charles City County. Not to split hairs, but given the fact that I have no source proving the date of William's birth, I have to assume that his family could be found in either Prince George or Charles City.

With that in mind, I turn to searching for records. Because I don't know much about either William or Julia Green, I decided to use the general search form (rather than searching a particular collection). I went to Ancestry.com's general search form and entered the terms seen in image **C**.

One of the search results was for a William Vaughn of Mecklenburg County. In his will, he names his wife as *Mildrage*, a far cry from Julia. Is this a mismatch, or a second wife? I kept reading. Further along, he mentions his daughter, *Sary Gregory*. I know that in my own research I've run across Vaughan-Gregory marriages, so this could be part of the family. Although I didn't list a Sary, I did have a Sally who also married a Gregory. The will also mentions sons Samuel, John, James, Peter, and daughters Milarson, Milley, and Elizabeth.

My prior research into this family reveals all the sons mentioned in the will, along with the daughters (although my records show Millicent and Milly instead of Milarson and Milley). Reading to the bottom of the will, all ten children are listed—finally, with the same names as in my prior research. It looks like this William is my William! Because the will mentions ownership of two plantations, I'm certain I'll be able to find land records for this family.

But what about Julia and Mildrage? In the same set of search results, I found records for both wives. Julia seems to have passed away fairly early in the marriage, making Mildrage

C

First & Middle Name(s)

William

☐ Exact...

Last Name

Vaughn

☐ Exact...

Place your ancestor might have lived

City, County, State, Country

Birth Year

1702

☐ Exact +/-...

SEARCH   Show fewer options ∧   ▣ Match all terms exactly

Add event: Birth   Marriage   Death   Lived In   Any Event   More ∨

| | Year | Location | |
| Birth | 1702 | Virginia | ✕ |

☐ Exact +/-... ☐ Exact

Add family member: Father   Mother   Sibling   Spouse   Child

| | First & Middle Name(s) | Last Name | |
| Spouse | Julia | Green | ✕ |

▣ Exact   ▣ Exact

Use a general search form when you don't have much information about an ancestor.

the mother of most of the ten children. But, I don't have proof of dates, so that's conjecture on my part.

USING MORE ANALYSIS TOOLS

Thanks to the boom in genetic genealogy, third-party services have developed tools to further help you understand and use your DNA results. These companies can provide you with new ways of looking at your AncestryDNA results, as well as expose you to a different pool of test-takers (hopefully increasing your chances of finding a match).

To take advantage of these companies' services, you'll need to download your AncestryDNA results as raw data. Go to Settings from your DNA home page, then click the Download Raw DNA Data button. You'll receive an e-mail with further instructions. Your data will be presented in a .txt file. Be sure to keep this information safe—as AncestryDNA notes, downloaded raw data is no longer protected by AncestryDNA's privacy policy.

In this section, we'll discuss three of the largest and most widely used services: DNA.land, GEDmatch, and DNAGedcom. You can learn more about these and other tools in *The Family Tree Guide to DNA Testing and Genetic Genealogy* by Blaine T. Bettinger

(Family Tree Books, 2017), or by consulting *Family Tree Magazine*'s article on the subject <**www.familytreemagazine. com/premium/free-dna-genealogy-websites**>

DNA.land

DNA.land <**dna.land**> is a joint research project between the New York Genome Center and Columbia University. In short, it uses crowd-sourced science to study genomes. After uploading your raw DNA file and waiting up to twenty-four hours, you can log back into the system to see your results as calculated by the site, with relative matches, relative-of-relative matches, your ancestry results, and trait predictions (e.g., what color your eyes might be based on your genetics). You can view your ancestry composition (similar to an ethnicity estimate; image **D**) in both chart and map formats, accompanied by brief explanations of each geographic area.

GEDmatch

Perhaps the most popular resource for uploading and analyzing DNA results is GEDmatch <**gedmatch.com**>, a free tool that boasts more 200,000 DNA samples. Like AncestryDNA, GEDmatch allows you to compare your DNA test results to those of other users, and it gives you ample tools to compare and visualize your data (image **E**). As an added bonus, GEDmatch accepts DNA data from multiple testing companies (such as 23andMe <**www.23andme. com**> and Family Tree DNA <**www.familytreedna.com**>), expanding your list of potential genetic matches to include those who haven't tested with AncestryDNA.

To use GEDmatch, simply sign up for a free account and upload your raw DNA data. Your data will be assigned a unique ID number (called a "kit number"), and you'll need to wait a couple days for your data to process before you can access certain tools.

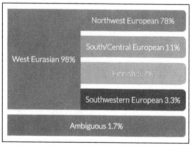

D

West Eurasian 98%
- Northwest European 78%
- South/Central European 11%
- Finnish 5.7%
- Southwestern European 3.3%

Ambiguous 1.7%

DNA.land allows you to view your ethnicity estimate in a different format.

The most useful of GEDmatch's many analysis tools is probably the "One-to-many" function, which compares your DNA sample (called a "kit") with all of those in GEDmatch's database. Once the analysis is finished, you'll receive a detailed breakdown of which users you share DNA with, including the amount of shared DNA (measured in centimorgans, or cM) and contact information. The similar "One-to-one" tool allows you to compare data to a single kit, providing charts and graphs visualizing the amounts (and locations) of shared DNA. Critically, both of these tools allow you to compare DNA results from multiple companies.

For more on using GEDmatch, check out Shannon Bombs-Bennett's article on analyzing DNA with GEDmatch <www.familytreemagazine.com/premium /tutorial-analyze-dna-with-gedmatch>.

DNAGedcom

DNAGedcom <www.dnagedcom.com> (image **F**) is relatively new to the scene (having been founded in 2013), but it's quickly proving itself to be a central resource for the experienced genetic genealogist. Here, you can download whole spreadsheets of information that can help you identify genetic matches or attempt an advanced genetic genealogy technique: triangulation, in which you use DNA information about two people to make inferences about a third. To begin, simply register for a free account.

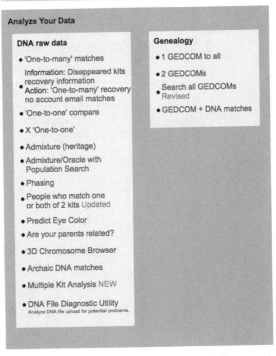

File Uploads

Raw DNA file Uploads
- Generic Upload *FAST*
  Do NOT open or un-zip raw DNA data files before uploading.

Genealogy - Family Trees
- GEDCOM genealogy Upload
- GEDCOM genealogy Upload Fast Beta version

Analyze Your Data

DNA raw data
- 'One-to-many' matches
  Information: Disappeared kits recovery information
  Action: 'One-to-many' recovery no account email matches
- 'One-to-one' compare
- X 'One-to-one'
- Admixture (heritage)
- Admixture/Oracle with Population Search
- Phasing
- People who match one or both of 2 kits Updated
- Predict Eye Color
- Are your parents related?
- 3D Chromosome Browser
- Archaic DNA matches
- Multiple Kit Analysis NEW
- DNA File Diagnostic Utility
  Analyze DNA file upload for potential problems.

Genealogy
- 1 GEDCOM to all
- 2 GEDCOMs
- Search all GEDCOMs Revised
- GEDCOM + DNA matches

Though its interface may look simple, GEDmatch offers several complex analysis tools that will allow you to dig deeper into your DNA results and compare your DNA with other users'.

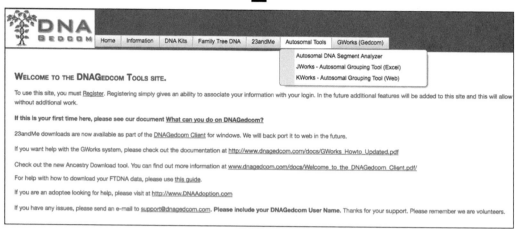

The tools on DNAGedcom (such as the Autosomal DNA Segment Analyzer and JWorks) are more suited for the experienced genetic genealogist, as they can provide incredibly detailed data about matches.

To work with AncestryDNA data, you'll need the DNAGedcom Client desktop app, which requires a small monthly subscription fee. The DNAGedcom Client app will download your AncestryDNA data (including matches and information about the ancestors you have in common with them) and format it into a spreadsheet. You can then use the formatted data in the site's other analysis tools, such as JWorks, KWorks, and GWorks (the latter of which can also analyze an uploaded GEDCOM file).

If you've already run your DNA data through GEDmatch (or if you've also tested with Family Tree DNA), you can also run the Autosomal DNA Segment Analyzer (ADSA) for free. This tool generates a table including match information and data about how your DNA overlaps with your matches.

For more on using DNAGedcom, check out the site's FAQ page **<dnagedcom.com/FAQ .aspx>** or its guides for individual tools.

PART 4

DIVING DEEPER INTO
ANCESTRY.COM

15

COLLABORATING WITH OTHER USERS

f you uploaded a family tree to Ancestry.com (see chapter 2 for details) and took a DNA test (chapter 12), you've probably already connected with other family researchers. Hopefully your connections have given you new data, stories, and even some photos. Most of all, though, you've probably seen the value of networking with other Ancestry. com users.

For myself, collaborating with other Ancestry.com users has resulted in some amazing discoveries: the first photos I've ever seen of some of my ancestors, the identity of my mom's father, and family stories that never managed to make their way down my branch of the family tree.

In this chapter, I'll examine even more collaboration opportunities that Ancestry.com can offer.

Community, located under the Help menu, is the jumping-off page for all things collaborative on Ancestry.com (image A). If you want to engage with other users or volunteer for projects, start here. You'll see three columns:

1. Get Help, Give Help
2. Collaborate
3. Contribute

One of the first things you'll want to do is set up your Community Preferences, which are located in your Member Profile. You'll find a link at the bottom of the Collaborate column. Once you've clicked over to your Profile Page, click the link to your profile and contact settings; this is where you'll find Community Preferences. Once you've completed

Welcome to the Ancestry Community
Collaborate with the largest online family history community.

❓ Get Help, Give Help

◎ Ancestry Support Community
VISIT NOW

Share tips. Give solutions. Start discussions. The Ancestry Support Community is *the* place for members to ask questions, share their family history, and connect with other users.

💬 Message Boards ›

Get help with your research whether you're interested in surnames and locations or DNA and folklore.

👥 Collaborate

Discover more about your family story by connecting with millions of other Ancestry members.

✉ Member Connect ›

Find out which Ancestry members are also researching your ancestors-and get updates when they discover new info.

◄▇ Public Member Trees ›

Search family trees created by other

➕ Contribute

Join thousands of members helping others discover their roots and preserve their family history.

📖 World Archives Project ›

All you need is a computer and a little time to help save the world's historical records. You create the index, and we give the public access for free.

⚑ Find A Grave ›

The Community page, under Ancestry.com's Help tab, has a number of resources that can connect you to other researchers. They're organized into roughly three groups: "Get Help, Give Help," Collaborate, and Contribute.

this set-up, go back to the main Community page (under the main toolbar's Help tab) and go through each of the three sections.

GET HELP, GIVE HELP: THE ANCESTRY.COM MESSAGE BOARDS

The first link at the top of the Get Help, Give Help will take you to the Support Center, which was covered in chapter 1. The next item in the column is a link to Message Board.

Message boards have been around since the earliest days of Internet genealogy. If you've never used a message board, here's how they work: After locating a message board of interest (a place, category, surname, etc.), search it for whatever information you seek, then leave a message asking for help or post a message in reply to someone else's query.

A common term you will see on a message board is *thread*. When someone posts a message and other people reply to that message, the whole group of messages is called a thread. In other words, a thread is a group of messages strung together.

Although you can find several message board sites around the Internet, Ancestry.com has the largest online genealogy community, boasting more than 198,000 message boards with twenty-five million messages and counting. Let's hop in and see what we can find.

Start by navigating to the Message Boards via the dropdown menu under the Help tab, located on the main toolbar. Click the Message Boards link and you'll be at the board's landing page (image **B**). From here, you have several options. You can search for a board

Message Boards

The world's largest online genealogy community with over 25 Million posts on more than 198,000 boards.

Search for content in message boards

Names or keywords

| e.g. John Smith or Civil War | | SEARCH | Advanced Search |

Find a board about a specific topic

Surnames or topics

| | GO |

Surnames

A B C D E F G H I J K L M N O P Q R S T U V W X Y Z

Categories

Localities Categories

Category	Sub-Categories	Boards
Australia	8	3
Canada	14	5
United Kingdom and Ireland	7	6
United States	2	2
Western Europe	14	2

More Localities Categories >

Topics Categories

Category	Sub-Categories	Boards
Cemeteries & Tombstones	8	6
Genealogy Software	1	32
Immigration and Emigration	8	11
Military	16	22
Research Resources	8	37

More Topics Categories >

The Ancestry.com Message Boards host years and years of discussion about a myriad of genealogical topics.

by content (e.g., names or keywords) or topic (e.g., surname), or you can browse message boards based on locality or category (e.g., record type).

Let's look at the different ways to find message boards.

Searching by Content

My family had lived in Lone Jack (Missouri) since the early 1830s, and I knew that some had joined the Union forces and some the Confederacy. Given that, I was interested in learning more about the battle. I decided to search the message boards for the keywords *Battle of Lone Jack*, and I punched that into the simple search field on the main Message Boards page. As you look at a list of search results, you'll see that Ancestry.com includes an excerpt of the original message, the date the message was posted, and the message board on which it was posted (image **C**). As you'll notice, search results also show you the navigation that each result is nested in—in this case, Localities>North America>United States>States>Missouri>Counties>Jackson.

The search turned up several mentions of the battle, among them a post on the Surname Board: Faulkenberry, which (as you know from reading this book) is one of my surnames. I went to that result first by clicking its name.

Once you view a board, you can view either the thread or individual messages. You'll see three separate areas (image **D**):

1. **Post Summary**: See a summary of the post, including the surnames mentioned and the number of replies. There's also a link to the Ancestry.com user who posted the message and a link to view other posts the user has made. You'll also see the post's "classification" (e.g., query, obituary).

2. **The Message**: The second portion of the board contains the message, in this case, a research query.:

> Hello: I am looking for info on a James Toliver Faulkenberry Born 1847 and died 1924 he was married Sarah Elizabeth Smith born 1849, Died 1932. James enlisted in the Conferated [sic] Army at Lone Jack, Mo in 1862 fought in the battle of Lone Jack and Wesport [sic], Mo. He is believed to have 7 children. My great grandmother was Matilida Ann Faulkenberry born 1868 Married James Vance Cline. Please contact me by e-mail if you have info.

What fascinated me about this message is that, on one of my trips to Missouri, I photographed the tombstone of James and Sarah Faulkenberry and three of their children. Of course, I contacted the person who posted the message to see if they wanted copies of the photos.

3. **Post Timeline**: The third section of the post page shows the original post, the date of the replies, and the names of the authors. If the author of a post has a public profile, you can click on his username to send a private message via the Ancestry.com e-mail system.

Searching by Surname

I'm quite interested in learning more about the Dearing side of my family, since I've done almost no research on it. I know when the family came to the United States, but I have no idea who they were and why they migrated from Virginia to Missouri. I have nothing more than a few names and dates. I decided to consult the Message Boards.

Fortunately, you can search for Message Boards based on topic or surname. This time, I used the Advanced Search form because I wanted to add both a surname and a place to

Search Results

Search the Boards

Names or keywords

| battle of lone jack | SEARCH | Advanced Search |

Search Results for "**battle of lone jack**" – 112 Messages

| 10 ▾ per page | | ‹ 1 of 12 › |

George Matthew Wright   Posted on: 31 Dec 1999, by Peggy Luce

Localities > North America > United States > States > Missouri > Counties > Boone

The following was taken from the "History of Boone County" by William Switzler, 1882. The subject of this sketch was born in Boone county, Missouri, April 3d, 1939. He was the son of Wesley and P...

KAYSER, Albert, biography   Posted on: 27 May 2002, by ⬛ Jeffrey Elmer

Localities > North America > United States > States > Washington > Counties > Klickitat

An Illustrated History of the State Of Washington, by Rev. H.K. Hines, D.D., The Lewis Publishing Co., Chicago, IL., 1893 ALBERT KAYSER, an enterprising citizen of Block House, Klickitat county, Washingto...

You can keyword-search Ancestry.com's massive collection of message boards.

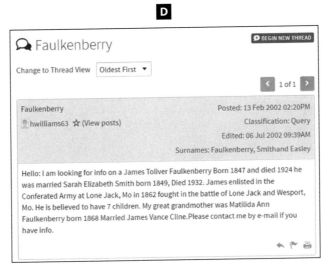

🗨 Faulkenberry

Change to Thread View   Oldest First ▾

‹ 1 of 1 ›

Faulkenberry	Posted: 13 Feb 2002 02:20PM
👤 hwilliams63 ☆ (View posts)	Classification: Query
	Edited: 06 Jul 2002 09:39AM
	Surnames: Faulkenberry, Smithand Easley

Hello: I am looking for info on a James Toliver Faulkenberry Born 1847 and died 1924 he was married Sarah Elizabeth Smith born 1849, Died 1932. James enlisted in the Conferated Army at Lone Jack, Mo in 1862 fought in the battle of Lone Jack and Wesport, Mo. He is believed to have 7 children. My great grandmother was Matilida Ann Faulkenberry born 1868 Married James Vance Cline.Please contact me by e-mail if you have info.

On a message board, you can view either an entire thread or an individual message.

Use Soundex

Did you notice a checkbox on the Advanced form titled Use Soundex? If you're new to genealogy, you may be scratching your head about what that could mean. In brief, Soundex is a phonetic coding system that groups together names that sound alike but are spelled differently. For example, the surnames Hendrickson, Hendrixon, Hendricksen, Hendrixson, and Hendricks all convert to the same Soundex code: H536.

If you want to learn more about Soundex, go to the Ancestry Support Center and search *Soundex*.

the search. As you can imagine, you may get hundreds (if not thousands) of irrelevant hits if you're searching messages for a fairly common surname and you don't add a location. Using the Advanced Search form definitely helps when it comes to getting more refined results.

For my search, I entered the location (town name) in the Names or Keywords box and *Dearing* in the Surnames box. The system found only two messages matching my search parameters. The messages didn't contain information about my direct ancestors, but it did contain an obituary. The obit listed the name of the deceased person's mother (including her maiden name, Dearing), and the fact that the deceased was born in Milan, Missouri. Since the town had a population of less than two thousand, I was pretty sure that this Dearing was part of the family.

Next, I changed the location to Sullivan County, Missouri, and had seven messages to review. This was a jackpot find, as it gave a lot of history about the Dearing family. One message mentioned the Wilhite Cemetery—a place I'd visited. I shared my photo of the Bailus Dearing tombstone in a thread.

I returned to the main message board page to search for another ancestor, Robert McClelland Hume. Follow along with me, and I'll show you how to do this search.

From the Message Boards home page, type the surname into the Surnames or Topics board. In this instance, I typed in *Hume*. This will bring up a new screen with several surnames that include Hume (e.g., Humeck, Humenik). I clicked on Hume. This took me to a third screen where I could search for Robert (image **E**).

This time, only five search results came back. One was an index to a genealogy book that didn't help, as I didn't recognize any of the names in the index, other than Hume. Three were queries, one of them containing a query about my direct line:

> per research Ancestry.com - John HUME born Virginia 1786 married Sarah McClelland - died after 1860 in Ohio. John son of William ll and Anne? and grandson of William l and Frances Pattishall - his brother Robert became his

Search for content in message boards

Names or keywords

| robert mcclelland hume | | SEARCH | Advanced Search |

○ All Boards ● Hume - Family History & Genealogy Message Board

I typed my ancestor's name in the search box and checked the Surnames option, not the All Boards option. This should help narrow my results.

legal guardian in Ohio after Frances died in 1803. I am looking for a link for my direct family line in Faquier [sic] County Virginia. Am directly descended from a John Hume born 1764 and married to Lysha? Am not sure how my great-great ties into William ll and Frances - there is a tax record of an unnamed son of Frances and William ll in 1802 in Stafford County Virginia. Also, your John had 4 brothers and 6 sisters - none remained in Virginia - all moved to Greenbrier, W Va or Ohio. John's son with Sarah McClelland, William Harrison born 1826 in Ohio married Mary Corns.

As you can see from the post, there is a massive amount of information to go through, and it will take some doing to untangle all of these lines. Fortunately, there were nine replies to this post, a few of which gave me even more information about my Hume line. Interestingly, I noted that Sarah and John's son, William, married a Corns. His brother, Robert (my third great-grandfather), also married a Corns. Now this is exciting news!

Searching by Locality

Under the Localities Categories section on the main Message Boards page, click the More Localities Categories link. This takes you to a landing page for localities. The basic search form here has the option to search all boards or just localities. I clicked to open the Advanced Search form and selected Localities instead of All Boards. After typing in *Shelby County Indiana* in the name/keyword field and *Hendrickson* in the surname field, the system returned fifteen hits.

The search results were a bonanza of information, particularly about a Hendrickson-Voyles family I knew next to nothing about. I contacted the author of the original post, as well as three who posted replies, and among us we've added many more people to our family trees and uncovered a previously unknown migration.

In all of the years I've done genealogy, I've learned to never underestimate the power of networking. This Hendrickson search was no exception.

F

You can also search or browse the Message Boards by topic, which range from family Bibles to census records. Some categories also have subcategories, and each category contains at least one message board.

Searching by Topics Category

From Adoptions to Volunteer Projects, the Topics Categories message boards at Ancestry.com have something for almost everyone. Although the Message Board home page lists a handful of categories, click the More Topics Categories link to expand the list.

Here, you can ask questions or learn a tremendous amount about research topics and challenges we all encounter. Among the topics:

- adoption
- census
- military
- medical
- methods
- newspaper research
- DNA research
- research groups
- slave trade

Each category is organized into message boards related to the topic (image **F**). Larger categories also have subcategories, which are then divided into message boards.

As someone who has ancestors who lived in early America, I selected the Pioneer Programs category, which has only one board, "Pioneer Certification" (image **G**). Many states have Pioneer Certificates available to people whose family lived in an area before a certain date. I searched the Pioneer Program board first for *Indiana*, then followed a link in the post to the Society of Indiana Pioneers where I learned my Hendrickson has already been proven to be an Indiana pioneer. How cool is that?

Next, I went to the Migration boards and choose the "Santa Fe Trail" board, because it's a place I've traveled and read about extensively. One of the queries asked about

Thread	Author	Replies	Last Post
Pioneer Certification — Threads: 40 · Messages: 97			
Tulsa Pioneers	magnoliasouth	0	11 Jun 2015 02:47PM
California Pioneer Register and Index	cestlamae	3	20 Jun 2012 06:34PM
TENNESSEE PIONEER/SETTLER CERTIFICATE	glenda1936	2	14 Mar 2012 10:54AM
Is there anything like this in Canada?	FMatchettSpri...	2	15 Dec 2011 03:55AM
Pioneer Certificates-Pennslyvania	Chuck	1	01 Sep 2011 02:49PM
THE OREGON EARLY SETTLER & PIONEER CERTIFICATES PROJECT	Kathi Stine	3	26 Jul 2010 05:31PM
Jefferson County Indiana Pioneers	Ericson1951	0	24 Jul 2010 09:48PM

Smaller categories may have only one message board. In this case, the Pioneer Programs category has just this Pioneer Certification message board.

sources for Santa Fe Trail information. I knew of two books that might help (both period diaries), and so I posted a reply.

How did I do that? If you look at the original post, you'll see three icons. Click the arrow to reply, the flag to report abuse, and the printer to print. Once you've clicked the reply arrow, a new box will appear in which you can add your response. You can check the box to be notified when another user replies to the thread.

What if you make a mistake and you've already posted a response to a thread? Just return to your message and click the pencil icon (it's in the lower right corner below your message) to edit. Click the trash can icon if you want to remove your message entirely.

Starting a Thread

Now that you know how to search for (and reply to) a thread, how do you start a thread of your own? First, go to the board where you want to leave a message. In this case, I went to the Keller surname board, as that's the name for which I have a lot of information and would like to be able to share with other researchers. Once you're on a specific message board, you can click the Begin New Thread link to the right of the board name.

CREATE A MEMBER PROFILE

If you followed along in chapter 1, you will have already set up your Member Profile. If you haven't done so, go back to chapter 1 and complete this task. Creating a member profile will make it much easier for other researchers to find and connect with you.

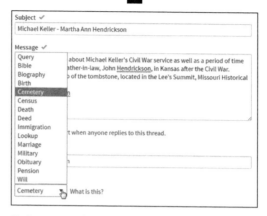

Begin your own thread by clicking the appropriate button on a message board's landing page. Be sure to select what your thread is discussing (e.g., a record or a particular question/query).

Next, a new screen will open and you can begin typing your message (image **H**). Choose a subject line that helps other users identify whether your message pertains to their family; if the subject line is too vague, it won't be that helpful to someone skimming through the messages.

From the dropdown Classification menu, select the item that best describes your message (e.g., query, deed, cemetery, etc.). You can also add a file to your message, but that's optional. For example, you may have a copy of a military record, a cemetery photo, or another type of document you want to attach to your message. In my case, I added a photograph of Michael Keller's tombstone.

Now that you've completed the message, you can either choose to preview the message (click the Preview link) or just go ahead and post it (click the Post link). Your message will now show up on the message board as a new thread.

People have lefts thousands of messages seeking information about a research problem or a dead-end challenge. Helping other researchers is something genealogists do. So, too, is posting information you have that you know will help other genealogists, as many of us have photos or stories that we know are hard to find. While you're in the message boards, consider leaving a little something to help the next person whose tree is difficult to climb.

COLLABORATE

The Collaborate section of the Ancestry.com Help page is where you'll find more ways to share information with other Ancestry.com members. Here, you'll find Member Connect, Public Member Trees, the Member Directory, and Member Profile.

With Member Connect, you have the option of either connecting with or ignoring other users researching the same ancestor.

Click Member Connect at the top of a profile to see all of your connections.

In this section, we'll discuss three of those four options. (We discussed the fourth, Public Member Trees, in chapter 2.)

Member Connect

The Member Connect link takes you to a landing page where you'll learn how to set up your own network of researchers. How this works is pretty nifty; Ancestry.com scans Public Member Trees to find people who are researching the same families in your trees. Once information is found, you can decide how much or how little you want to connect to your own tree.

To begin, go to the profile page of any of your ancestors. At the top of the profile page is a menu, with the last item being Member Connect. Click the link, and a list will appear of other Ancestry.com members who are researching this same person. You'll see individual research items and sources beneath each member who is researching your family. For each connection that seems to match your ancestor, click the Connect button (image **I**). This user will then be added to your list of connections (image **J**).

Next, you'll now be notified of anytime your connection adds information relative to your shared ancestor. You can also find Recent Member Connect Activity on your Ancestry.com home page.

L

Information on your profile can be seen by other Ancestry users — SEE PUBLIC VIEW

Can you help other members? [EDIT]

Tell us if you are able to help other members who may be doing similar research.

Research Interests [EDIT]

You have not yet added any research interests. When you do, it helps us suggest useful resources to you and also helps similar researchers find and contact you so that you can help each other in your research.

Add a research interest now

Your profile and contact settings [EDIT]

You can customize your settings about how other members can contact you, as well as what displays on your public profile.

Edit your preferences

K

Research Interests

Name	Location	Date Range
McLary's	Brown/Morgan County Indian	1830 - 2011
Burcham	Hendricks, Indiana, USA,	1830 - 2000
Hendrickson	Hendricks, United States of America	1830 - 2000
Herring	Hendricks, United States of America	1830 - 2000
Luckey or Lucky	Oconee, United States of America	1860 - 1880

You can view other users' stated research interests, which can help you determine if they are researching the same ancestors or locations as you are.

Edit your Ancestry.com profile preferences to make it easier for other users to find and connect with you.

Member Directory

Did you know that you can search for other Ancestry.com members using the Member Directory? In addition to being on the Help menu, the directory is located under the Search tab. Click over there now and walk through the process with me.

But first: Why would anyone want to search the Member Directory? Primarily because you can search for other members by their research interests, username, location, age, gender, and experience level. You can use wildcards in your searches here. The more fields you enter, the more narrow the search results; the fewer fields, the broader the search results.

When you're on the Member Directory page, you can search for a particular Ancestry. com member by his or her name, or you can search by the surname, location, and year of users' research.

Searching for users this way will allow you to view a list of users who have listed something as a research interest. Of the three, year is perhaps the least frequently included in research interests, but searching using these categories can be efficient. I entered *Hendrickson* in the Last Name box and *Indiana* in the Location box. This returned four hits, with one exactly fitting my search criteria.

In the search result, I clicked on the Ancestry.com username to go to the member's Profile page, showing me the user's research interests (image **K**), contribution(s) to message boards, basic demographic information, and whether the user is able to help other people (assuming the user has filled in all of the information on their Profile). The Profile box also has a link to contact the user or view the profile.

By the way, don't always go by the "last log in" date that is listed in search results; in this case, the user had logged in one day (not one year) earlier.

SETTING UP YOUR PROFILE

At this point, you may be wondering how to set up your own profile so other researchers can get a sense of your areas of interest and expertise. It's easy. From any page on Ancestry.com, click your account's name on the top right corner of the screen, then select Your Profile from the dropdown menu. Here, you can edit your profile or see how your profile looks to other users (image **L**).

By clicking Edit in the Can You Help Other Members? box, you can indicate whether you're willing to assist other users in their research should they contact you. Next, under Research Interests, click the Add a Research Interest Now to add the areas in which you're interested in researching. This will open a new page. At the top of the page, you'll find a green plus sign and the link to Add a New Interest. Click that link, and you'll see a new form in which to add information.

First, you'll need to enter either a last name or a location. Next, enter a date range and add any comments you feel would be helpful to someone searching the Member Directory. Be sure to check the box at the bottom of the form to allow other members to see your research interests.

The last item under the Profile page is where you set your contact preferences. This is where you tell the Ancestry.com system how people can contact you:

1. anonymously via Ancestry.com's online message feature
2. via your e-mail address that you can display to other members
3. none—other members cannot contact you

Because one of the great benefits of creating an Ancestry.com user profile is the ability to connect with other members, I highly recommend you do not pick option three.

CONTRIBUTE

If you like volunteering, this is the section of Community where you'll find two ongoing projects: World Archives and Find A Grave.

On the Ancestry World Archives Project, you can view what communal projects Ancestry.com has in progress, giving you an opportunity to contribute to the genealogical community.

Ancestry World Archives Project

The Ancestry World Archives Project (image) **<www.ancestry.com/community/awap>** is a collaborative effort of volunteers who key in information from digitized historical records to create free record indexes. Once you register as a volunteer, you'll download and install a free software program and begin inputting information. Then, you type in the data you see on a record. Records needing indexing in this way can be either machine-printed or handwritten.

Once the software is installed, you can either pick the project you want to work on from a list of all projects, or you can let Ancestry.com pick its highest priority project. The Ancestry World Archives Project has excellent help files and a variety of records from which to choose.

If you like helping other genealogists and you have the time to volunteer, this might be a worthwhile project for you to investigate.

Find A Grave

Most genealogists have been using Find A Grave **<www.findagrave.com>** for years, but it's become a Community Project now that it's an official Ancestry.com property. Click the link to the Find A Grave Project, and you'll go directly to the Find A Grave home page.

Ancestry.com members are encouraged to add photographs, stories, locations, and biographies of family members to the website. Membership at Find A Grave is free. Create an account and log in (this is separate from your Ancestry.com membership login information). Once on the site, you can easily add information or find burials for your ancestors. You can also create an online memorial for a deceased individual by adding photos, flowers, or notes. If you want to remove banner ads from your memorial, you can pay a one-time fee. Other members can add flowers, photos and notes to the memorial. In the case of the memorial created for my dad , other people have left virtual flowers.

If you're as much of a cemetery-buff as most genealogists, I think this is a project you'll really enjoy working on.

16

BRANCHING OUT WITH NEWSPAPERS.COM AND FOLD3

Now, we've covered just about every major record group on Ancestry.com, plus AncestryDNA and the many collaborative opportunities available to users on the site. But these features are just the tip of the Ancestry.com iceberg. Newspapers.com <www.newspapers.com> and Fold3 <www.fold3.com> are Ancestry.com-owned subscription sites you can subscribe to, either with or without an Ancestry.com subscription. (An All Access Ancestry.com subscription includes both services, plus Ancestry.com.)

In this chapter, I'll give you an overview of the records on each site, plus how to navigate the sites and search for your ancestors within them.

NEWSPAPERS.COM

The leading name in digitized historical newspapers, Newspapers.com contains more than five thousand newspaper titles, with dates ranging from the 1700s through the 2000s. And this database continues to grow, with more than one million pages added each month. The site boasts a collection of publications from US states and territories (with Pennsylvania, Florida, and California among the best represented states), but the site offers some international offerings as well. Image **A** shows the geographic distribution of the collection as of this book's publication. Non-US publications include those from Canada, England, Ireland, Northern Ireland, and Panama, plus an impressively large collection from Australia.

Newspapers.com specializes in US newspapers, but the site boasts newspapers from around the world. This map shows the geographic distribution of newspapers the site has digitized.

Why Newspapers?

Newspapers.com boasts thousands of historical newspapers, but why should researchers care? Let's take a look at the history (and usefulness) of newspapers.

Newspaper content has changed over the centuries. The front page of a 1786 edition of *The Belfast Evening Post*, for example, had little news but lots of ads. Cognac, rum, buckles, locks, and hinges seem to be particularly popular, as were notices of ships' sailings. My favorite, of course, was the brigantine *Nancy*, which was said to be bound for New York. Potential passengers were assured that there would be an abundance of provisions of the "best kind." Contrast that front page with the 1916 *The Weekly Messenger*, published in Louisiana (annual subscription rate $1.00). This publication still has ads (for groceries and trips on the Southern Pacific), but now you'll find more of a local focus: sugar cane news, state fair events, and the results of a hometown football game.

Not only did the types of printed news change, but so, too, did article content. Take obituaries as an example. Today, an obituary—especially in a large urban area—will typically include information about the deceased, their family, career, (possibly) the cause of death, and any charity the family selected for donations. Earlier obituaries could include even more information, such as the character of the deceased as is evidenced in this 1939 obituary: "[He] lived a beautiful life free from envy, jealousy, or a worldy spirit." Or a poetic send-off from 1940: "[He] slowly sailed away with the angel of death and about 11:45 Sunday evening Oct. 6th, while skill, love and affection ministered by physician and loved ones, death drew near the pillow of our loved one and draped its sable garment about his weakened form and whispered, come."

Another major shift is in personal information that was once printed. Up until mid-twentieth century or so, it was not unusual to read an article that included the person's home address. While newspapers today would never print a home address (or at least I hope they wouldn't!), old mentions of them can help in your genealogy research. For example, if an ancestor's last known address was in the 1940 census and they seem to have disappeared from further records in that location, you could find them (and their new address) in a newspaper article.

By now, you may be wondering what difference it makes to understand a little about the evolution of newspapers and even the idea of "news." By glimpsing into the past, you can get a better sense of what you're apt to discover in newspapers, plus how best to go about searching them. For example, if you want to know as much as possible about an ancestor who lived more than one hundred years ago, you're going to have to search newspapers differently than you would for someone who passed away within the last decade.

To put it another way: Newspapers served a different role in days' past than they do today. Unless your ancestor did something extraordinary, had a well-known and successful business, committed a crime, or traveled with celebrities, he won't likely be mentioned in today's papers (except, of course, in obituaries). The exceptions to this might be high school or college sports reports or wedding announcements. However, in the early part of the twentieth century (and even up to the 1950s), newspapers reported out-of-town visitors, the adventures of locals abroad, religious cemeteries, and who was sick at the local factory. As a result, genealogists should search Newspapers.com, not just for obituaries, but also more broadly.

What can you expect to find in an historical newspaper? The answer is just about anything. Here is a sampling:

- local, national and international news
- sports (local, regional, national)
- commerce (prices of goods, names and addresses of local businesses)
- travels
- details of accidents (such as automobile crashes or deaths via runaway cart)

From the Newspapers.com home page, you can navigate to specific sections of the site or search the site straightaway using the search box.

- ships' sailings and arrivals
- illnesses
- engagements and weddings
- college acceptances
- poetry
- bank assets
- elections
- criminal cases
- law suits
- reunions

For more on why you should use historical newspapers in your research, check out James M. Beidler's book *The Family Tree Historical Newspapers Guide* (Family Tree Books, 2018) <**www.familytreemagazine.com/store/historical-newspapers-guide**>.

C

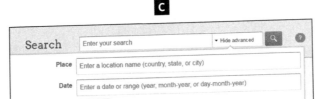

Show more search options (including place and date) by clicking Show Advanced.

D

COUNTRY (7)	STATE (52)	CITY (23)	NEWSPAPER (1)	YEAR (66)
United States of America	Alabama	Arizola	Casa Grande Dispatch	1912
Australia	Alaska	Bisbee		1913
Canada	Arizona	Casa Grande		1914
England	Arkansas	Clifton		1915
Ireland	California	Douglas		1916
Northern Ireland	Colorado	Flagstaff		1917
Panama	Connecticut	Florence		1918
	Delaware	Fort Whipple		1919

When you browse newspapers by location, each choice will open a series of options (beginning with state for US newspapers, then city, newspaper, and year).

Navigating Newspapers.com

When you first log in to your account, you'll be directed to the Newspapers.com home page (image **B**). From here, you can access search either via the links at the top of the page (Search, Browse, Papers, Clippings) or straight from the search box at the center of the page.

Let's start with the options in the Newspapers.com toolbar. Here's what you can do under each of the first three:

- **Search**: Click this link to go to a search box. To add more search options such as date and place, click the Show Advanced link on the right side of the search box (image **C**). From here, you can search by surname, date or place, or keywords.
- **Browse**: The Browse function lets you drill down to newspapers in specific locales at specific dates. First, select the country of interest, then (for the United States) the state, city, the names of newspaper, and year (image **D**). If you select a non-US country, your next choice will be city, then newspaper and year. Note, Guam newspapers fall into the column of US states.

Narrow by Newspaper Title

| Type paper name keywords | ✕ |

Date

1688   1869   2028

📅 Enter a date or range...

Location

US   World   Click a state

Type a state...

▦ Pennsylvania   25,260,032

▦ Florida   20,044,764

▦ California   17,990,591

▦ Illinois   17,561,645

▦ Ohio   16,676,196

> See more...

The left column on the Papers page allows for search filtering. Here, you can narrow your results by date or location.

- **Papers**: Here, you'll find a listing of all newspapers in the collection by name. You can also elect to change the display to show newspapers that are newly added or updated. The third option, Map, shows the geographic distribution of items in the collection. Notice that, once you're on the Papers page, you'll see a new column (image **E**). This is where you can filter the papers to be searched by date range, location, and/or name. Once you click on a state, either by name or via the map, the right column will change to display only the newspapers in that particular state.

- **Clippings**: Clippings are a great way to keep track of newspaper items you've found and want to save. Once you've found an article of interest, click the Clip button, then move and/or resize the clipping box around the article. You can also add a note; once you've clipped several articles, notes make it a lot easier to remind yourself of what you captured in the article (image **F**). To see all of your clipped articles, click the Clippings link at the top of the page. Once clipped, you can save the article to Ancestry.com, Twitter, Facebook, or your computer, or send it via e-mail. If you have a genealogy blog, you can also embed the article into your site.

A handy option to take notice of is that each of the newspapers, when displayed as a thumbnail, will note both the number of pages of that particular paper in the collection, as well as the date range available for searching (image **G**). Once you click on the name of any newspaper, you can search directly within the pages of that particular paper.

Have you found a newspaper article of interest? Be sure to use the top right menu to either clip, print/save, share, or save to your Ancestry.com family tree. When you elect to Save an article, you'll have the option of saving the entire page or just a portion of it, and whether to save it as a JPG (image) or a PDF.

Maximizing Your Newspapers.com Search

Of course everyone wants to find a newspaper mention of their ancestor. But even if your ancestor was never written about, you can use newspapers to fill in a lot of blanks in your family history. Using newspapers, you can read about the things that were important during your ancestor's lifetime, get a sense of what everyday items cost, find out which way the political wind was blowing, and discover family connections through simple mentions of weddings, travel, sports, and even police reports. I've found family clues throughout the years in reading newspaper accounts of a burglary or attempted break-in.

You can do newspaper research using a variety of approaches, such as name, place, or event. Use the filters in the left column to narrow down to a date range, state, or name of newspaper.

Part of your success (or failure) is going to be determined by whether a particular newspaper for a particular

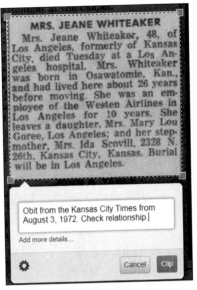

Newspapers.com allows you to create "clippings," short excerpts from newspapers that you can easily save for later reference.

The Daytona Gazette-News

Daytona Beach, Florida

1901–1902   439 pages

The DeLand News

DeLand, Florida

1903–1909   1,390 pages

The DeSoto County News

Arcadia, Florida

1905–1916   1,195 pages

Search results display the location, date ranges, and number of pages for each paper. Check the date ranges, in particular, to be certain issues are available during the time your ancestor lived in the area.

date range has been digitized. Although Newspapers.com has millions of pages online (and adds thousands of pages each day), it's possible the one newspaper you need to search may not be added as of yet.

If your ancestor's town newspaper hasn't been digitized, search for a newspaper from the closest large town. It's possible your ancestor's town didn't have a newspaper (or, if it did, it was only published weekly or monthly), so widen your geographic search. For example, a newspaper for a town I'm interested in—Lone Jack, Missouri—isn't available. However, because Lone Jack is close to Kansas City, I broadened my search to include K.C., then searched for Lone Jack. Among the many results was a 1963 article about the little town and its history. Bingo!

If you're not getting the results you hoped for, try widening your search to larger geographic areas or use multiple search phrases. Also, be sure to use quotation marks around a name or phrase (e.g., *"george webster"*) to force the system to search instances where those two words appear together. Otherwise, the search will return instances of any time "George" and "Webster" are mentioned in an article, even if they're referring to different people.

Also, be sure to make use of wildcards. The question mark (?) can be used to replace a single letter, while the asterisk (*) can replace several letters. Also, don't forget to be creative in how you do word searches. For example, a search for *world war ii* returned more than ten million hits, while *wwii* returned only six million.

Lastly, don't give up hope if you can't find an ancestor mentioned by name, because you can discover something about their world. Branch out and search by town, church name, organization (e.g., the Ladies Aid Society or the Boy/Girl Scouts), sports team names, schools, etc. I can almost guarantee you'll find something to help with your genealogy research.

FOLD3

Fold3 is Ancestry.com's military arm. Launched in 2007 under the name Footnote.com, it was acquired by Ancestry.com in 2010 and rebranded as Fold3 in 2011, in reference to the triangular shape of a folded flag used to honor deceased veterans. While you may begin your military search at Ancestry.com (see chapter 6), you'll typically move over to Fold3 to access more detailed records.

As of this writing, the site contains more than 491 million records that date from the Revolutionary War to the modern era (including the Persian Gulf War and the wars in Iraq and Afghanistan). As you might imagine, the largest single group of conflict records relate

Search Fold3 by the veteran's name and the name of the conflict he or she served in.

to World War II. By 1945, more than 12 million Americans served in the Armed Forces, which amounted to nine percent of the US population. The site also has more than 57 million international military records (primarily from the United Kingdom) and nearly 290 million non-military records (including censuses, homestead records, naturalization records, and documents relating to the Dawes Act).

You can immediately begin searching by name and/or conflict, or spend a little time reading the latest military articles on the home page (image). You also have the option of watching a video from Ancestry Academy on using Fold3 <**www.ancestry.com/academy /course/military-vets-fold3**>.

Records Overview

The types of records available depend on the conflict. For example, Revolutionary War records contain items such as service records, pensions, and imprisonments, as well as George Washington's correspondence. It's interesting to note the level of governmental detail Washington was involved with (probably, in part, because he was building a brand new government). Imagine having to make decisions on things like coinage, soldier disputes, and instructions on what to do in his absence!

Among some of the most valuable Revolutionary War records are pension files. These can be quite lengthy; my ancestor's runs a full eighteen pages. In them are statements of service and affidavits from people who knew my ancestor and attested to his identity and

Even pension record indexes, like this one from Fold3, can provide you with valuable information.

When browsing records, click the name of a war to view available records.

Draft registration cards, like this one from World War II, are among the most reliable sets of records.

service. Note that, while viewing any record on Fold3, you can save it to your Ancestry.com tree by clicking the green button in the top left part of the screen.

Pension files are also available for the War of 1812 and the Civil War. A Civil War widow's pension file can include information about the marriage and children. A pension file for the veteran, himself, is only an index (image **I**). However, the index card contains the name of the regiment, the date of death, and the certificate number.

In addition to saving a record to your Ancestry.com account, you can use the top right menu to bookmark it, add an annotation or a comment, download, print, share, or add to a memorial.

If you want to see all records available for each conflict, click on the name of any war from the home page and a second panel will slide out showing you the names of digitized records (image **J**). At the bottom of the list is a link to Browse All Titles. Be sure to click this, as there can be more than a dozen additional record groups not shown in the initial list.

Of particular interest to those searching twentieth-century records are WWI draft registration cards, which can be a genealogy jackpot. Information includes whether the individual was a natural-born or naturalized citizen, the type of work he did, the name of his employer, and his marital status, date and place of birth, and physical

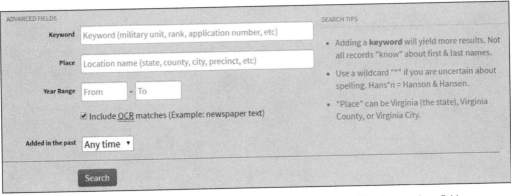

As on Ancestry.com and Newspapers.com, you can use additional fields when searching for records on Fold3.

description. A WWII draft registration card (image) is similar, although it asks for the name and address of "someone who will always know your address." In addition, the physical description portion is now a checklist with choices such as "freckled complexion" and race (White, Negro, Oriental, Indian, and Filipino).

If your ancestor served in any conflict, you'll likely find at least some type of military record on the site.

Navigating Fold3

When you log in to your Fold3 account, you'll be presented with a simple search box that has options to select the conflict as well as add advanced fields. You can search from that menu or the Search link at the top of the page.

You can use Advanced fields to add keywords, place, and date ranges (image). Keywords can come in handy if you're searching for ancestors who have common surnames and you know the name of a regiment or military unit (e.g., the 328th Infantry). The Browse function will give you the option of searching all titles.

If you don't know anything other than the names of the person and conflict, start with a simple search, then add additional fields (such as date range or state) as you can. In some instances, the more you can narrow down the search, the better. As you can imagine, trying to find a John Smith without additional input is almost impossible.

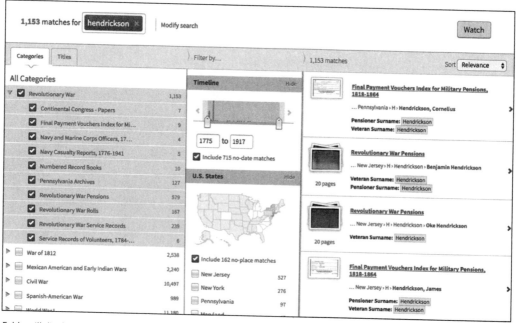

Fold3 will display your search results, allowing you to filter down your results by category, time, or location.

Once you've filled in the name and any additional fields, the results page will display the documents that are a match (image **M**). You'll also see tools to narrow the search. You can select specific record types, categories, location, and date ranges. Click on a search result to slide open a viewer to see the document and its source.

Depending on the record or record type, you may have to navigate through several screens when browsing records. For example: Vietnam War > Veterans Affairs Death File > Surname Starts With (i.e. H), then a more finite Starts With Letter (Ha, Hd, He, etc) > given (first name) > sort by date of birth.

In addition to search, you'll probably use the Memorial tab in the main toolbar. This is where you'll have the chance to create a Memorial page for any of your military ances- tors. Click the Add a Memorial Page link, search for your ancestor, and then add photos or documents to the Memorial page (image **N**). Photos can be those found on Fold3 or uploaded from your own system.

Don't forget to save your finds to your Ancestry.com account.

Fold3 allows you to create memorial pages for your military ancestors, giving you and other users a place to remember them.

Maximizing Your Fold3 Search

In my experience, the more information I have about an ancestor, the better. Here's a sample search to show you how adding as much information as possible can really narrow down your search.

I have a Civil War ancestor with a fairly common name (John Knox). By searching for his name and service dates (1861–1865), I received nearly three thousands matches—far too many. However, I also know that he enlisted from Missouri and that he served in the 18th Infantry Regiment. Going back to the search box I modified the search to: *John Knox, 18th, Missouri, 1861–1865*. I now had just twelve matches. Of the twelve, five were of city directories and weren't a match for my ancestor. Interestingly, when I changed one of the search parameters to 18th Infantry, I got seven matches, all for family members. Lesson: Experiment with search phrases.

Once you've found a record of interest, take advantage of the options at the bottom of a record page. Click the filmstrip icon to toggle the filmstrip of individual pages off and on

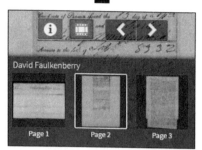

When viewing records, you can switch between individual pages of a record.

(image). Displaying the filmstrip makes it easy to skip from one image to another image further along the strip. The i icon opens another section at the bottom of the page with information on any comments or annotations to the record. This is the section where you'll also find Source information including publication number, source place (such as National Archives), and a brief descriptive summary.

Don't forget to save your military discoveries to your Ancestry.com account.

APPENDIX

ANCESTRY.COM QUICK LINKS

Ancestry.com's Quick Links module lets you bookmark web links that you'd like to save for future reference, including those on Ancestry.com and other genealogy websites such as FamilySearch.org **<www.familysearch.org>** and USGenWeb **<www.usgenweb.org>.**

To add a Quick Links module to your home page, click the Customize Your Homepage link in the upper right corner. Select Quick Links from the list of available modules, then click the Add to Your Homepage button.

While on your Ancestry.com home page, you can create a Quick Link by clicking the Add a Link button located at the top of the My Quick Links module. Then type in the website address (URL) of a favorite site or page, then name the link. Click Save, and the site will appear in your list of Quick Links.

Here are a few Ancestry.com links you may want to save in the My Quick Links module:

- Ancestry Academy **<www.ancestry.com/academy>**
- Blog **<blogs.ancestry.com/ancestry>**
- Card Catalog **<search.ancestry.com/search/CardCatalog.aspx>**
- Facebook **<www.facebook.com/Ancestry.com>**
- Family History Wiki **<www.ancestry.com/wiki>**
- Message Boards **<boards.ancestry.com>**
- My Account **<secure.ancestry.com/myaccount>**

My Quick Links

ADD A LINK

- Ancestry Card Catalog 🗑
- Birth, Marriage & Death Records 🗑
- U.S. Census Records 🗑
- Immigration & Emigration Records 🗑
- Military Collection 🗑
- Family Tree Magazine website 🗑
- Family Tree University 🗑

Ancestry.com allows you to save shortcuts called Quick Links, making your most-used resources more accessible.

- News and updated collections **<www.ancestry.com/cs/recent-collections>**
- Search **<search.ancestry.com>**
- Support **<support.ancestry.com>**
- YouTube how-to videos **<www.youtube.com/user/Ancestrycom>**

You can also add quick links for other websites, such as FamilyTreeMagazine.com **<www.familytreemagazine.com>** and FamilySearch.org **<www.familysearch.org>**.

ANCESTRY.COM SHORTCUT KEYS

Shortcut keys (aka "hot keys") are keyboard strokes that you can use to save time when searching and viewing results on Ancestry.com. Here's a look at the most common keyboard shortcuts you'll use. (Note: PC users need to hit the Ctrl button along with the shortcut key, and Mac users may need to hit the Command button along with the shortcut key.)

Shortcut	Purpose
n	Launches a new search by opening a new search form
r	Refines your search (Note: It will launch a search form that's pre-populated using the data you just searched; it also enables you to edit information in a search form without using the back keys or the Edit link.)
p	Previews current record in search result
>	Highlights next record
<	Highlights previous record

INDEX

ABOUT THE AUTHOR

Nancy Hendrickson is a genealogy author, blogger, and instructor at Family Tree University <www.familytreemagazine.com/university>. A contributing editor at *Family Tree Magazine*, Nancy writes almost exclusively about Internet genealogy, research, and American history. She's a member of Western Writers of America and a long-time photography buff. Nancy is active on Facebook <www.facebook.com/genealogyteach>, Twitter (*@genealogyteach*) and Pinterest <www. pinterest.com/genealogyteach>. You can find her at her website <www.ancestornews.com> or contact her via e-mail: *genealogyteach@gmail.com*.

DEDICATION

Dedicated to my mom, Marjorie Grace Hendrickson Dunn, 1922–2017. About her, my brother, Mark, said it best:

My mom was the most open and tolerant person I've ever known. Not the easy tolerance that comes after something becomes "acceptable," but the innate sense of goodness that made her accept everyone for what they are, offering her love and friendship without conditions. It was that spirit that made my mom feel privileged to have been one of the few people who were able to vote for Franklin D. Roosevelt and Barack Obama. It was that spirit that opened her welcoming arms to people of different races, religions, and sexual orientation in her family and when they joined her family.

Mom never whined about how things used to be better, that the "good old days" were lost and everything new bad. For her, the old days were when you lived in fear that your child would contract polio or die from a simple infection because antibiotics didn't exist. She was optimistic, welcoming change, but holding strong to core values.

She is so missed.

ACKNOWLEDGMENTS

While writing this book, I was reminded of the first events that inspired my love of gene-alogy. When I was seven or eight, my grandmother told me how her Civil War grandfather had been shot in the knee at Shiloh. Years later, after receiving records from the National Archives, I was thrilled to learn that her stories were true.

Another grandmother, along with my aunts, mom, and sister, added to the stories until—even as a child—I had a strong sense of who I was and where I fit in the long line of generations. Looking back, it's clear that everything I've written about genealogy, including this book, had its origins in childhood. So to all of those who kept the stories alive, my thanks.

My appreciation extends as well to Andrew Koch, my exceptionally talented editor. Andrew managed to catch my many missteps, making this book far better than it would have been without his guiding hand.

Lastly, a thank you to all the family who came before. Your lives and your stories propel me onward.

UNOFFICIAL GUIDE TO ANCESTRY.COM, SECOND EDITION. Copyright © 2018 by Nancy Hendrickson. Manu-factured in the United States of America. All rights reserved. No part of this book may be reproduced in any form or by any electronic or mechanical means including information storage and retrieval systems without permission in writing from the publisher, except by a reviewer, who may quote brief passages in a review. The content of this book has been thoroughly reviewed for accuracy; however, the author and the publisher disclaim any liability for any damages or losses that may result from the misuse of any product or information presented herein. Readers should note that websites featured in this work may have changed between when the book was written and when it was read; always verify with the most recent information. Published by Family Tree Books, an im-print of F+W Media, Inc., 10151 Carver Road, Suite 300, Blue Ash, Ohio 45242. (800) 289-0963. Second edition. All other trademarks are property of their respective owners. This book is not authorized or sponsored by Ancestry.com or any other person or entity owning or controlling rights to Ancestry.com, its name, trademark, or copyrights. This guide has not been reviewed, edited, or approved by Ancestry.com or any of its employees or affiliates.

ISBN: 978-1-4403-5326-0

Other Family Tree Books are available from your local book-store and online suppliers. For more genealogy resources, visit <www.familytreemagazine.com/store>.

22 21 20 19 18   5 4 3 2

DISTRIBUTED IN THE U.K. AND EUROPE BY
F&W Media International, LTD
Brunel House, Forde Close,
Newton Abbot, TQ12 4PU, UK
Tel: (+44) 1626 323200,
Fax (+44) 1626 323319
E-mail: enquiries@fwmedia.com

PHOTO CREDITS

Cover (left to right): Courtesy Getty Images, Shutterstock, private collection

All other images courtesy their respective copyright owners, including Ancestry.com and its subsidiary websites.

a content + ecommerce company

PUBLISHER AND COMMUNITY LEADER: Allison Dolan
EDITOR (SECOND EDITION): Andrew Koch
EDITORS (FIRST EDITION): Dana McCullough and Kelsea Daulton
DESIGNER: Michelle Thompson | Fold and Gather Design
PRODUCTION COORDINATOR: Debbie Thomas

4 FREE

FAMILY TREE templates

- decorative family tree posters

- five-generation ancestor chart

- family group sheet

- bonus relationship chart

- type and save, or print and fill out

Download at <www.familytreemagazine.com/familytreefreebies>

MORE GREAT GENEALOGY RESOURCES

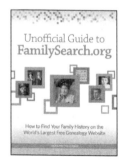

UNOFFICIAL GUIDE TO FAMILYSEARCH.ORG

By Dana McCullough

UNOFFICIAL ANCESTRY.COM WORKBOOK

By Nancy Hendrickson

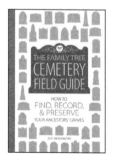

THE FAMILY TREE CEMETERY FIELD GUIDE

By Joy Neighbors

 Join our community! <facebook.com/familytreemagazine>